RACE, COLOR, AND THE YOUNG CHILD

RACE, COLOR, and the Young Child

by John E. Williams
and J. Kenneth Morland

The University of North Carolina Press
Chapel Hill

Copyright © 1976 by The University of North Carolina Press
All rights reserved
Manufactured in the United States of America
ISBN 0-8078-1261-7
Library of Congress Catalog Card Number 76-812

Library of Congress Cataloging in Publication Data

Williams, John E   1928–
  Race, color, and the young child.

  Bibliography: p.
  Includes index.
    1. Race awareness.   2. Prejudices and antipathies
(Child psychology).   I. Morland, John Kenneth, joint
author.   II. Title.
BF723.R3W54   301.45'1'042   76-812
ISBN 0-8078-1261-7

To KATHY and MARTEE

CONTENTS

Preface / ix

Acknowledgments / xiii

1. Perspectives on Race: Past and Present / 3

2. Color Usages and Evaluative Meanings in Contemporary Culture / 33

3. Attitudes Toward the Colors Black and White / 62

4. Racial Attitudes / 95

5. Modification of Color and Racial Attitudes / 134

6. Racial Acceptance and Preference / 166

7. Perception of Racial Similarity and Classification / 193

8. Interrelationships Among Racial and Color Concepts / 214

9. Synthesis and Interpretation of Research Findings / 237

10. A Developmental Theory of Color and Race Bias / 260

Appendixes:
   A. Future Directions for Research / 285
   B. Technical Summaries of Research Procedures / 317

References / 341

Index / 351

PREFACE

This book represents the collaborative efforts of a social-developmental psychologist and a social anthropologist to describe what is known—and what needs to be investigated—concerning the development of race and color concepts in young children. In planning the book, we had several objectives in mind. We wanted to summarize our own research findings extending back over a period of more than fifteen years. We wished to integrate our findings with those of other investigators to provide, in a single source, a summary of the research literature on this topic. As a third objective, we wanted to attempt a more comprehensive theoretical analysis than had yet been done—one which would adequately embrace all of the research findings to date. Finally, we hoped to encourage and stimulate other investigators to undertake research which would answer the many remaining questions concerning race and color concepts in young children.

In an effort to avoid creating either an overly popularized or an overly technical book, we have aimed our writing at the person with a general grasp of the concepts and research strategies of empirical behavioral science but without extensive advanced training in this area. We believe that the book will be comprehensible to persons who have had an introductory course or two in psychology, sociology, or anthropology, or have developed a comparable behavioral science background in other ways. In the college setting, the book is relevant to courses dealing with race relations and/or child development in the disciplines of psychology, sociology, anthropology, and education. In some courses, it will be particularly useful because of its substantive subject matter, and in others because of its illustrations of research methods and theory construction in the behavioral sciences. Beyond the college scene, the book should be of interest to professional persons who work with young children, and to lay persons who wish to keep abreast of current findings in the social sciences—particularly those persons who are themselves parents of young children.

The book is organized into four main sections and two appendixes. In the first section we are concerned with race and color concepts in the adult world which provide the general cultural framework within which the child's learning occurs. The second and third sections are composed of reviews of the research literature dealing with race and color concepts among young children. Section four is devoted to a synthesis of research findings and their theoretical interpretation. Appendix A contains a discussion of methodological issues and substantive questions for future research. Appendix B consists of a technical report on the principal measurement procedures employed in the research studies cited in the book.

Throughout the book we refer to the two major American racial groups as Euro-Americans and Afro-Americans —Euros and Afros, for short. We have used this particular racial nomenclature quite deliberately and we believe for very good reasons. We feel that the designations "Caucasian" and "Negro" now have unfavorable connotations for many Americans, and this book itself cites evidence that the currently popular "white person," "black person" nomenclature promotes racial bias. We like the terms Euro-American and Afro-American because they are reasonably descriptive of the distinction intended, emphasizing as they do the fact that, while the racial groups have some different antecedents, they are both a part of American society and culture. The other racial designation terms are used only in historical contexts, in quotations, or in descriptions of research procedures in which these terms were employed.

Do a psychologist and an anthropologist look at things the same way? Not always—but we believe the book is more interesting because of this. Workers in the subdisciplines of behavioral science too often go their own way, speaking their own language to their own fellow specialists. In writing this book, we have had to communicate with one another across disciplinary lines, which has been an exciting and instructive experience for us. We hope it will be for the reader.

ACKNOWLEDGMENTS

The authors wish to express appreciation to the children who have participated in our research studies, and to the parents and teachers whose cooperation makes such research possible. We are particularly indebted to the kindergarten directors and school principals who have supported our work and have been willing to risk the controversy which sometimes arises in conducting research in an area of high social significance.

The first author is appreciative of the support given to his work by Wake Forest University through a faculty research leave, regular grants from the faculty research and publication fund, and the use of the facilities of Wake Forest's Casa Artom in Venice, Italy, while working on this book in the summer of 1973. During the years 1967–74, the first author's research was supported by grant HD-0281 from the National Institute of Child Health and Human Development. Much of this research would not have been accomplished without this assistance, and appreciation is expressed herewith. The first author notes with greatest gratitude the contributions of his colleague Deborah L. Best whose creativity, organizational skill, and persever-ance have facilitated all of the Wake Forest research studies conducted since 1971. The special contributions of our former colleague Donna A. Boswell also are noted with appreciation.

The second author acknowledges with appreciation

grants that made much of his research possible: from Randolph-Macon Woman's College, the University Center of Virginia, the Southern Fellowships Fund, the Mutual Educational and Cultural Exchange Act of 1961 (Fulbright-Hays Act), and the U.S. Office of Education. He is also grateful to Randolph-Macon Woman's College for a sabbatical leave which provided time to work on the manuscript. The second author is particularly indebted to his students, Ellen Suthers, Lea Saute, and Julia Wolfe, who helped with various aspects of the research.

We acknowledge our debt to the many undergraduate and graduate students, at our institutions and elsewhere, who have conducted studies using our research procedures, and whose names are mentioned as their work is described throughout the book. The number of persons who have contributed to the research we discuss provides a classic documentation of the cooperative nature of scientific research.

Finally, we express our warmest thanks to Jane Reade for her assistance in the preparation of the manuscript. Her superb technical skill, unfailing good spirits, and enthusiasm for the project have contributed greatly to its completion.

RACE, COLOR, AND THE YOUNG CHILD

1.
Perspectives on Race: Past and Present

Young children have a remarkable ability to learn from experience, and such learning is particularly extensive in the preschool years. Given the importance attached to race and color in American society, it is not surprising that American children begin to develop racial and color awareness at an early age, as the studies that we report later will show. Much of this development is the result of direct and indirect influences that come from social norms and social structure. Attitudes toward and ideas about race and color are conveyed to the young American child by parents, playmates, teachers, mass media, and other communicators of the culture. We therefore need to be reminded of the kinds of messages about race and color that American society is giving to its children before we look at the responses of the children themselves. We need to do this in terms of past as well as present influences, for it is difficult to understand the renewed emphasis today on the importance of race and color unless we see it as a reaction, in part, to past attitudes and treatment.

Making broad generalizations about any aspect of American society and culture, including attitudes and ideas about race and color, is risky, for there are variations in belief and behavior. It seems safe to say, however, that

America is a society in which racial differentiation has long been considered of fundamental importance. Certainly in the past, and continuing into the present, categorization by race has been a crucial factor in patterns of marriage, friendship, neighborhood of residence, social relations, religious affiliation, schooling, employment, political power, and recreational pursuits. This emphasis on the importance of race is basic in the technical meaning of "racism," which can be defined as the belief that race is a primary determinant of human behavior and capacities. American children, then, absorb their attitudes toward and ideas about race in what might be termed a racist society.

We are aware that children differ in the ways in which they encounter beliefs and feelings about race and color in American society. Social and cultural influences are transmitted primarily through the words and actions of others, who may amplify, suppress, or distort patterns in line with their own knowledge, need, and perceptions. Moreover, children are not empty vessels into which societal messages are poured; rather, they are active participants in their own learning, and they screen messages in terms of their own needs. While recognizing this individuality in learning, as well as variations in the cultural patterns themselves, we find it essential to describe the general sociocultural framework in which American children learn about race and color.

EARLY VIEWS

Although our primary concern is with the present-day setting in which American children learn about race, a look at the past can give needed perspective on current attitudes, beliefs, and practices that surround children. In this brief treatment, we shall be able to present only a few of the views found in religion, science, literature, and law as this country began to struggle with the matter of race and color differences.*

Slavery and Its Consequences

From its beginning America was a country in which racial differences were present and had to be dealt with. First there were Indians from whom the land was wrested, and soon came Negro slaves from Africa. Initially, Indians and Negroes were set apart from the European settlers because of their "savagery" and "uncivilized" condition. As time went on, however, racial differences per se were relied on more and more as a justification for unequal treatment, if, indeed, it was felt that justification was needed. There is general agreement among historians that slavery itself was a crucial factor in generating this emphasis on race as a rationale for differential treatment. Winthrop Jordan calls the enslavement of Negroes in America "the unthinking decision," for at the start of settlement in America by Europeans "no one had intended to establish the institution of slavery. Yet in less than a century the foundations of a peculiar institution had been laid" (1968, p. 44).

For the first twenty years or so after the arrival of Negroes in America little is known about their status. It was not until 1640 that laws began to be passed that led to the conception of slavery as being perpetual for life, both for adults and their offspring. The result was that English immigrants to America created a condition of chattel slavery that ran counter to English law. New statutes were formulated and passed that permitted greater and greater control over slaves by their masters, until Negroes were treated as property. Jordan notes that by the end of the seventeenth century chattel racial slavery was found throughout the American colonies, a condition that Elizabethan Englishmen would have found strange and

*For fuller accounts the reader should see Gossett (1963), Jordan (1968), Smith (1972), Stanton (1960), Snyder (1962), and Wood (1970).

unfamiliar. However, for Europeans in American colonies in the eighteenth century slavery was an aspect of culture that was taken for granted as a normal part of life. As Jordan puts it: "English colonials of the eighteenth century were faced with full-blown slavery—something they thought of not as an institution but as a host of ever-present problems, dangers, and opportunities" (1968, p. 98).

Until the American Revolution, slavery and freedom co-existed without serious challenge. With the development of the revolutionary movement and its condemnation of British control, antislavery groups became vocal, pointing out the inconsistency of demanding freedom for some but not for all. Such protests helped to abolish slavery in six northern states in the late 1700s, and the abolition movement grew in the upper South at that time. But the great expansion of cotton production made possible by the invention of the cotton gin in 1793, the massacre of Europeans by Negroes in the Haitian revolt around the turn of the century, and slave revolts in America, all gave impetus to the continuation of slavery throughout the South.

Religious Views

In both its pronouncements and structure, organized religion in America tended to support and to express the importance of race. At the same time, there was strong opposition to slavery and to the unequal treatment of races. Both proslavery and antislavery groups sought religious justification and utilized religious arguments. One of the early disagreements was whether or not slaves should be given religious instruction and converted. On the one hand, it was argued that slaves should be converted, since one justification for slavery was that it offered an opportunity to save those who would have otherwise remained heathen; on the other hand, there were fears that such conversion might make slaves less efficient workers and more desirous of freedom. When slaves were brought into churches, they were usually segregated in such a way as to demonstrate their lower status. Also, they and the rest of the congregation were often reminded that slavery was decreed by God. H. Shelton Smith has quoted from a sermon given by an Episcopal minister of Maryland around the middle of the eighteenth century and directed toward slaves: "Almighty God hath been pleased to make you slaves here, and to give you nothing but Labour and Poverty in this world. . . . If you desire *Freedom*, serve the Lord here, and you shall be his *Freemen* in Heaven hereafter" (Smith, 1972, p. 12). The minister went on to tell the slaves that their owners were "God's Overseers" and that any wrongs committed against them were also committed against God and would be punished in the life to come.

After the mid-1700s concern about the compatibility of slavery and Christianity grew stronger in a number of churches. The Society of Friends was one of the first religious organizations to condemn slavery. In its 1754 yearly meeting in Philadelphia, the Society voted to disown members who bought or sold slaves, and by 1800 it had cut its ties completely with slaveholding. However, as Smith points out (1972, pp. 35–36), the Friends frequently discriminated against Negroes by denying most of them membership in the Society, not receiving them as social equals, and often refusing to let them be buried in their cemeteries. In the 1780s the Presbyterians, Baptists, and Methodists, among other denominations, made moves against slavery at their annual meetings, and a number of their influential leaders declared that human bondage was contrary to the tenets of their faith. However, strong opposition to the abolition of slavery prevailed within these denominations, so that by the beginning of the nineteenth century, they did not, as a rule, oppose slavery but began to give it official sanction.

Such sanction was built upon several premises. One was Biblical, in which it was contended that both the Old and New Testaments approved of slavery. In the Old Testament, the curse of Noah upon his son Ham, believed to be the ancestor of Africans, was used to show that God had ordained slavery. In regard to the New Testament, it was pointed out that Jesus had not spoken explicitly against the institution of slavery, and that Paul had given it at least implicit support when he advised a Christian slave, Onesimus, to return to his master, Philemon. The Reverend Josiah Priest in a book first published in 1843 in Albany, New York, was among those giving formal expression to this position. His book was entitled *Bible Defense of Slavery*, and it went through five editions. Another sanction of slavery came from belief in the racial superiority of the Euro-American and the inferiority of the Afro-American, a belief that we shall note several times in this chapter. Thus, slavery was considered a necessary societal arrangement adapted to the inherent nature of the races. Finally, it was asserted that slaves were better off in America than in Africa, for in this land they could be elevated above the "savagery" of the land of their ancestors. According to a Presbyterian minister of Virginia, writing in 1857: "In the history of nations it would be difficult to find an instance in which people have made more progress upward and onward than the African race has made under the operation of American slavery" (quoted in Smith, 1972, p. 145). Not only had slaves benefited, in the view of these defenders of slavery, but so had all mankind, for slavery was considered the means whereby a benevolent and all-knowing God had made the development of civilization possible.

Although most of the sanctioning of slavery came from churches in the South, there was also support in northern churches. While this support was given, in part, to avoid schisms, it also came from basic agreement with the racial views of slaveholders. But in the 1840s the issue of slavery, along with disagreement about principles of governance, openly divided northern and southern churches. Methodists split into northern and southern bodies in 1844, Baptists in 1845, and Presbyterians during the Civil War. While there were other important matters involved, it is significant that differences in how the Negro race should be treated were paramount in these divisions, illustrating again how important the matter of race has been in American life, even in Christian churches purporting to believe in and promote the brotherhood of mankind.

Almost from the start, racial separation characterized American religion. Initially, Negroes were segregated within a congregation or they were placed in separate churches. Later, most of them formed separate denominations. The latter first emerged in a formal way with the establishment in Philadelphia of the African Methodist Episcopal Church in 1816, as a reaction against racial discrimination in the Methodist Episcopal Church. Afro-Americans organized other separate Methodist and Baptist groups until division by race became quite extensive. E. Franklin Frazier (1964) has pointed out how the separate Negro churches functioned to provide Afro-Americans with organizations which were truly their own, in which they were completely accepted, and where they could avoid subordination in a Euro-American-dominated society.

This religious separation, along with discriminatory treatment against Afro-Americans in all areas of life, contributed to what H. Shelton Smith termed "the triumph of racial orthodoxy" among southern churches during the first decade of the twentieth century (Smith, 1972, pp. 258–305). This orthodoxy included a firm belief by Euro-Americans in their own inherent superiority, the inferiority of Afro-Americans, and in the consequent necessity for racial segregation.

Additional support for this "racial orthodoxy" came from scientific and other writings of the nineteenth and early twentieth centuries. At the beginning of the 1800s the scientific argument revolved around the question of whether or not races were separate species. An early champion of the basic unity of man as a single species was Samuel Stanhope Smith, professor of moral philosophy and later president of what became Princeton University. He sought to explain racial differences as superficialities which were entirely the result of climate. The first serious challenge to this thesis was made by Samuel George Morton, a Philadelphia physician and professor of anatomy at Pennsylvania Medical College. His *Crania Americana*, published in 1839, claimed that races were separate species, endowed with quite different physical and moral characteristics. The notion of races as a separate species was supported by Josiah Nott, a physician in Mobile, Alabama, and George Gliddon, the United States vice-consul at Cairo. Together in 1854 they produced a book entitled *Types of Mankind*, to which the renowned biologist, Louis Agassiz, contributed a chapter. This book argued strongly for great difference in races and sharply questioned the basic unity of mankind. The first printing of this book sold out immediately and the book went through nine editions.

The view that races were different species permitted the argument that some races were more advanced than others. The contention that Negroes were a less advanced species gave justification to their enslavement, for they could not be considered "men" within the meaning of the Declaration of Independence. While the discoveries of Darwin eventually decided the issue of multiplicity of species in favor of the unity of mankind, racial differences continued to be looked upon as basically important and related to inherent inferiority and superiority. Some scientists maintained that within the same species there could be "advanced" and "backward" races. They did this by utilizing a form of social Darwinism, expressed in the notion that those who were in superior positions were there because they were the most "fit." As Gossett (1963, pp. 144–57) points out, the evolutionary theories of such social scientists as Herbert Spencer could be applied to show that the more advanced societies were made possible by the more advanced races. The writings of other scientists, including the biologist Francis Galton, the sociologist William Graham Sumner, and the psychologist G. Stanley Hall, were utilized to show that there were more advanced and less advanced races. While there were scientists at the time who challenged the notion of the superiority of races, the idea that "superior" cultures were created by "superior" races had a strong appeal to Euro-Americans, who were invariably classified as belonging to the superior race.

Literary Views

Far more widely read than the scientific treatises were the novels and nontechnical expositions dealing with race. Gossett (1963, p. 198, pp. 239–42) illustrates how James Fenimore Cooper's characters tended to follow racial stereotypes, with Negroes being inferior to Indians, who were, in turn, inferior to Americans of European background. More explicit in their use of race to explain fictional characters were such novelists as Jack London, Frank Norris, and Owen Wister, who glorified "Anglo-Saxons" in their writing. This was done primarily through the heroes of their stories, who, Gossett points out, were almost always "tall and athletic blonds, with blue or gray eyes." These novelists also disseminated a form of social Darwinist racism, which accounted for the superior place of Anglo-Saxons through their "fitness" to triumph over persons of less able races.

The novels of Thomas Dixon, Jr., promoted belief in the inferiority of Afro-Americans even more directly. His trilogy of *The Leopard's Spots*, *The Clansman*, and *The Traitor*, all published within the first seven years of the 1900s, sold many copies and were widely read. They glorified Euro-Americans and expressed fear and hatred for Negroes, who were referred to as "the black death." For example, *The Clansman* is a story of Reconstruction days in South Carolina which attempted to justify the violent activities of members of the Clan against Negroes who tried to utilize the power they gained briefly during Reconstruction. The book was later made into a film, *The Birth of a Nation*, which reinforced belief in the innate backwardness of Negroes and the danger they posed if they ever moved out of their subordinate position.

The expressions about race and race differences in the nineteenth century and at the beginning of the twentieth century were not systematic presentations of the fundamental importance of race as a factor in behavior. Rather, the majority of those who wrote about the issue assumed or implied that race was the key factor in determining such things as temperament, character, and intelligence, and that these were fixed by racial heredity. However, in the early 1900s several explicitly racist treatises became available to Americans. We shall look briefly at the work of four prominent writers who were highly influential in promoting the idea of the importance of race. Two were from Europe and two from America.

Houston Stewart Chamberlain was an Englishman who became a German citizen and a son-in-law of the composer Richard Wagner. He utilized a survey of history to propound the preeminence of the Teutons, or Germanic tribes, who were descended from the Aryans. His two-volume work, *The Foundations of the Nineteenth Century*, which developed this thesis, was first published in German in 1899 and translated into English in 1910. Chamberlain elaborated race into a mystique: "Race lifts a man above himself; it endows him with extraordinary—I might say supernatural—powers . . ." (1912, 1:269). He claimed that races differed markedly in creativity, and that the most highly gifted of all were the Germanic races or the European Aryans. Chamberlain believed that even though the Teutons were not necessarily the only ones who molded history, ". . . they unquestionably deserve the first place: all those who from the sixth century onwards appear as genuine shapers of the destinies of mankind, whether as builders of States or as discoverers of new thoughts and of original art, belong to the Teutonic race. . . . Physically and mentally the Aryans are pre-eminent among all peoples; for that reason they are by right . . . the lords of the world" (1912, 1:lxvi, 542).

Another European, Arthur de Gobineau, a Frenchman, wrote *The Inequality of Human Races* in the 1850s, and it was published in this country in 1915. In the preface he described his position: "I was gradually penetrated by the conviction that the racial question overshadows all other problems of history, that it holds the key to them all, and that the inequality of the races from whose fusion a people is formed is enough to explain the whole course of its destiny" (1915, p. xiv). Gobineau traced the fall of civilizations and the death of societies, arguing that these failures were not primarily the result of the type of government, or internal corruption, or the forms of social institutions, or physical environment, or religion. Rather they were due to the character of the people and their creative capacity, and that these, in turn, were a function of race. For him, history revealed a racial hierarchy, with whites at the top, blacks at the bottom, and yellows in between. He concluded: "Such is the lesson of history. It shows that all civilizations derive from the white race, that none can exist without its help, and that a society is great and brilliant only so far as it preserves the blood of the noble group that created it . . ." (1915, p. 210).

Two of the most prominent and influential American

proponents of the importance of race were Madison Grant and Lothrop Stoddard. Both made references to Chamberlain and Gobineau, sometimes to question their methodologies and Chamberlain's claim of Teutonic superiority, but not to contest the idea that race was preeminent in understanding history and human behavior. Grant carried high credentials. He was a graduate of Yale, with a law degree from Columbia, and he served in such distinguished positions as chairman of the New York Zoological Society, trustee of the American Museum of Natural History, and councilor of the American Geographical Society. His most influential publication, *The Passing of the Great Race*, first published in 1916, sold well over 20,000 copies and supported and fed the belief in white supremacy. The preface was written by Henry Fairfield Osborn, a renowned paleontologist who taught at Princeton and Columbia. In the preface, Osborn stated the theme of Grant's book: "European history has been written in terms of nationality and of language, but never before in terms of race; yet race has played a far larger part than either language or nationality in moulding the destinies of men" (1918, p. vii). The subtitle of Grant's book is "The Racial Basis of European History," and in tracing racial history he credited whites, especially Nordics, with the inherent virtues that made European civilization possible. In contrast, he believed Negroes to be a subservient race who were valuable as long as they remained in lower status, "but once raised to social equality their influence will be destructive to themselves and to the whites" (1918, p. 87). Grant was alarmed at the possibility that "the Great Race," that is, the Nordics, would be swept into a "racial abyss" in America if our "maudlin sentimentalism" blinded us to racial distinctions.

The other American writer who wrote fervently in support of white supremacy, Lothrop Stoddard, was also an accomplished person. He held a law degree, a master's degree, and a doctorate, all from Harvard University. He wrote some twenty-two books and numerous articles for popular consumption. Among his most influential writings was *The Rising Tide of Color Against White World-Supremacy*, which was published in 1920 and which carried an introduction by Madison Grant. In his preface to the book, Stoddard explained his stance: "More than a decade ago I became convinced that the key-note of twentieth-century world politics would be the relations between the primary races of mankind" (1920, p. v). Stoddard had a very pessimistic outlook, as did Grant, for fear that the white race would be inundated by the colored races. To him World War I was the first "White Civil War," which so weakened the white race that cataclysmic possibilities were opened. He feared that the "white dikes" holding back the "rising flood of color" would be broken and that whites would be deluged by "dusky waves." His book is filled with a conviction of urgency and impending tragedy: "Ours is a solemn moment. We stand at a crisis—the supreme crisis of the ages" (1920, p. 299). Stoddard felt this way, because for him:

. . . the white races which emerged out of prehistoric shadows forged a high civilization, and thereby provided in a myriad ways their fitness for the hegemony of mankind. . . . All of these marvellous achievements were due solely to superior heredity, and the mere maintenance of what had been won depended absolutely upon the prior maintenance of race-values. Civilization of itself means nothing. It is merely an effect, whose cause is the creative urge of superior germ-plasm. Civilization is the body; the race is the soul. Let the soul vanish, and the body moulders into the inanimate dust from which it came (1920, p. 299).

In summarizing the views of the period of 1880 to 1920, Gossett has stated that there were some writers who disagreed with the widely accepted notion that Afro-Americans were inherently inferior and therefore had to be treated differently, but these writers stood against the majority. Gossett went on to say:

Most of the people who wrote about Negroes were firmly in the grip of the idea that intelligence and temperament are racially determined and unalterable. They concluded, therefore, that the failures of Reconstruction, the low educational status of the Negro, his high statistics of crime, disease, and poverty, were simply the inevitable results of his heredity. The defenders of the Negro were thus cast in the role of sickly humanitarians who refused to face facts (1963, p. 286).

Laws about Race

Beliefs about the primacy of race were long upheld and reinforced by law and by informal codes. Indeed, the sanctity of law gave support to the importance of racial differences by requiring that races be treated differently. Prior to the Civil War, laws kept the status of slaves fixed, and Negro freedmen were restricted in both the South and the North by legal, as well as extralegal, means. There was little need for those in power to worry about "keeping Negroes in their place," for such a place was clearly defined by law, and by informal "understandings."

Even after the Civil War and the adoption of the Thirteenth Amendment abolishing slavery, Negroes continued to have few rights. In the South, "Black Codes" were passed by legislatures to control the several million slaves who had been freed. These codes were rigorous and had the effect of reestablishing the master-slave relationship. When federal statutes eliminated the Black Codes, the South entered a period of uncertainty about the structure of race relations according to law. But toward the end of the nineteenth century the region began to put into effect the kinds of Jim Crow laws that had been developed in the North after slavery had been abolished there. Decisions by the United States Supreme Court supported the legality of segregation. The *Plessey* v. *Ferguson* decision of 1896 permitted racially separate facilities and treatment as long as they were equal. In this decision the Court contended that "legislation is powerless to eradicate racial instincts." In *Williams* v. *Mississippi* in 1898, the Court completed the basis for permitting legally enforced racial segregation and disfranchisement by upholding Mississippi's law, which, in effect, kept Negroes from voting.

Such decisions encouraged certain politicians at the turn of the century to employ racist appeals in their campaigns for election. James K. Vardaman of Mississippi, Benjamin R. Tillman of South Carolina, and Tom Watson of Georgia were among those who built much of their support by denouncing Afro-Americans and declaring them to be something less than human. Concurrent with these anti-Negro appeals, laws and state constitutional provisions that were enacted to restrict the voting rights of Afro-Americans developed in a number of southern states. Regulations were adopted that made it necessary for voters to read and understand the state constitution, that required the payment of poll taxes, and that set up the so-called "grandfather clauses." The latter were designed to make it possible for illiterate whites to vote while keeping Negroes from voting. This was done by exempting from any sort of literacy or educational tests those eligible to vote at a time prior to which Afro-Americans could not vote, and also by exempting the descendants of those eligible to vote at that prior time. Thus if a person had a grandfather or father eligible to vote, he was also eligible, without having to submit to a test. However, Afro-Americans were subjected to such stringent tests that they could seldom pass. Another means of preventing Negroes from having a meaningful vote was to bar them from participating in the primary elections, for it was in these "white primaries" that the real choice of candidates took place.

After the *Plessey-Ferguson* decision of 1896 which legalized segregation in public facilities, a number of southern states began to require separation of the races in schools, public transportation, restaurants, public assemblies, recreational events, and hospitals. The extremes to which racial segregation was required are seen in a South Carolina law of 1915 prohibiting whites and blacks from working in the same room, using the same entrances, exits, paywindows, or stairways at the same time, and from using at any time the same lavatories, toilets, or drinking buckets. Other examples of extreme segregation are seen in the requirement in Atlanta courts for separate Bibles for Negro and white witnesses, and in a 1930 Birmingham ordinance which prohibited Negroes and whites from playing dominoes or checkers together. Separate taxis for the races were required by Jacksonville in 1929, Birmingham in 1930, and Atlanta in 1940. By 1944 Gunnar Myrdal, the Swedish social scientist who studied race relations in America, was able to state that the separation of the races in the South was so complete that white southerners had contact with Negroes almost exclusively as servants or in other highly formalized caste-like situations. The conviction developed that the laws requiring racial separation were somehow in accord with the "nature of things" and that to try to change such laws would involve grave dangers to both races. C. Vann Woodward illustrates this conviction by quoting an article in the *Atlantic Monthly* of January 1944 by David L. Cohn of Mississippi, who wrote: "It is William Graham Sumner's dictum that you cannot change the mores of a people by law, and since the social segregation of the races is the most deep-seated and pervasive of the Southern mores, it is evident that he who attempts to change it by law runs risks of incalculable gravity" (Woodward, 1966, p. 104).

Thus, by requiring certain kinds of behavior between the races, the laws themselves were instruments of education in the importance of race. And since these laws discriminated against nonwhites, handicapping them economically, politically, educationally, and socially, they promoted the belief in the superiority of Euro-Americans and the inferiority of Americans in other racial categories. Persons growing up in this situation would assume that such distinctions on the basis of race were inherent and inevitable.

RECENT VIEWS

Recent views and practices regarding race and race relations differ considerably from those of the past. Yet racial classification continues to be important in America, due, in part, to reactions against beliefs, attitudes, and social practices which have come down to us from previous generations.

Court Decisions and Laws

Even as states were passing laws resulting in unequal treatment on the basis of race, the federal courts were challenging the constitutionality of many of these laws. In 1915 the Supreme Court declared the grandfather clauses to constitute unequal treatment in violation of the Fifteenth Amendment. After a series of decisions regarding the "white primary," the Supreme Court in 1944 established finally and conclusively that prohibition from voting in primaries on the basis of race was a violation of the Fifteenth Amendment. The Supreme Court also declared unconstitutional subsequent attempts to prevent Afro-Americans from voting. For example, it declared unconstitutional the 1946 Boswell Amendment in Alabama, which permitted the registration only of those persons who could "understand and explain" any article of the United States Constitution, because this was used as a device to prevent Negroes from voting. The restrictive covenant, requiring the purchaser of a house to agree not to sell to minority races, was held by the Supreme Court in 1948 to be unenforceable, since it was a violation of the equal protection clause of the Fourteenth Amendment.

In its 1954 decision on school desegregation, the Supreme Court reversed the 1896 *Plessey-Ferguson* decision, which had permitted legally established racial segregation as long as the facilities were equal. In stating that racial segregation in public education could no longer be required by law, the Court concluded: ". . . in the field of public education the doctrine of 'separate but equal' has no place. Separate educational facilities are inherently unequal. Therefore, we hold that the plaintiffs and others similarly situated for whom the actions have been brought are, by reason of the segregation complained of, deprived of the equal protection of the laws guaranteed by the 14th Amendment." In reaching its decision, the Court relied on the testimony of social scientists in regard to the psychological and social effects of forced racial segregation: "To separate them [children in grade and high schools] from others of similar age and qualifications solely because of their race generates a feeling of inferiority as to their status in the community that may affect their hearts and minds in a way unlikely ever to be undone." In their book dealing with the 1954 Supreme Court decision, Blaustein and Ferguson declared this ruling to be ". . . the most important legal decision of the twentieth century, and it may well have been the most important legal decision ever rendered by an American court" (1957, p. ix). For legal authorities to react in such a way to a decision regarding racial segregation supports the idea that race and race relations have been and continue to be of crucial importance in American life.

Federal legislation guaranteeing equal treatment of all Americans began to be passed in the late 1950s and continued through the 1960s. The Civil Rights Act of 1957 was the first civil rights law passed by Congress since the post-Civil War Reconstruction period. It prohibited action that prevented persons from voting in federal elections, created a Civil Rights Commission, and set up a Civil Rights Division in the Department of Justice. A 1960 act strengthened provisions of the 1957 act to provide for court reinforcement of voting rights. One of the most far-reaching laws affecting race relations was the Civil Rights Act of 1964. This act required equal access by all citizens to hotels, restaurants, places of amusement, and retail establishments. It also gave authority to the Attorney General of the United States to initiate suits against public schools that did not desegregate, it required nondiscrimination in employment, and it contained a provision to cut off federal funds or federal contracts from organizations that continued to practice racial discrimination. The Voting Rights Act of 1965 suspended literacy tests and other devices found to be discriminatory as qualifications for voting in eight states, and it provided for federal examiners to conduct voter registration and observe voting in these states. The 1968 Civil Rights Act prohibited discrimination in housing because of race, including discrimination in the granting of loans and the buying and selling of houses by real estate firms.

Clearly, the strong trend in federal court decisions and laws has been toward the elimination of racial discrimination in all forms of public life. However, the effects of past laws and practices involving racial discrimination are still felt by minority group members, and it has been necessary to focus on the racial classification of individuals in order to be sure nondiscrimination laws are being carried out.

Scientific Views

In contrast to the speculations about race by the social Darwinists, and by such writers as Chamberlain, Gobineau, Grant, and Stoddard, present-day scientists have engaged in carefully devised empirical studies of race and race differences. Most of the work has been done by anthropologists, although psychologists, sociologists, geneticists, and others have also made contributions. In general, the research findings do not agree with earlier views of racial inferiority and superiority, although there are a few scientists who appear to believe that such exist.

A major problem in trying to compare races in terms of ability, or on any other human trait, is due to the difficulty in scientific delineation of races. Physical anthropologists, who specialize in racial classification, state that all classification systems have arbitrary features. According to Buettner-Janusch, "Classifications are not immutable, and the ones we use must be appropriate for the occasion" (1966, p. 616). He points out, for example, that if one is studying gene flow between Americans of European and African ancestry, race is defined in one way, but when studying the frequency of certain alleles in younger and older persons in the same population, race is defined in another way. At one time it was thought that the human species could be readily divided into three major races, Caucasoid, Mongoloid, and Negroid, along with several other groupings related in some way to these three. Most anthropologists now feel that such a typology is so over-simplified and abstract as to be meaningless. Buettner-Janusch states why he does not use such terms: "We have carefully avoided words such as negroid, mongoloid, caucasoid, and the related expressions: colored, black, yellow, white. We do not find these are biologically useful terms. They are not usually defined with any degree of precision or consistency by those who use them. Those who use them seldom make an attempt to determine whether Mendelian populations are being referred to. These expressions are probably best kept out of the language of science" (1966, p. 612).

Some anthropologists use a classification suggested by Stanley Garn (1965), in which there are "major geo-graphical races," from nine to twelve in number, "local races" within these major divisions, and "microraces" within the local races. Other anthropologists believe that the term "race" should be abandoned in science, for they believe that it hinders scientific investigation and a genuine understanding of human variation. C. Loring Brace, a physical anthropologist, has gone so far as to say: "The reality of races as biological entities, then, is to be found in the human conviction that they exist. . . . They are real because people believe they are, and social reality —the human world—is determined by human belief" (1971, p. 5). Most anthropologists, however, feel that the concept of race can be used scientifically to designate systematic biological variations within a species. Buettner-Janusch is among these. He defines race in the following way and in so doing supports our point of the complexity involved in identifying a race:

A race of Homo sapiens is a Mendelian population, a reproductive community of individuals which share in a common
gene pool. The level at which we define the reproductive
community depends upon the problem we are investigating.
. . . The implication is that there are an infinite number of
possible races within the species Homo sapiens. Species are
closed systems; Mendelian populations or races are open
systems. A genetic system which is not closed may be defined at
any particular level. All members of our species belong to one
Mendelian population . . . [which] is divisible into smaller
Mendelian populations, an almost infinitely large number of
them (1966, pp. 612–13).

The scientific designation of races as populations that vary in the frequency of certain genes bears little relationship to the social and legal designations employed to categorize a person racially in the United States. And it must be remembered that almost all studies of race have utilized the popular, not the scientific, designation of race. To show how this nonscientific designation operates, we can look at the way in which the Census Bureau arrived at its racial classification of Americans in the 1970 decennial census. Respondents were asked to indicate the racial category with which they identified themselves. Thus, some persons of Mexican or Puerto Rican descent classified themselves as "white," while others classified themselves as "nonwhite." For persons of mixed parentage who did not know how to classify themselves, the race of the father was used. In the 1960 census this had been done differently; those whose mixed parentage was "white" and any other race were assigned to the other race, regardless of which parent was "nonwhite."

But the problem of trying to determine whether or not races differ in innate ability does not stop with the confusion in racial designation. Even if it were possible to set up relatively homogeneous racial groupings, there is the question of whether the variations in the genetic characteristics by which the groupings are determined are those which affect ability, or are invariably found in combination with genetic characteristics that do affect ability. In other words, do the genes which determine such racial characteristics as the color of the skin, shape of the nose, eversion of the lips, etc., determine anything else about the person? There is no empirical evidence from scientific research that they do.

Still another problem concerns environmental influence. In scientific studies of race, we think in terms of groupings that differ in the frequency of certain genes, that is, in terms of biological categories of the human species. But whatever the genes represented in a racial category, they do not operate in a vacuum. There are also matters of opportunity and motivation, which are environmental in nature. It is exceedingly difficult to equate these so that racial factors in behavior can be measured.

Finally, there are the problems of the measuring instruments used to determine superiority and inferiority. The use of intelligence tests as objective measures of innate capacity has come under sharp criticism. Anthropologists have shown that such tests invariably involve biases toward particular kinds of learning, and opportunities for learning. The use of one's own culture or aspect of one's culture to determine the "advancement" of a race usually does little more than demonstrate ethnocentrism and the lack of knowledge of the many variables that go into the formation of a culture.

One of the most serious and carefully devised recent studies related to the question of racial superiority and inferiority was carried out by Arthur R. Jensen, an educational psychologist. Jensen's propositions, and the reactions which they engendered, provide an illustration of some of the problems that arise in trying to relate racial differences to differences in behavior. After a discussion of tests that purport to show which factors are associated with variation in IQ scores and the manner in which IQ can be separated into genetic and environmental components, Jensen concluded, in regard to the factor of race, that his evidence supported the hypothesis "that genetic factors are strongly implicated in the average Negro-white intelligence difference" (1969, p. 82). Furthermore, according to Jensen, environmental differences could not account for the average differences between racial groupings. Jensen's hypothesis was immediately subjected to criticism by other scientists. C. Loring Brace, a physical anthropologist, criticized Jensen's definition of race as "a breeding population" by stating that it is "so vague that it provides no basis for differentiating between a clan and a village, a tribe and a whole continent, or even between two nuclear families" (1971, p. 7). It might be added that in the tests reporting racial differences in IQ scores, social-legal rather than biological criteria were used to delineate races. Martin Deutsch, a psychologist, has claimed that Jensen relied in a too uncritical way on IQ tests as a measure of innate intelligence:

Standard intelligence tests measure essentially what children have learned, not how well they might learn something new. Intelligence tests have been constructed within a certain kind of society and a certain kind of cultural milieu, basically white middle-class America. During a period of dynamic social change, tests have remained static and have become increasingly irrelevant for understanding the nature and evolution of an organism's intellectual behavior (1969, p. 82).

Two sociologists, Arthur Stinchcombe (1969) and Rosalie Cohen (1971), have criticized Jensen's assumptions about the way in which environment affects behavior. Stinchcombe argues that environment contains many variables, that it has a cumulative effect, and that until more is known about these characteristics, it is not possible to speak of the relative effects of heredity and environment. Cohen notes that conceptual styles may differ systematically in particular environments and need to be taken into account when assessing environmental influence on learning.

It might be assumed from the foregoing discussion that all that present-day scientists have succeeded in doing is to show the enormous problems and pitfalls that arise when trying to relate differences in behavior to genetic differences between populations termed races. However, by pointing out the difficulties, scientists have made positive contributions. First, they have undermined the simplistic approach to race and race differences often taken in the past, especially the belief that races can be readily delineated on a genetic basis. Second, they have pointed out the far-reaching effects of discriminatory treatment against races, however they are designated. Finally, they have called for more sophisticated studies of how environment and heredity combine to affect behavior.

It is difficult to know what effects scientific studies of race have had on attitudes toward race. Evidently very little scientific or other information about race is taught in a direct way in elementary and high schools. However, it is possible that the impact of the scientific views is reflected in responses to public opinion surveys which indicate that there are comparatively few Americans who say they believe in innate racial superiority or inferiority, or show a ready acceptance of unfavorable racial stereotypes (CBS News, 1968, p. 2–3).

Religious Views

During the civil rights struggle of the 1950s, which led to the Supreme Court decision on public schools and to federal legislation requiring equal treatment of all Americans, every major religious denomination in the United States made pronouncements against racial prejudice and discrimination. For example, the 1952 General Conference of the Methodist Church adopted the following: "Ours is a world church. As such, its responsibility is to unite in one fellowship men and women of all races and nations. As Christians, we confess ourselves to be children of God, brothers and sisters of Jesus Christ. This being true, there is no place in the Methodist Church for racial discrimination or racial segregation." When the Supreme Court handed down its decision of 1954 declaring racial segregation in public schools to be unconstitutional, the decision was openly supported by all major religious groups. In June 1954, for example, the Southern Baptist Convention approved of the following recommendation: "That we recognize the fact that this Supreme Court decision is in harmony with the constitutional guarantee of equal freedom to all citizens, and with the Christian principles of equal justice and love for all men." The National Council of Churches has repeatedly spoken out against unequal treatment of races. In a 1952 statement the Council stated that it "renounces and earnestly recommends to its member churches that they renounce the pattern of segregation based on race, color, or national origin as unnecessary and undesirable and a violation of the Gospel of love and human brotherhood." In its 1972 triennial meeting, the National Council elected an Afro-American as its president. An interfaith group, the National Conference of Christians and Jews, has promoted National Brotherhood Week since 1934 as a means of reducing religious and racial prejudice and increasing understanding and equal treatment.

51507

Not all religious organizations have issued declarations favoring equal treatment of races, for some of the smaller denominations and sects have openly opposed racial integration, or at least have not promoted it. However, as Harrell points out (1971), it is difficult to generalize about such groups, for some encourage all races to join their churches and they have integrated congregations. For our purposes, it is sufficient to note that the official position of the great majority of churches today is in marked contrast to the earlier one in which slavery was supported and Euro-American superiority proclaimed. Attention continues to be paid to race, not to justify separation but to acknowledge racial equality and the basic unity of mankind. However, as we shall see in the next section, official church statements have done little to change the racial segregation characteristics of most American churches.

PRESENT-DAY EMPHASES ON RACE

We have summarized the sociocultural aspects of race in America, in earlier and more recent times, and have seen that some fundamental changes have taken place. In the past, racial prejudice and discrimination against non-Euro-Americans were buttressed by legal, scientific, and religious views, and embodied in a societal structure of unequal status and power. More recent court decisions, scientific findings, and religious statements have repudiated these past views, and racial minorities have organized to play a major part in bringing about change. Steps are being taken to rectify the effects of past mistreatment which has handicapped members of racial minorities. In this movement away from overt racial discrimination and belief in racial inferiority, however, there is a continued and even heightened emphasis on the importance of race.

Court decisions and laws attempting to remedy past discrimination require that special attention be given to race in order to insure that racial discrimination is no longer practiced. Thus, in order to eliminate racial discrimination in public education, the courts have required some school districts to institute racial balance which necessitates the children and teachers being assigned to schools primarily on the basis of their race. The extent to which such practices can make children aware of the race of their classmates is illustrated in the following incident which took place in a Virginia school system which was in the process of being racially balanced. In a Euro-American family, the father asked his fifth grade daughter who had just returned from a day at school how everything had gone. The daughter replied that one of the first things the teacher did was to count those in the class and that she had discovered there were too many of "them" and not enough of "us." When asked what she meant by "them" and "us," the daughter responded, "The blacks and the whites, of course." The father then inquired about what had been done, and he was told that several of "them" had been sent to another room and several of "us" had been brought into her room. And, she added, "Susie doesn't know what race she belongs to, because she stood up when the teacher counted the blacks, but she is really white." The father found out later that Susie was a very light-skinned Afro-American.

Despite the pronouncements of American religious bodies calling for equal treatment of races and for the elimination of racial segregation, American churches and synagogues largely are segregated by race, at both the national and local levels, a separation that reflects the past development of denominations along racial lines. In those denominations and interdenominational groups, like the National Council of Churches, which are multiracial, racial caucuses have been formed and officers chosen so that the races have proportionate representation. Such actions call for special attention to racial affiliation.

Proportionate representation by race has also been adopted by some political organizations. Special attention is paid to the race of eligible voters when cities propose to annex surrounding areas. For example, an annexation by Richmond, Virginia, was recently challenged in the courts on the grounds that it brought in so many Euro-Americans that it diluted the black vote.

As we noted previously, the relation of race to behavior is of questionable biological significance. Genetically speaking, races are not fixed, established categories; instead, they are rather arbitrary constructs. And the legal-social designation of race actually used to classify persons into races bears little relationship to biologically constructed categories. Nevertheless, there is a strong emphasis in America at present on the importance of racial pride, racial political power, and cultural differences that are believed to be race related. These emphases are seen in such expressions as "black power," "white society," "Indian self-determination," "Chicano culture," and so forth. In each of these expressions, the focus is on racial difference, along with cultural differences believed to be related to racial experience. A part of this focus comes from organizations of racial minorities established to gain equitable power. To be effective these organizations promote racial solidarity. Another part of the focus derives from a search for individual and group identity. There is a new espousal in America of racial and cultural pluralism, with an accompanying criticism of the accuracy and desirability of America's being a "melting pot" in which various racial and cultural groupings are "blended." This promotion of what has been termed "ethnicity" is an indication of the current emphasis on the importance of recognizing and accepting one's racial identity, as defined by the society, and acknowledging the differences in culture that are thought to be related to racial background. Fields such as Black studies, Indian-American studies, and Mexican-American studies have been instituted in colleges and universities to point up racial and cultural variations and to emphasize the part non-Euro-Americans have played and are playing in American society.

A final example of the present-day emphasis on the importance of race is seen in affirmative action programs required by the federal government in business, industry, higher education, and other areas. These programs are designed to ensure that members of racial minorities are recruited and put into positions of authority and prestige. They require action, not neutrality. Officials must do more than announce a nondiscriminatory policy; they must actively seek out and attract those in racial minorities, and compliance with nondiscrimination laws is judged in terms of the extent to which minority members have actually been added. To fulfill the goals of proportionate representation by race called for by executive orders and guidelines, the racial affiliation of workers, students, and executives has to be carefully noted and reported. As a result of affirmative action programs, there has been an increase in the number of racial minority members admitted to colleges, graduate schools, and training programs, and employed in high wage and high prestige positions. The implementation of certain affirmative action programs has brought the charge that race is being considered as more important than any other attribute, and as a result there is "reverse discrimination," that is, discrimination against those in the majority race category solely because of their race (Epstein and Forster, 1974). Even so, Afro-Americans and other racial minorities continue to be significantly underrepresented in positions of authority and prestige, and to have a significantly lower standard of living than members of the Euro-American majority.

This, then, is a brief description of the sociocultural context within which young American children learn about race. It is a setting in which racial categorization is an important aspect of life, with every person expected to accept and feel positively about his own racial identity, and with persons of all races promised equal treatment. In spite of efforts toward equality, it is a setting in which non-Euro-Americans, generally, are still at a disadvantage economically, politically, and socially, while Euro-Americans, generally, remain in the advantaged position. It is this general sociocultural background that we must keep in mind as we attempt to understand the development of racial concepts and attitudes in young American children.

2.
Color Usages and Evaluative Meanings in Contemporary Culture

The concept of race is inextricably intertwined with color and color symbolism and a proper appreciation of the manner in which young children respond to race and color requires a consideration of the general usages and meanings of colors—particularly the colors white and black—in contemporary adult culture. This discussion of the symbolic usages and affective meanings of colors among adults is intended to provide further background for the interpretation of the research findings with children which will constitute our focus in the remainder of the book.

There are two major ways in which color is implicated in the matter of race. First, there is the unavoidable fact that human beings differ in skin color, and that color differences constitute highly salient stimuli to the visually oriented Homo sapiens. Humans show differential attention to the brightness of stimuli during the first days of life (Hershenson, 1964), and make discriminations on the basis of hue by the age of six months (Fagan, 1974). In this sense, man is naturally "color-conscious" and disposed to attend to color differences. Further, there is evidence suggesting that humans are particularly sensitive to differences along the light-dark color dimension. In terms of the evolution of language, anthropologists have shown that color names representing "white" and "black" (and "red") are found among nonliterate groups who have no other color vocabulary. Related to this is the fact that the color names "white" and "black" are usually found to be the most frequently used color terms in all languages (Hays, Margolis, Naroll, and Perkins, 1972). These findings seem to support the idea that humans are particularly attuned to light-dark color differences such as those found in the variations of human skin tone. Since people find skin-color differences so compelling, they also seem likely to consider them to be "important," and to come to believe that persons who are colored differently must be fundamentally different. In this way, variations in human skin color contribute significantly to the notion of "race." One is almost tempted to believe that if it were not for the variations in human skin color, and the differential geographic distributions of this characteristic, the concept of race might never have been invented.

In addition to skin color, there is another important way in which color is involved in the matter of race, which comes about through the custom of designating racial groups by color names: Euro-Americans are called white people; Afro-Americans are called black; Orientals are called yellow; and Indian-Americans are called red. A moment's reflection will indicate that these designations are inaccurate: the skin color of Euro-Americans is not white but some shade of pinkish-tan; the skin color of Afro-Americans is not black but some shade of brown. Orientals do not have yellow skins, nor do Indian-Americans have red skins. Thus, the "color-coding" of racial groups is quite inaccurate if the color names employed are supposed to be at all descriptive of skin color.

One might argue that the racial color-code was never intended as an accurate physical description and that the practice is warranted because it is more convenient to designate racial groups in this way than it is to employ unwieldy names such as Euro-American, Afro-American, Oriental, etc. This argument contends that the use of white, black, and yellow to designate racial groups is equivalent to calling them X, Y, and Z. We can respond to this by admitting that the color-code *is* convenient, and if the use of color names had no more impact than using X, Y, and Z, there would be no quarrel with the color-coding practice. We will see, however, that color names have many nonracial applications which influence the meanings which they carry into the area of racial designation.

There are two major observations concerning the color-coding practice. First, the use of color names to designate groups of people carries an implicit suggestion that the groups so designated must be different types of people. This can perhaps be traced to the experiential basis of color names. Since the visual perception of white and black are such distinctive experiences, we may assume, quite unconsciously, that persons designated as white are basically different from those designated as black. The same point can be made in the case of the other colors used to code human groups where the distinctive visual experiences of yellow, red, and brown provide the subtle suggestion that the human groups designated by the words must also be different from one another. The color-coding practice thus seems to promote the idea of human races as being fundamentally different types of human beings.

The second major observation concerning the color-coding practice is the real possibility that the use of color names to designate racial groups may influence the way we feel about these groups. As noted above, color names are used in a great variety of situations which have nothing to do with race. If the color words acquire certain affective meanings in their nonracial use, and are then used as labels for groups of people, these nonracial meanings may generalize to the groups and influence the manner in which we respond to them.

Before going on to a consideration of some of the general, or nonracial, meanings of color names, it may be helpful to discuss the phrase "affective meaning" as it will be used in the following remarks. As the word *affective* implies, we are talking about the emotional qualities or feelings which words evoke in us, apart from their denotative or "dictionary" meanings. For example, if we look up the word communist in the dictionary, we will find it defined somewhat as follows: "A person who subscribes to the theory of a social system in which everything is held in common, private property being abolished." What the dictionary does not tell us is that, to the typical American ear, the word communist is a bad word rather than a good word, a strong word rather than a weak word, and an active word rather than a passive word. These latter meanings are affective, or connotative, meanings. If you were told that there was a Communist outside who wanted to speak to you, perhaps you might go to the door saying to yourself, "This person believes that property should be held in common," but you are much more likely to say, "Why does this bad, strong, active person want to talk to me?" The affective meanings of words are important in determining our feelings and behaviors in many situations.

When we speak of an interest in the meanings of color names, we are not interested in their formal, denotative meanings but in the affective meanings which have come to be associated with them. These feeling qualities concern us because they may become associated with a group of people who are designated by a particular color name. If, for example, we find that the color name red carries an affective meaning of strength, while the color name yellow carries a meaning of weakness, we might wonder about the effect of referring to Indian-Americans as "red men," or Orientals as the "yellow race." Do the meanings of the color names generalize to the groups of persons and lead us to feel that Indian-Americans are strong persons, while Orientals are weak? We will attempt to answer this question later in the chapter after we have examined the meanings associated with the color names which we use to designate racial groups. We will proceed first to a general discussion of the ways in which the terms *white* and *black* are employed as cultural symbols, and then we shall consider the results of research studies dealing with the affective meanings of color names.

BLACK AND WHITE
AS GENERAL CULTURAL SYMBOLS

It takes only a few moments' reflection for one to realize that there is a wide variety of situations where white is used to symbolize goodness and black to symbolize badness. This usage can be seen in idiomatic speech, religion and the supernatural, literature, and the mass media.

Idiomatic Speech

Everyday speech abounds with usages of the word black in a manner which implies negative evaluation or "badness." A black mark is an indication of censure or failure; a blacklist is a catalog of undesirable persons; a black sheep is a dissolute member of a respectable family; a black market refers to illegal trade; a blackball is a negative vote or exclusion; blackmail is extortion of money by threat; blackhearted means evil intentioned; a blackened reputation is a ruined one; etc. The negative evaluation associated with black in each of these examples can be seen by the fact that the substitution of the word bad for the word black leaves the meaning of the phrase essentially unchanged. There are, of course, things which are positively valued and happen to be colored black, such as the black ink of the bookkeeper, or the black pearl. It is difficult, however, to think of any nonliteral uses of black that do not carry the negative evaluative meaning. One might think that the recent adoption of the term black as an identity term by some Afro-Americans would constitute an exception to the rule. Surely, if a word is chosen as an identity term, it must carry a positive evaluation. A careful analysis suggests that such was not the case in the choice of black by Afro-Americans. Rather, the word seems to have been chosen because of its strength, and because of its "oppositeness" to white, the majority identity term. This analysis suggests that the use of the slogan "black is beautiful" was not so much a statement of current feelings as a recognition that black must lose its negative meaning and become "beautiful" if it was to function as an effective identity term.

In contrast to the negative use of the word black, the word white is used in idiomatic speech to convey the idea of positive evaluation, as in the phrase, "that's white of you," meaning "that's good of you," and in the designation of a promising person as a "white hope," "white knight," or "fair-haired boy." This usage is especially obvious in the case of something which is otherwise bad, and which we want to make good, as in the case of "a white lie"—a harmless fib—or "whitewash" —to conceal errors or faults. What about the "white flag" or the "white elephant"? These seem to be the counterparts of the black pearl, where something, which happens to be light in color, is associated with a negative situation. In the former case, a light-colored flag is more visible when one wants to surrender. In the latter case, light-colored elephants were considered sacred in India, hence of no practical use and only a financial burden to the person who received one as a gift.

A more extensive list of speech idioms involving the use of white to symbolize goodness and black to symbolize badness has been compiled by John Stabler and Faye

Goldberg (1973). The difficulty of finding bona fide examples of reversed symbolism was demonstrated by the results obtained when Paul Chance (1974) asked the readers of *Psychology Today* to "reverse the bigotry of language." Although the response was enthusiastic, the results were quite meager and consisted largely of expressions which had their origin in the literal usages of the colors (as in black ink and white elephant) and not in their symbolic usages. Generally, then, white is used to signify goodness and black to signify badness in popular speech. These usages contribute to the general language context within which the young child learns to interpret the world in which he lives.

Religion and the Supernatural

The areas of human experience concerned with religion and the supernatural make extensive use of symbolism, and no symbols are more regularly employed than the colors white and black, or light and darkness. In Judeo-Christian religion, the conflict between the powers of good and evil is portrayed as a struggle between the powers of light and the forces of darkness. Angels are conventionally symbolized as white, while Lucifer is known as the prince of darkness. On a more personal level, the wayward soul is urged to repent of his black sins, to be cleansed, and to become as "white as snow." A primitive application of this symbolism is illustrated in an experience of a research associate of one of the authors. While asking a kindergarten director for permission to conduct a study of white-black color meanings with her children, the researcher was surprised to be told by the director that she was certain her children knew the evaluative meanings of white and black. When the puzzled researcher asked how the director could be so confident of this, she was shown a teaching aid called "The Wordless Book." This commercially produced booklet, consisting of several colored pages, was used in religious instruction in this church-related kindergarten. In the use of the booklet, the child was told that the black page represents sin, the red page represents the blood of Jesus, and the white page "stands for our hearts washed clean when God saves us." While the typical child's exposure to the white-black symbolism of Christianity is rarely so specific, the message which he receives if he attends Sunday school and church is probably much the same.

It is not only in the symbols of its formal religions that Western culture employs the black-white symbolism. It can also be seen in other activities dealing with the supernatural, such as the practice of witchcraft and the "black arts." In religious practices centering around the worship of the devil, black is employed as a principal symbol of allegiance to the forces of evil, as in the "black mass" in which the participants attempt to negate and desecrate the symbols of the Catholic mass.

The use of white-black symbolism in religious practice is not confined to Western cultures. Evidence of the same symbolism can be found among many nonwestern groups. With reference to this point, Kenneth Gergen has written:

For the Chiang, a Sino-Tibetan border people, a sacred white stone is a leading feature of worship. The anthropologist studying this culture notes the people's basic tendency to equate white with goodness, and blackness with evil. Among the Mongour, descendants of the Mongols, black is the color of mourning, and white betokens good fortune. The Chuckchees of Siberia utilize black to symbolize the Kelets, or evil spirits. Germaine Dieterlen has observed that for the Bambara, a West African Negro tribe, white is used to symbolize wisdom and purity of the spirit. A piece of white cloth is sometimes hung over the door of a home where the inhabitants have just made a sacrifice; white is also the regal color. The dark tones of indigo, on the other hand, connote obscenity, impurity, and sadness. Black is also identified with the North and the rainy season. Similarly, Negroes of Northern Rhodesia are observed to associate good luck with cleanness and whiteness. A hunter smears a white substance on his forehead to invoke the powers of fortune; a person who has met with disaster is said to be "black on the forehead." In Nigeria, the Nupe tribe represents bleak or frightening prospects, sorcery, or evil by black, while white implies luck and good prospects. The Yorubas, also in Nigeria, wear white when worshiping, as they believe the deities prefer white. Among the Creek Indians of North America, white betokens virtue and age, and black implies death. Although the present examination did reveal irregularities, these were extremely few and limited largely to instances in which white was associated with funeral rites. In short, the major volume of the evidence suggests widespread communality in feelings about black and white (Gergen, 1967, pp. 397–98).

It seems justifiable to conclude, then, that there is a general, cross-cultural tendency toward the symbolization of the supernatural forces of good with the color white, and the forces of evil with the color black. One can wonder what it is about these particular colors which makes them so universally acceptable in this way, and we will consider possible answers to this question in a later chapter. For the moment, let us simply note that in many and perhaps most parts of the world, children are learning religious beliefs and practices in which goodness is symbolized with the color white, and evil with the color black.

Literature

Considering the pervasiveness of the religious symbolism just discussed, and the powerful influence of religion upon literature, it is not surprising to find the white-black symbolism widely employed in literature, both at the adult and children's level. Harold Isaacs, in discussing this point, has written: "The carry-over of the Bible's imagery into the common usage, visible in Chaucer and Milton, is richly illustrated in Shakespeare, whose own impact on the English language has hardly been less great than that of the Bible itself. 'Black is the badge of hell/The hue of the dungeons and the suit of night,' says the King in *Love's Labor's Lost*. . . . In quite another tone, in *Macbeth*, we come on: 'The devil damn thee black—,' again the symbolic joining of sin, the devil and the blackness of skin which runs continuously from Job and the prophets through centuries of our literature" (Isaacs, 1963, p. 76). Harry Levin (1960) in his book *The Power of Blackness* discusses the same symbolism in the works of Hawthorne, Poe, and Melville. Thus, it can be shown that many of the major authors of Western literature make extensive use of white-black symbolism as they attempt to grapple with the problems of good and evil in human existence.

Young children, of course, are rarely exposed to great literature in a direct fashion, and are probably more influenced by the use of the black-white symbolism in children's stories, nursery rhymes, and fables. Harold Isaacs has noted the white-black symbolism to be found in Hugh Lofting's Dr. Dolittle stories which first appeared in 1920.

Dr. Dolittle, an animal doctor who travels with an entourage of a dog, a duck, a pig, an owl, a monkey, and a parrot, goes to Africa to cure monkeys of a plague. Dolittle and his animal helpers become the prisoners of a black king. In the king's garden the parrot and the monkey meet the king's son, Prince Bumpo, who is pictured as an ugly, gnomelike black man with a huge nose that covers most of his face. They hear him yearn aloud: "If only I were a *white* prince!" The parrot promises that Dr. Dolittle will change his color if he helps them escape. To Dr. Dolittle the unhappy prince tells his story:

"Years ago I went in search of The Sleeping Beauty, whom I had read of in a book. And having traveled through the world many days, I at last found her and kissed the lady very gently to wake her—as the book said I should. 'Tis true indeed that she woke. But when she saw my face she cried out, 'Oh, he's black!' And she ran away and wouldn't marry me—but went to sleep again somewhere else. So I came back, full of sadness, to my father's kingdom. Now I hear that you are a wonderful magician and have many powerful potions. So I come to you for help. If you will turn me white, so that I may go back to The Sleeping

Beauty, I will give you half of my kingdom and anything besides you ask" (Isaacs, 1963, p. 79).

The use of the black-white symbolism in more recently published children's stories is often more subtle, but still quite detectable. Consider the following excerpts from Eth Clifford's delightful book, *Red Is Never a Mouse*,* published in 1960:

"Do you know what WHITE is?
WHITE is a lily, or sugar or thread.
WHITE is a cloud floating by overhead.
WHITE is a beard or a bottle of milk.
WHITE is a bride dressed in satins and silk.
WHITE is a ghost or a swan, or the snow,
BUT WHITE IS NEVER, NO NEVER, A CROW!"
"Do you know what BLACK is?
BLACK is the night when the stars are not out.
BLACK is the crow who is flying about.
BLACK is the coal or an ant crawling past.
BLACK is a shoe or a witch's mean laugh.
BUT BLACK IS NEVER, NO NEVER, A GIRAFFE" (Clifford, 1960).

In the foregoing, the ominous quality associated with the color black, in contrast to the color white, is communicated generally through the choice of examples— only the "witch's mean laugh" represents a clear symbolic use of black as bad. The message, however, is probably quite clear to the young listener, particularly when read expressively by an adult who is himself a conveyer of the white-black symbolism.

The Mass Media

Popular journalism abounds with the use of the white-black symbolism. This is understandable, of course, because of the general literary influences upon the

*From *Red Is Never a Mouse* by Eth Clifford, copyright © 1960 by Ethel Rosenberg, reprinted by permission of the publisher, The Bobbs-Merrill Company, Inc.

journalist, and his need to communicate with the masses. The necessity of saying a lot to everyone in a few words makes the use of generally understood symbols a necessity—and no symbolism seems more generally understood than that a white something is a good one, and a black something is a bad one. A well-chosen metaphor is worth a thousand words, and the popular journalist makes extensive use of those which employ the white-black symbolism.

The moving pictures and television use black-white idioms in their dialogue and, in addition, employ the black-white, light-dark, symbolism in their visual effects. The classic formula of the good guy with his white hat fighting the bad guys with their black hats is still alive in the modern "adult" western, where the moviemaker dresses the hero in black and thus titillates his audience with the prospect of the good-bad guy, such as Paladin, the "have gun, will travel" bounty hunter in the television series of the 1960s. The same symbolism is employed, in a more playful form, in television commercials such as those involving the "Dodge Boys" whose status as good guys is presumably validated by the fact that they wear white hats. In the area of children's programming, light and darkness are regularly employed to produce emotional effects. Although Walt Disney inherited some of the symbolism of his movie Snow White from the classic children's story, the visual effects of darkness and black associated with the evil queen and her destructive intent will never be forgotten by those who saw the movie as young children—or even as adults. Such experiences seem likely to provide a strong reinforcement of the link between darkness and negative feelings.

Our discussions of idiomatic speech, religion and the supernatural, literature, and the mass media, have attempted to sketch the ways in which our general culture is permeated with the symbolism of white as good, and black as bad. As noted, this symbolism is not confined to

American or Western culture but is also evident in the East. Faye Goldberg and John Stabler (1973) have made an extensive examination of black and white symbolism in the Japanese language and religion and have concluded that ". . . the associations to black and white found in the West are present in Japan; however, the polarization of these associations is much less, and black and white are more often seen as complementary opposites which exist within an individual and in nature" (p. 42). Faye Goldberg (1973) has also documented the strong dislike of dark skin color among the Japanese—an aversion which is evident in classical Japanese culture which antedates any contact with dark-skinned foreigners or with prejudiced Europeans.

In the next section, we will discuss the findings of our research studies of the affective meanings of colors to young adults. In addition to a careful assessment of the evaluative meanings of black and white, we have been concerned with other important questions. Evaluation is only one—albeit, the primary—dimension of affective meaning, and the colors white and black may differ in potency or activity meanings in ways which are not easily discerned by the anecdotal method. In addition, there is an interest in understanding the affective meanings of the other color names used to "code" groups of people, i.e., red, yellow, and brown. These questions can only be answered by objective research methods which can penetrate the myriad uses of color names and can describe the general affective meanings which the color names have come to possess. Once these meanings are understood, we can raise again the question of the possible effects of using color names to designate groups of human beings.

RESEARCH FINDINGS ON THE
AFFECTIVE MEANINGS OF COLOR NAMES

In this section, we will summarize the findings from our research on the affective meanings of color names. We will first consider studies done in the United States and see whether color meanings vary with geographic region, or with race of the subject. We will also consider whether color meanings have changed in the last few years, during the period of the development of the Black Identity movement among Afro-Americans. We will then consider the question of cross-cultural similarity in color meanings by comparing the research findings from studies of young adults conducted in a variety of different cultural settings. Before turning to the research findings, it may be helpful to explain the research method used in these studies—the semantic differential.

The Semantic Differential

The semantic differential is a sophisticated rating procedure devised by Charles Osgood and his associates at the University of Illinois (Osgood, Suci, and Tannenbaum, 1957). The procedure was developed in order to provide a method for the assessment of the affective meanings of words and other stimuli. In brief, the procedure requires the subject to consider a particular word (e.g., black), and to describe his feelings about the word by choosing an appropriate point along a series of seven-point scales, each of which is defined at the extremes by a pair of opposite adjectives, e.g., good-bad, weak-strong, active-passive. An example of the rating sheet used in most of the research to be described here is shown in Figure 2-1. For purposes of illustration, the rating sheet shows the responses made by a college student who rated the term black. It will be noticed that twelve adjective scales are used in this particular form of

Figure 2-1. Sample Semantic Differential Rating Sheet

BLACK

	1	2	3	4	5	6	7	
unpleasant		X						pleasant
strong		X						weak
good						X		bad
slow		X						fast
foul			X					fragrant
small						X		large
clean					X			dirty
dull			X					sharp
nice			X					awful
active					X			passive
sacred					X			profane
heavy	X							light

the procedure, with six of the scales (the odd-numbered ones) being "evaluation" scales, i.e., unpleasant-pleasant; good-bad; foul-fragrant; clean-dirty; nice-awful; sacred-profane. If we number the blanks on each scale from one to seven, with one always indicating the positive end of the scale and seven the negative end, we can then average the six scores made by a subject and get a score which represents his average evaluation response (or evaluation score) for the concept being rated. In Figure 2-1, the subject's evaluation score was 5.0 indicating a somewhat negative response to the concept black. The remaining six adjective scales are nonevaluation scales with three scales representing the *potency* dimension (strong-weak; small-large; heavy-light) and three representing the *activity* dimension (slow-fast; dull-sharp; active-passive). The subject's potency score is obtained by averaging his ratings on the three potency scales, with a score of one indicating the "weak" end and a score of seven indicating the "strong" end. The subject's activity score is obtained in like manner from the three activity scales, with a score of

Color Usages and Meanings in Contemporary Culture / 47

one representing the "passive" end and a score of seven the "active" end of each scale. For example, the subject in Figure 2-1 received a potency score of 6.0 and an activity score of 3.0 which indicate that he viewed the concept black as quite potent or strong, and somewhat passive. In this way, a subject's evaluation, potency, and activity scores are obtained for the concept he has been asked to rate. If we are interested in the typical response of a group of subjects to a particular concept, we can compute a group mean (average) for the evaluation scores, the potency scores, and the activity scores. Most of the data from the studies which we will describe have been of this sort, i.e., the mean evaluation, potency, and activity scores which were obtained when a particular group of subjects rated familiar color names or other related concepts.

Our review of the research literature deals with the general affective meanings of color names as these are judged in a nonracial context. For example, subjects are asked to express their general feelings about the words white and black with no suggestion that they should respond to these terms in the context of racial designation. The reader needs to keep this fact before him if he is to appreciate the significance of the research findings. Colors and color names are used in many contexts which have nothing to do with race and it is their general affective meanings which we will consider here.

Color Meanings in the United States

The first study was conducted in 1963 using two groups of Euro-American and one group of Afro-American college students (Williams, 1964). The 110 Afro students and a group of 116 Euro students were from universities in North Carolina, while the second group of 70 Euro students was from a university in Kansas. All subjects rated five "race-related" color names (black, white, yellow, red, and brown) and five "non-race-related" color names (blue, green, purple, orange, and gray), presented in a random order, with an experimenter of the same race as the subjects reading the instructions and supervising the general administration of the procedure. The instructions presented the task in a general nonracial context and no mention was made of color as it relates to race.

The first analyses of the data were to determine whether the Euro groups from North Carolina and Kansas were responding differently to the color names. It was found that their responses were highly similar and it was thus shown that the difference in geographic region had no appreciable effect upon the students' responses. This enabled the two Euro groups to be pooled for comparison with the Afro group.

The main findings of the study are shown in Figure 2-2, where the mean race-related color scores obtained in the pooled Euro student group and the Afro student group are displayed. The top portion of the figure shows the evaluation scores, with the potency scores shown in the middle portion, and the activity scores at the bottom. The overall impression from Figure 2-2 is that the Euro and Afro students rated the color names in a highly similar fashion. On the evaluation dimension, both groups rated white most positively, then yellow, red, brown, with black rated most negatively. As the figure suggests, however, the color names black and brown were not rated as negatively by the Afro subjects as they were by the Euro subjects.

On the potency dimension, both groups of subjects rated the color names in the same order, from weakest to strongest: yellow, white, brown, red, and black. The activity ratings again revealed a high agreement between the two groups of subjects, with brown and black being rated somewhat passive, white and yellow as somewhat active, and red as quite active.

The results of the foregoing study were interpreted as

Figure 2-2. Mean Semantic Differential Scores of Euro- and Afro-American College Students for the Race-Related Color Names: White (W), Black (BL), Brown (BR), Red (R) and Yellow (Y) (Williams, 1964)

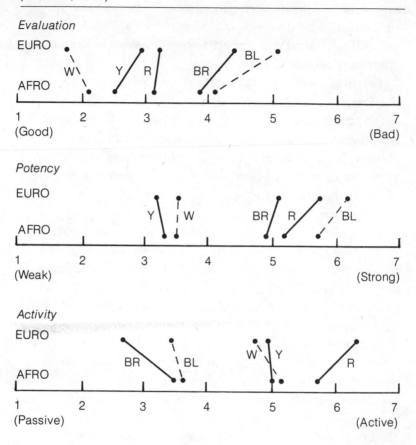

demonstrating several phenomena concerning the affective meaning of color names. First, the different color names evoked widely different affective responses along all three dimensions of meaning. Thus, black was not only more negative in evaluation than white, as expected, but it was also stronger and more passive. Second, the color meanings were shown to be quite similar across both geographical and racial lines, providing strong support for the notion that the affective meanings of colors had been learned via experiences common to most persons in the general American culture.

The study just described was conducted prior to the development of the Black Identity movement as a major force among Afro-Americans. In 1963, it was still uncommon for either Afro-Americans or others to use the word black to designate members of this racial group. During the middle and late 1960s, however, there was a rather dramatic change in the willingness of Afro-Americans to be designated as "black." The dynamics of this change have been described as follows:

Under the impetus of a heightened need for a sense of racial identity, and following the lead of the Black Muslim movement of the early 1960s, a new racial identity movement developed, with the designation black used as a rallying point. This choice of the term black in preference to others (e.g., Afro-American) seems due, at least in part, to its being opposite to the name (white) by which the majority group was designated, thus making it particularly effective as an identity term. Serving to counteract the "bad" and "passive" connotations of black were such slogans as "Black is Beautiful" and "Black Power." In this way, the term black has become acceptable to many Negro Americans and is often preferred to the term Negro, which is viewed as old fashioned, at best, and insulting, at worst. In addition to the acceptance of black, the rhetoric of the new identity movement involved a rejection of "whiteness," which was associated with the general culture and with the oppression of Negro persons" (Williams, Tucker, and Dunham, 1971, p. 223).

In order to assess possible changes in the general affective meanings of black and white occurring during the middle and late 1960s, a study using the same general procedure was conducted in 1969 (Williams, Tucker, and Dunham, 1971). The subjects in this study were 99 Euro and 239 Afro students from two universities in North Carolina. For Euro students, there was no change in the affective meanings of white, black, or any other color name; thus, the 1969 findings were essentially the same as those shown for the 1963 Euro group in Figure 2-2.

Figure 2-3. Mean Semantic Differential Scores of Afro-American College Students for the Race-Related Color Names: White (W), Black (BL), Brown (BR), Red (R), and Yellow (Y) (Williams, Tucker, and Dunham, 1971)

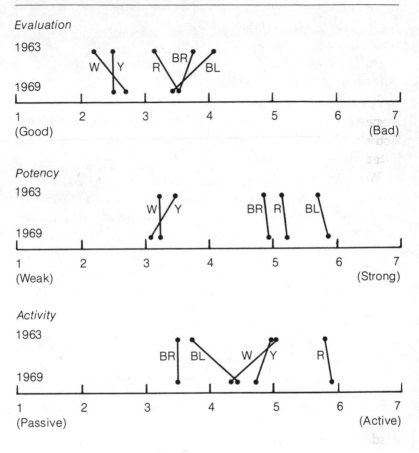

For Afro students, there were some changes in color meanings from 1963 to 1969. Figure 2-3 shows the mean race-related color scores for the 1963 and 1969 Afro subjects. On the evaluation dimension, it was found that white had become less good, and black had become more good, across the time interval studied; however, white was still rated more positively than black by the 1969 group. Regarding activity, black was found to have become more active and white less active so that there was no longer any difference in activity meanings for the two color words. There were no changes in the potency meanings across the time interval—black remained quite strong, and white remained somewhat weak. The observed changes in the meanings of black and white were even more pronounced when the 1969 Afro students were categorized according to their degree of identification with black separatism. Among those students identified as high separatist, the evaluation difference between black and white disappeared, with both colors rated moderately positive. The activity change was even more dramatic with black being rated more active than white.

While there has been no study of black and white color meanings among Afro-American college students since 1969, studies conducted with Afro high school students in 1972 and 1973 indicated that black was being rated more positively than white, although both color names were still rated positively in absolute terms. These high school findings, which we will discuss in greater detail in chapter 3, suggest that the trend seen in the Afro college student data between 1963 and 1969 has continued, and that the color name black has assumed a positive meaning among young-adult Afro-Americans.

We interpret the findings of the studies just reviewed to indicate that the Black Identity movement has had an impact on black and white color meanings among Afro students but not among Euro students. Thus, it can be seen that the meanings of black and white are dependent not only on general cultural factors, but also on the particular use—and significance of that use—among certain groups of persons.

Color Meanings Outside the United States

Are the color meanings that we have observed among American students specific to American culture, or Western culture? Or can they also be demonstrated among non-Western groups? The study which we designed to answer this question employed data obtained from groups of university students in Germany, Denmark, Hong Kong, and India (Williams, Morland, and Underwood, 1970). For the first three groups, the semantic differential was translated into German, Danish, and Chinese, respectively. For the Indian group, we used the regular English language version, as English is the language of Indian university students. All subjects rated the usual five race-related and five nonrace-related color names, presented in random order. Scores for the two American groups (Euro and Afro) from the 1963 study were included for comparative purposes.* For each of the six subject groups, mean evaluation, potency, and activity scores were computed for each of the ten colors. When the data were analyzed, a high degree of similarity was found in the order in which the ten color names fell along each of the three affective meaning dimensions. Thus, there was a high degree of cross-cultural agreement as to which colors were relatively good and which were relatively bad, which were weak and which were strong, and which were passive and which were active.

The mean evaluation scores for the German, Danish, Chinese, and Indian groups for the five race-related color names can be seen in Figure 2-4, together with the more recently obtained mean scores of English-speaking college students in Thailand and the Philippines. An examination of the scores in Figure 2-4 indicates that all groups rated white as quite positive, while black was rated from neutral to moderately negative.

Frances Adams and Charles Osgood (1973) have recently published a landmark study of the affective meanings of seven color names in 23 different language-culture groups in Europe, Asia, and the Americas. Among the color names rated were the four "race-related" color names: white, red, yellow, and black. When the evaluative meanings of these color names were averaged across all 23

*This cross-cultural study was conducted prior to the 1969 study noted above.

Figure 2-4. Mean Evaluation Scores Obtained from Seven Groups of College Students for the Color Names White (W), Yellow (Y), Red (R), Brown (BR), and Black (BL)

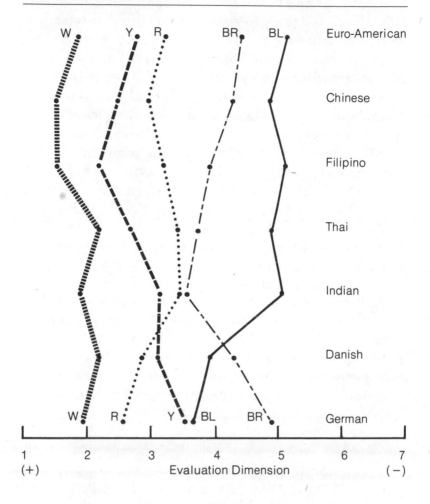

cultures, it was found that white was rated most positively, and black was rated most negatively, with red and yellow occupying intermediate positions. When the cultures were considered individually, white was evaluated more positively than black in all 23, and black was rated most negatively of all 4 race-related colors in 21 of the 23 groups. With regard to the affective meaning dimensions of potency and activity, white was generally found to be "weak" and "active," while black was found to be "strong" and "passive." In addition, among all colors rated, black had the lowest average "cultural instability" score, i.e., it had the most consistently agreed upon meaning among the individual persons within each cultural group. In summarizing their findings, the authors concluded that "there are strong universal trends in the attribution of affect in the color domain" and they speculated that the tendency to evaluate white more positively than black may be due to the common experiences of humans in all cultural settings where ". . . clean, light-colored things, and (for a diurnal animal) lightness is more benevolent than darkness" (p.135, p.151).

The cross-cultural findings regarding the evaluative meanings of white and black are remarkably consistent in view of the cultural diversity in the groups studied. That such diverse groups respond to white and black in a similar fashion suggests the operation of some broad pan-cultural influences on the development of these color meanings. In chapter 10, we will propose a theoretical explanation for this finding in terms of the diurnal nature of Homo sapiens and a tendency to develop aversive responses to the dark of night.

RESEARCH FINDINGS ON THE COLOR-CODING OF RACIAL GROUPS

We are all familiar with the language usage which designates racial groups by a color-code in which Euro-Americans are called white, Afro-Americans are referred to as black, and the color names yellow, red, and brown are used to designate Orientals, Indian-Americans, and Southeast Asians, respectively. Having seen the different affective meanings which these color names possess, we can now raise the question of the possible influence of the color-coding practice upon the way persons respond to racial groups. We have conducted a number of studies with young adults which provide evidence on this point.

If the color name by which a racial group is designated acts to influence our affective response to the group, we should find some similarity between our affective responses to the group and our affective responses to the associated color name. This proposition was tested (Williams, 1966) by using three research groups: the first group rated the five race-related color names; the second group rated five "color-person" concepts (white person, black person, red person, yellow person, brown person); and the third group rated five ethnic concepts (Caucasian, Negro, American Indian, Oriental, Asiatic Indian). It is obvious that some of these concepts are linked by the color-coding practice, and some are not. For example, the concepts white, white-person, and Caucasian are associated concepts and we might expect to find some meaning similarity among them. The same could be said for: black, black-person, and Negro; for yellow, yellow-person, and Oriental; for red, red-person, and American Indian; and for brown, brown-person, and Asiatic Indian. On the other hand, no meaning similarity would be expected in clusters of concepts which are not linked by the color-code (e.g., white, black-person, Oriental; or black, red-person, Caucasian). When the data for the Euro-American subjects were analyzed in this way, it was found that the meaning similarity among the clusters of color-code-linked concepts was much greater than among the clusters of concepts not linked by the color-code. In other words, how the subjects felt about the color-person and ethnic concepts could be predicted to a substantial degree from their feelings about the associated color names. This was particularly true on the evaluation dimension where the order of the color names was the usual white, yellow, red, brown, black; the order of the color-person concepts was white person, yellow and red persons (tie), brown person, black person; and the order of the ethnic concepts was Caucasian, Oriental and American Indian (tie), Asiatic Indian, and Negro. Thus, the evaluative meanings of the color-person and ethnic concepts were as one would predict from a knowledge of the evaluative meanings of the associated color names. This study, which was done in 1963, also included groups of Afro-American subjects who generally agreed with the Euro-American subjects' ratings of color names, but showed marked differences in their ratings of color-person and ethnic concepts. For example, they rated the concept Negro more positively than the concept Caucasian, and the concept brown person more positively than the concept white person. Thus, the hypothesis that the color-coding of racial groups influenced the way the groups were perceived was supported only among the Euro-American subjects. Some evidence of cross-cultural generality of the Euro-American findings has been shown by the replication of the color-coding effect among German university students who are also "Caucasian" (Williams and Carter, 1967).

When the American study just described was repeated with Euro-American subjects in 1970 (Williams, Best, Wood, and Filler, 1973), the same general findings were obtained, e.g., the order of the color-person and ethnic concepts along the evaluative dimension was predictable from the evaluative meanings of the associated color names. In addition, it was shown that, while the meanings of the color names and ethnic concepts had not changed from 1963 to 1970, the 1970 color-person concepts were more closely identified with their respective ethnic concepts than had been the case in 1963. This result suggested that the effect of the Black Identity movement on Euro-American students had been to create a greater equivalency between white person and Caucasian, and black person and Negro, without altering their feelings about the ethnic concepts themselves. Taken together, the results for the Euro students in the two studies were clearly consistent with the hypothesis that the affective meanings of color names tend to generalize to the racial groups with which they are associated.

The findings just described suggested that when we associate the color name white with something, we come to view it more positively, and when we associate the color name black with something, we come to view it more negatively. This proposition has been tested in two experimental studies which have the advantage of permitting the assessment of cause-effect relationships in a manner not possible in correlational studies of the type which we have been considering. In the first experimental study (Harbin and Williams, 1966) each of ten color names was associated with one of ten "nonsense syllables" in what is known as a paired-associate learning task. The subject's task was to learn which color name was associated with which nonsense syllable so that when the color name (e.g., "white") was presented to him he was able to give the associated nonsense syllable (e.g., KAZ). After the subject had learned the associations, he then rated each nonsense syllable on the semantic differential. The analyses of these data indicated that the evaluative ratings of the nonsense syllables showed a significant correlation with the evaluative ratings of the associated color names so that, for example, the syllables which had been associated with white were rated more positively than the syllables associated with black. Thus, it appeared that the evaluative meanings of the words white and black had, in part, transferred to the associated syllables.

In the second experimental study (Filler and Williams, 1970) the paired-associate method was used once again with each of the five race-related color names being associated with a drawing of a different human figure. When the human figures were subsequently rated on the semantic differential, it was found that the rank order of the evaluative ratings of the figures was identical to that of the color names with which they had been associated, e.g., the human figures were rated most positively when they had been associated with white and least positively when they had been associated with black. Thus, the evidence from the two experimental studies provides additional support for the theory that the systematic association of color names with groups of persons may condition the affective meanings of the former to the latter. In this way, the color coding of racial groups may serve as one of the many determinants of racial attitudes.

RESEARCH FINDINGS CONCERNING THE RELATION OF COLOR NAMES TO COLOR HUES

Important to an understanding of color concepts and attitudes is the relationship between color names and the actual colors which they represent or, in more technical terms, between the *signs* and the *significates* in the area of color meaning.* All of the color research findings discussed above have dealt with the affective meaning of color *words*, not of colors themselves, and we must ask how similar the responses are to these two different types of stimuli. This question was examined in a study of Euro-American college students (Williams and Foley, 1968) in which one group of subjects rated ten color names on the semantic differential, while a second group rated ten color patches each of which was placed at the top of a rating sheet. The results of the study were quite clear; the affective meanings associated with the color patches were highly similar to the meanings associated with the corresponding color names, along all three meaning dimensions. For example, consider the following evalua-

*We are indebted to Robert C. Beck for his insistence on the importance of exploring this relationship.

tion scores for the five race-related color names, with the evaluation scores for the corresponding color patches given in the parentheses: White, 1.91 (2.00); Yellow, 2.56 (2.44); Red, 3.49 (3.10); Brown, 4.57 (4.84); Black, 5.42 (5.04). The high degree of affective meaning similarity for color hues and corresponding color names suggests that in many situations one may be able to interchange color signs and color significates with the assurance that the meanings of the two types of stimuli are essentially the same. This conclusion provides a useful bridge between our young adult studies and our studies of preschool children, in which we have assessed evaluative responses to figures colored black and white.

Our review of the evaluative meanings of colors and the use of color names to designate groups of persons provides a background for an examination of color and racial attitudes in young children. This, then, is the general cultural scene—the "colorful" world, in the midst of which young children develop their conceptions of the meanings of color names, and their attitudes toward groups of persons who differ in skin color and in the color names by which they are designated.

3.
Attitudes Toward the Colors Black and White

The pervasive use of white and black as cultural symbols, and the evidence among young adults of a tendency toward the positive evaluation of white, and negative evaluation of black, lead naturally to questions concerning the childhood development of this tendency. As we review the studies in this chapter, we shall see that there is a general similarity in the evaluative responses of young adults and preschool children to these colors. Although it may seem "obvious" from this that the preschooler has already learned the conventional evaluative meanings of black and white as a result of contact with the symbols of the adult culture, there are other logical possibilities to be considered. Perhaps the pro-white/ anti-black bias of preschool children is a reflection of a pro-light/anti-dark bias which is learned in very early childhood as a result of experiences with the light of day and the dark of night. In this case, the cultural symbols and the color evaluations of adults could be seen as a continuation and elaboration of shared feelings from childhood, constituting a result, not a cause, of the preschooler's pro-white/anti-black bias. And, of course, there is the possibility that an adequate explanation may require a joint consideration of both early experience and cultural learning in which an initial bias established on the basis of early personal experiences is further shaped and conceptualized as a result of cultural influences. As we review the research findings, we will make occasional reference to these possible explanations and will return to give careful attention to this matter in chapters 9 and 10.

In reviewing the studies of white-black color attitudes in young children, our attention will be directed first, and primarily, at children in the kindergarten and early school years with whom the preponderance of research has been conducted. After considering the findings regarding color bias at this age level, we will review the much more limited evidence on this topic among younger children at the two- and three-year-old level. Finally, we will describe the findings of some studies at the junior and senior high school level which provide a bridge between the color meaning findings among young children and among young adults.

A word of caution is advisable. The studies in this chapter tell us how children respond to the *colors* black and white presented in a nonracial context. We must take these data at face value and not leap to the conclusion that the children are trying to tell us something about their racial attitudes toward "white" and "black" people. The question of the relationship of black and white color meanings to racial attitudes is an important one which we can attempt to answer only if we proceed carefully and conservatively as we interpret the test behaviors which the children demonstrate.

COLOR ATTITUDES IN THE PRESCHOOL AND EARLY SCHOOL YEARS

The majority of the studies which we will review have employed a procedure known as the Color Meaning Test, designated CMT. The CMT is an outgrowth of a technique first developed by Cheryl Renninger Minton

(Renninger and Williams, 1966) in order to assess the evaluative meanings associated with the colors black and white by children who are not yet capable of taking a pencil and paper test. The initial 12-item form of the test—designated CMT I—was originally described by Williams and Roberson (1967); the revised 24-item form—CMT II—has been described by Williams, Boswell, and Best (1975) and is also described in detail in Appendix B.

In the CMT procedure, the child is presented with a picture which displays drawings of two animals, one colored white and one colored black but otherwise identical. The child is then told a story in which an evaluative adjective is used, and is asked to indicate which animal is the one described in the story. The following are two sample stories: (1) "Here are two lambs. One of them is a good lamb. She does what her mother tells her to. Which is the good lamb?" (2) "Here are two cats. One of them is a bad cat and scratches on the furniture. Which is the bad cat?" In each case, the child chooses the white or the black animal in response to the examiner's question.

In CMT I, a total of twenty-four stories are told, twelve of which are nonscored "filler" items, and twelve of which involve black and white animals and evaluative adjectives. Of the twelve evaluative adjectives used, six are positive evaluative adjectives (good, clean, nice, pretty, smart, kind); and six are negative evaluative adjectives (bad, dirty, naughty, ugly, stupid, mean). Six animal pictures are used: horses, dogs, kittens, rabbits, cows, and teddy bears. Each of the pictures is used twice in the procedure with a different adjective of the opposite evaluative type being used the second time. CMT I, thus, gives the child twelve response opportunities, which are scored by counting one point for selecting the white animal when a positive adjective is used, and counting one point for selecting the black when a negative adjective is used. The scores range from 0–12, with high scores indicating a consistent tendency to associate the white figure with the good words and the black figure with the bad words (i.e., W+/B−). A low score would indicate the reverse, that is, a consistent tendency to associate white with negative words and black with positive words (B+/W−). A score in the midrange of the scale (around 6) indicates that the child shows no consistent choice in response to the positive and negative words. Statistically speaking, whenever a child obtains a score of 9 or up, he is demonstrating a significant tendency toward W+/B− bias; conversely, a score of 3 or down shows a significant tendency toward a B+/W− bias.

In the revised version of the Color Meaning Test, CMT II, the nonscored filler items have been eliminated and the number of evaluative adjectives has been doubled by the addition of six more positive adjectives—friendly, happy, healthy, helpful, right, and wonderful—and six more negative adjectives—cruel, sad, selfish, sick, unfriendly, and wrong. The number of animal pictures has also been increased from six to twelve by the addition of ducks, pigs, chicks, mice, sheep, and squirrels, with each picture again being used twice. The 0–24 score range of CMT II allows for a more sensitive assessment of individual differences than does the 0–12 score range of CMT I. On CMT II, a score of 17 or higher (i.e., 17–24) is indicative of a significant degree of W+/B− bias; a score of 7 or lower (i.e., 0–7) is indicative of a significant degree of B+/W− bias; and scores around 12 represent an unbiased performance. CMT II was designed so that, when desired, the 24-item procedure can be divided into two equivalent 12-item short forms known as series A and series B. In the CMT II standardization study, described below, the correlation between scores on the two short forms was found to be .46, which enables us to estimate the internal consistency reliability of the total 24-item scale at about .63. While not as high as one could wish, the finding indicates that about two-thirds of the variability in CMT II scores is due to individual differences in color bias, and about one-third to various chance factors.

Before proceeding to our discussion of color attitudes as assessed by the CMT procedures, we need to comment on a major point concerning the interpretation of CMT scores. CMT is a forced-choice procedure which requires the child to make a response to each of the picture-story presentations. If the story contains a positive adjective, the child must choose either the white or black animal; if the story contains a negative adjective, the child must again choose. Under these conditions, the child's responses indicate his *relative* evaluation of the white and black animals, not his absolute evaluation. When a child obtains a high CMT score, he indicates that white is evaluated more positively than black, and not necessarily that black is evaluated negatively, in absolute terms. This characteristic of the forced-choice procedure is examined in more detail in our consideration of methodological issues in Appendix A.

Proceeding to a discussion of the research studies in which CMT I and II, and certain other research procedures, have been employed to assess the evaluative meanings of the colors white and black to young children, we will first consider the findings among Euro-American children, and then among Afro-American children. To reduce confusion as we move back and forth between the two versions of CMT, the reader may find it helpful to remember that CMT II is twice as long as CMT I, so that if CMT I scores are doubled they are generally equivalent to CMT II scores.

Color Attitudes Among Euro-American Children

The first study employing CMT I (Williams and Roberson, 1967) was conducted in North Carolina in 1966 and involved 111 Euro preschoolers with a mean age of five years, four months (5-4) who were tested by female Euro examiners. The mean CMT I score in this group was 10.0, with 74% of the children showing evidence of

W+/B— bias (scores of 9–12), 24% scoring in the unbiased (4–8) range, and only 2% scoring in the B+/W— range (0–3). Although it is obvious from the high mean score that the children were choosing the white and black animals in a consistent manner, it is interesting to examine the children's responses to the individual positive and negative adjectives. The results of these analyses are displayed in Table 3-1, where it can be seen that the frequency of choice of the white figure to the six positive adjectives ranged from 75.7% to 87.4%, while the black figure was chosen in response to negative adjectives from 82.9% to 90.1% of the time. Thus, we can see that the two sets of adjectives functioned as groups, with little variation among the adjectives comprising a particular group. Considering the wide variation in denotative meaning within each group of adjectives, the data provide impressive evidence of a broadly generalized tendency to associate white with "goodness," and black with "badness," on the part of these preschool children.

Table 3-1. Percent of 111 Ss Responding to Adjectives by Indicating White or Black Figure on the Color Meaning Procedure (Williams and Roberson, 1967)

Evaluative Adjective	Figure Chosen	
	% White	% Black
Pretty	87.4	12.6
Clean	84.7	15.3
Nice	83.8	16.2
Smart	82.0	18.0
Good	81.1	18.9
Kind	75.7	24.3
Ugly	17.1	82.9
Dirty	16.2	83.8
Naughty	18.0	82.0
Stupid	18.0	82.0
Bad	15.3	84.7
Mean	9.9	90.1

The mean CMT I score for the 111 children in the study just described is shown as the first entry in Table 3-2 in which are also shown the mean scores obtained in other CMT I studies of Euro children. For each group, the table lists the average age, the race of the examiner, and the state and year in which the study was conducted.

Several observations can be made concerning the data seen in Table 3-2. First, all mean scores are on the high side of the 0–12 score range and, thus, indicate a tendency toward W+/B− bias in all groups. Second, there is no consistent evidence that the degree of W+/B− bias is related to region of the country—the mean scores of children from Ohio and New York are quite similar to those of the North Carolina groups, although the Illinois group is somewhat lower. Third, there is no consistent evidence of any age trend in the data—the mean score of 10.2 in Tse's group of four-year-olds is not appreciably different from the mean score of 9.8 in Skinto's group of seven-year-olds. Fourth, the lower scores seen in the Figura study, where both Euro and Afro examiners were employed, suggest a possible race of examiner effect. We

Table 3-2. Mean CMT I Scores in Various Studies of Euro-American Children

Investigator(s)	N	Av. Age	Race of E	State-Year	Mean CM
Williams and Roberson (1967)	111	5–4	Euro	N.C. ('66)	10.0
Williams and Edwards (1969)	84	5–6	Euro	N.C. ('67)	9.2
Skinto (1969)	28	7–6	Euro	W. Va. ('69)	9.8
Keller, K. S.*	24	5–9	Euro	Ohio ('70)	10.2
Figura (1971)	23	5–0	Mixed	Ill. ('71)	8.3
Tse, M.*	30	4–4	Euro	N.Y. ('71)	10.2

(Mean of Means = 9.6)

*Throughout the book, studies without a formal citation are unpublished investigations conducted under the sponsorship of the authors.

should note another interesting finding from the Skinto study—the CMT I scores of her first and second grade subjects were not significantly correlated with IQ, as measured by the Peabody Picture Vocabulary Test. This finding, and the evidence of minimal correlation of CMT I scores with age, have important theoretical implications which we will examine in chapter 9.

We will now consider studies conducted with CMT II. The first data are from the CMT II standardization study conducted in 1972 and 1973 in Winston-Salem, North Carolina (Williams, Boswell, and Best, 1975), in which 160 Euro preschoolers were administered CMT II and the Peabody Picture Vocabulary Test. The children ranged in age from three years, four months (3-4) to seven years, one month (7-1),* with a mean age of five years, one month (5-1). Half the children were male and half female. Half of the children in each sex group were administered the procedure by Euro examiners, and half by Afro examiners. Analyses indicated that neither the sex of subject nor race of examiner variable had a significant effect on CMT II scores. In the latter case, the 80 subjects with Euro examiners obtained a mean score of 17.3 while the 80 subjects with Afro examiners had a mean of 16.9.

The frequency distribution of CMT II scores for all 160 Euro subjects is shown in Figure 3-1 where it can be seen that the scores fell into a reasonably symmetrical distribution centering toward the high or W+/B− end of the scale. In Table 3-3, the scores of the children have been classified into the following categories: 0–7, Definite B+/W− bias; 8–9, Probable B+/W− bias; 10–14, No bias; 15–16, Probable W+/B− bias, and 17–24, Definite W+/B− bias. An examination of the findings seen in Table 3-3 indicates that they are generally consistent with the findings of the CMT I studies. The large majority of these Euro subjects showed at least probable evidence of a

*The oldest children were enrolled in a postkindergarten, school-readiness class. None had yet entered the first grade.

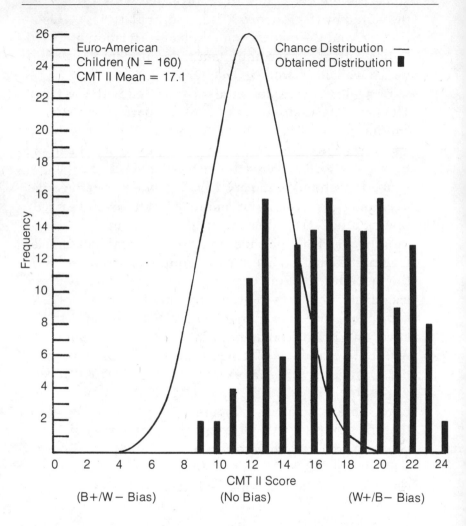

Figure 3-1. Frequency Distribution of Color Attitude Scores for 160 Euro-American Preschoolers in CMT II Standardization Study (Williams, Boswell, and Best, 1975)

W+/B− bias with 74% of the subjects obtaining scores of 15 or above while only 24% obtained scores in the nonbiased (10–14) range. It can also be noted that only 2 of the 160 children tested showed any evidence of B+/W− bias and these both scored in the probable rather than definite score range.

Table 3-3. Number and Percent of CMT II Scores of 160 Euro-American Preschool Children Falling into Each of Five Categories (Williams, Boswell, and Best, 1975)

Score Range	Category	Number	Percent	Chance Expectancy (%)
0–7	Definite B+/W− bias	0	0	3.3
8–9	Probable B+/W− bias	2	1.2	12.1
10–14	No bias	39	24.4	69.2
15–16	Probable W+/B− bias	27	16.9	12.1
17–24	Definite W+/B− bias	92	57.5	3.3

Table 3-4. Mean CMT II Scores of Euro-American Children Tested by Euro-American Examiners in Various Studies

Investigators	N	Av. Age	State-Year	Mean CMT II Score
Williams, Boswell, and Best (1975)	160	5–1	N.C. ('73)	17.1
Collins (1972)	60	5–0	Tenn. ('72)	17.6
Graves, D. J.*	60	5–8	N.C. ('72)	18.7
Shanahan (1972)	14	6–7	Wash. ('72)	18.5
Traynham (1974)	20	5–6	Ark. ('73)	18.5
Traynham (1974)	20	8–6	Ark. ('73)	17.3
Boswell (1974)	50	5–7	N.C. ('73)	18.7
Young, B.*	23	4–6	Ontario, Can. ('74)	16.3 (est.)†

*Unpublished studies.
†Young administered only half of CMT II and obtained a mean of 8.15.

The general picture of a high degree of W+/B− bias among Euro-American children has been confirmed by several additional CMT II studies. These are summarized in Table 3-4 which lists the average age of the children, the place and year of the testing, and the mean CMT II score obtained. It can be observed that the mean CMT II scores were remarkably consistent in spite of the variations in age and geographic locality.

It is interesting to note that CMT II scores of the 160 Euro children in the standardization group were found to correlate only .11 with vocabulary IQ, and only .20 with chronological age. These low correlations indicate that there was little tendency for the brighter children to score higher than the duller children, or for the older children to score higher than the younger children. These findings are of considerable theoretical import, because they cast doubt on the idea that the W+/B− tendency is learned as a simple result of the child's contact with the black-white symbolism of the general culture.

The evidence of the development of the W+/B− concept discussed thus far has been obtained in studies using the method of the Color Meaning Test. It is always desirable to be able to demonstrate a phenomenon by more than one research method, since this establishes the generality of the phenomenon and demonstrates that one's evidence is not somehow a function of a particular methodology. John Stabler and his associates have also been interested in the W+/B− phenomenon in young children, but have approached its assessment *via* several different routes. These researchers first had preschool Euro children sort a number of small objects to determine which of the objects were positively evaluated and which were negatively evaluated; thus, a lollipop, a toy watch, a balloon, a nickel, etc., were found to be "good" objects; and a rubber snake, a plastic skull, a spider, a cigarette butt, etc., were found to be "bad" objects. Having thus "scaled" the objects for their evaluative associations, the researchers then tested the hypothesis that good objects would tend to be associated with white, and bad objects with black. This was done by placing each object before the child, showing him a white box and a black box, and asking him which box contained a duplicate of the object placed before him. The results of the study showed that the preschoolers tended to say that the good objects were in the white box, and the bad objects in the black box (Stabler, Johnson, Berke, and Baker, 1969).

Another method employed by Stabler and his associates involves the use of two "talking boxes," one colored white, the other black, which are in fact speaker enclosures attached to a tape recorder. The child is trained for the task by first having it demonstrated that each of the boxes can "talk," and that the child can discriminate from which box the voice is coming. Following this training, the child is asked to indicate whether it is the white or black box which is making each of a series of statements when, actually, the sound is being emitted from both speakers with equal intensity. The statements read through the speakers reflected either a positive "self concept" (e.g., "I am good," "I am nice," "I am smart") or a negative "self concept" (e.g., "I am stupid," "I am mean," "I am sad"). When the procedure was employed with a group of Euro preschoolers (median age = 5-9), it was found that the positive statements were more frequently attributed to the white box, while the negative statements were more frequently attributed to the black box (Stabler, Johnson, and Jordan, 1971). An extension of this experiment, in which such recorded statements as "You are good," "You are nice," "You are smart," etc., or "You are stupid," "You are mean," "You are sad," etc., were broadcast, yielded similar results: i.e., the children reported hearing positive statements originate from the white box and negative statements originate from the black box (Hepler, 1974). In still another study, Stabler had preschool Euro children choose which of three boxes they thought contained a prize for them: a white box, a black box, or a "neutral" colored (orange or green) box. The results indicated that 60% of the children chose the white box, 30% chose the neutral box, and only 10% chose the black box.

The methodological ingenuity of Stabler and his associates is also seen in a field study method employed with elementary school children on the school playground. Stabler provided the children with plastic bats and gave them the opportunity to hit black and white Bobo dolls, or black and white cardboard boxes. The behavior of the children was filmed and later scored with regard to the frequency with which the children attacked the white and black targets. Using this technique, it was found that Euro children tended to hit the black objects first, and to destroy the black boxes first. The findings of this study are important because of the suggested link between negative evaluation and aggression, i.e., there appears to be less constraint against aggression toward the "bad" colored black objects, than the "good" colored white objects (Stabler and Johnson, 1972).

In sum, the Stabler studies add much to our knowledge of the responses of Euro-American children to the colors black and white. When Stabler's findings are combined with those from the Color Meaning Test studies, there is an impressive array of evidence of a pervasive tendency toward positive responses to the color white and negative responses to the color black among young Euro children.

Color Attitudes Among Afro-American Children

In beginning our examination of the evaluative responses of Afro-American children to the colors black and white, it may be well to repeat our earlier warning: the responses of Afro children to the colors black and white are just that—and should not be assumed to have any relevance to race until such has been demonstrated. We must not let ourselves be led into an intellectual racism which insists that the response of Afro-American children must be telling us something of racial significance. We must let the findings speak for themselves and later determine what, if any, bearing the findings have on the matter of racial bias or self concept development among Afro children.

The first investigation to be summarized here was conducted in North Carolina in 1970 (Williams and

Rousseau, 1971). This was a CMT I study involving 89 Afro-American children with a mean age of 5-2 who were tested by young Euro-American women. In addition to CMT I, each child was also given the Peabody Picture Vocabulary Test (PPVT), and an interview procedure which examined the child's ability to name the colors black and white, and his tendency to identify personally with the black and white animals used in the test procedure. The mean CMT I score was found to be 8.9, with 64% of the children displaying W+/B− bias (scores 9–12), 3% showing B+/W− bias (scores 0–3), and 33% being unbiased (scores 4–8).

An analysis of the responses of the 89 subjects to the individual positive and negative adjectives yielded the results in Table 3-5 where it can be seen that the children responded to the adjectives in the same general manner as the Euro preschoolers described earlier, i.e., a majority chose the white animal in response to positive adjectives and the black animal in response to negative adjectives. The only nondiscriminating adjective was "kind," which

Table 3-5. Percent of 89 Afro Subjects Responding to Positive and Negative Evaluative Adjectives on Color Meaning Procedure by Indicating White or Black Figure   (Williams and Rosseau, 1971)

	% White	% Black
Positive Evaluative Adjectives		
Pretty	77.5	22.5
Clean	85.4	14.6
Nice	85.4	14.6
Smart	64.0	36.0
Good	75.3	24.7
Kind	51.7	48.3
Negative Evaluative Adjectives		
Ugly	29.2	70.8
Dirty	22.5	77.5
Naughty	32.6	67.4
Stupid	23.6	76.4
Bad	19.1	80.9
Mean	25.8	74.2

the children associated with the white and black figures with about equal frequency.

Several other findings from this study are noteworthy. When the CMT I scores were correlated with IQ scores from the Peabody Picture Vocabulary Test, no relationship was found; thus, the individual differences in color meaning scores were not related to individual differences in intellectual ability, measured in this way. The color identification procedure demonstrated that the children were quite accurate in picking the black and the white animal when asked to do so, indicating that they were aware of the color names associated with the animal figures. In the self-identification procedure, the examiner said to the child, "You are a little boy (girl) but let's make believe you are one of these two doggies. Which doggie are you?" with six such questions being asked. It was found that, in general, the white figure was chosen more frequently than the black figure. Of the 89 children, 27 made a consistent choice of the white animal on all six trials, while only 6 children made a consistent choice of the black animal. It was also found that the tendency to iden-tify with the white animal was positively related to CMT I scores, i.e., children with the strongest W+/B− bias showed the greatest tendency to identify with the white figure. Overall, the results of the study just described indicated that the Afro children tended to evaluate the colors white and black in a manner generally similar to Euro children, with a majority showing clear evidence of W+/B− bias. On the other hand, the degree of bias appeared to be somewhat less than that found among Euro children of comparable age.

One question not dealt with in the previous study was the possible influence of the race of the Euro examiners upon the responses of the Afro subjects. This variable was studied in an investigation conducted in South Carolina in 1970 by Jacqueline Vocke (1971). In the Vocke study, 90 Afro children, mean age 5-5, were administered CMT I:

for half of the children, the examiner was a Euro woman, and for the other half, an Afro woman. Among the children tested by the Euro examiner, the mean CMT I score was 9.4 with 62% showing W+/B— bias, and 2% showing B+/W— bias. Among the children tested by the Afro examiner, the mean CMT I score was 8.4, with 53% showing W+/B— bias, and 4% showing B+/W— bias. While the one point difference in the CMT I means was statistically significant, the high percent of W+/B— bias in both examiner groups indicated that race of examiner was not a variable of major consequence in the performance of these Afro-American children on CMT I. When all 90 of the subjects are considered as a single group, it was found that 58% showed a W+/B— bias, 3% showed a B+/W— bias, and 39% were unbiased. Thus, the Vocke study supported the findings of the previous study in indicating a general tendency toward W+/B— bias among Afro preschool children.

In Suzanne Skinto's (1969) study of first and second grade school children noted earlier, data were obtained from Afro children, as well as from Euro children. The 26 Afro children, with a median age of 7-6, obtained a mean CMT I score of 8.4 when tested by a Euro examiner. The similarity of this mean to that obtained from the preschool subjects in the two preceding studies suggests that W+/B— bias among Afro children persists into the early school years.

We will now turn to a consideration of the performance of Afro-American children on the CMT II procedure. The reader will recall that CMT II has a score range of 0–24, with a neutral midpoint of 12. The principal study of CMT II with Afro children is the 1972–73 standardization study (Williams, Boswell, and Best, 1975) in which this procedure and the Peabody Picture Vocabulary Test were administered to 160 Afro children ranging in age from 3-4 to 7-7,* with a mean age of 5-1. Half of the children were

*See footnote on page 69.

male and half female, with half of each sex group tested by Euro examiners and half by Afro examiners. When the data were examined for sex of subject and race of examiner effects, no significant differences were found. For example, the children tested by Euro examiners obtained a mean score of 14.8, while the children tested by Afro examiners had a mean score of 14.9. Thus, race of examiner effects were not found for either Afro or Euro children in the CMT II standardization study.

The frequency distribution of CMT II scores for all 160 Afro children is shown in Figure 3-2. The percents of the children falling in the various score categories are shown in Table 3-6. An examination of Table 3-6 leads to several interesting observations. A comparison of the obtained percents with the chance expectancy percents reveals a clear tendency toward high, or W+/B−, scores among these Afro children. Fifty percent of the children obtained scores of 15 and up indicating some evidence of W+/B− bias, 6% scored 9 and down indicating some evidence of B+/W− bias, and 44% scored in the 10–14 range indicating no consistent bias. If we use the more demanding categories of "definite" bias, about one-third of the children displayed a W+/B− bias while only one child of the 160 tested displayed a B+/W− bias. Having seen this

Table 3-6. Number and Percent of CMT II Scores of 160 Afro-American Preschool Children Falling into Each of Five Categories (Williams, Boswell, and Best, 1975)

Score Range	Category	Number	Percent	Chance Expectancy (%)
0–7	Definite B+/W− bias	1	0.6	3.3
8–9	Probable B+/W− bias	9	5.6	12.1
10–14	No bias	70	43.8	69.2
15–16	Probable W+/B− bias	28	17.5	12.1
17–24	Definite W+/B− bias	52	32.5	3.3

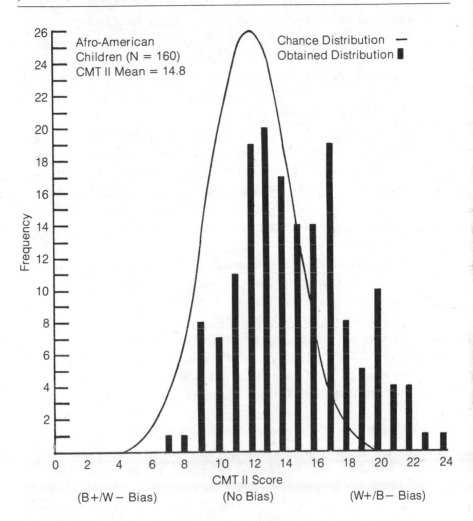

Figure 3-2. Frequency Distribution of Color Attitude Scores for 160 Afro-American Preschoolers in CMT II Standardization Study (Williams, Boswell, and Best, 1975)

evidence of W+/B− bias, we can ask whether the degree of bias is as high among Afro children as among Euro children. The answer is in the negative. The mean CMT II score for the 160 Afro children in the standardization study was 14.8 which is significantly lower than the mean of 17.1 which was found for the 160 Euro children from the same study. Thus, while the W+/B− bias is present in both groups, it is less evident in the Afro group than in the Euro group. This in turn suggests that the subcultural experiences of the Afro child may act partially to offset the general determinants of the W+/B− tendency in young children.

Before leaving our discussion of CMT II findings among Afro preschoolers, let us note the nonsignificant correlations of the color meaning scores with age (r = .11) and IQ (r = .09). This indicates that the individual differences in color meaning scores have little relationship to the age differences or IQ differences among the children. As noted earlier, this type of finding casts doubt upon the notion that the presence of W+/B− bias in Afro children can be explained as a simple result of their exposure to general cultural norms.

In considering the responses of Afro children to the colors white and black as assessed by procedures other than CMT, we turn again to the work of John Stabler and his associates. In the good and bad objects study, Afro preschoolers displayed a tendency toward the association of good objects with the white box and bad objects with the black box, but the tendency was not as consistent as that found among Euro preschoolers. In the "talking boxes" studies where Euro preschoolers "heard" positive "self-concept" statements coming from the white box, and negative statements coming from the black box, the findings for Afro children have been somewhat inconsistent, but in some cases have indicated a slight tendency toward the reversal of the foregoing effect. On the other hand, in the "prize guessing" study, Afro children (with an Afro examiner) chose the white box twice as often as the black box when asked to select the one which contained a prize which they had been promised.

Afro-American children have also been included in Stabler's school playground studies. When Afro children were given plastic bats and encouraged to attack two cardboard boxes, one colored white and the other black, there was an initial tendency toward striking the white box, with a later shift toward a concentration on the black box. Thus, while both Euro and Afro children tended to destroy the black box, they differed in their choice of initial target, with the Euro children first attacking the black box and the Afro children first attacking the white box. When the children were subsequently interviewed as to their black and white preferences, it was found that verbal and behavioral measures were generally consistent, i.e., children who had concentrated on hitting black targets stated they disliked the color black. Generally, the results of the Stabler studies of Afro children are consistent with the results of the Color Meaning Test studies. Young Afro children's responses to the colors black and white indicate that black usually elicits negative responses while white tends to elicit positive responses.

In our view, the simplest type of explanation for these findings is that there are some general influences which act toward the development of W+/B− bias in all young children and that these influences are offset, in part, by certain subcultural influences acting on the Afro child. This explanation seems more parsimonious than to propose that the Afro child has a natural tendency toward the positive evaluation of black which is completely overridden by general cultural influences. On the other hand, one finds proponents of the latter view who puzzle at length over the Afro child's failure to demonstrate his "natural" tendency to view black positively, and offer complicated hypotheses, often involving racial self-rejection, in an effort to explain why the Afro child does not act as he should. It seems to us that this type of theorizing grows out of an intellectual racism which places an exaggerated emphasis on racial membership, coupled with the naive view that the colors white and black have meaning to the young child only in the context of racial designation. This theory says, in effect: Afro-American children are different, and are called black; therefore, they should respond positively to the color black; and, if they don't, they are showing evidence of racial self-rejection. This type of theorizing seems to be unnecessarily convoluted and to constitute an unwarranted violation of the law of parsimony. Racial membership appears to have only a modest influence on the way young children respond to the colors white and black, and the search for the explanation of the W+/B− phenomena should be pursued in terms of general factors, which act upon all young children and which cause the development of the W+/B− tendency in the great majority of them. We will return to a further discussion of the origins of this tendency in chapters 9 and 10.

Color Attitudes Among French and Italian Preschoolers

Cindy Naylor employed translated versions of CMT II to study white-black color bias among preschool children in Dijon, France, and Venice, Italy (Best, Naylor, and Williams, 1975). The sample of 65 French children, mean age 5-11, obtained a CMT II mean of 15.7, with 55% of the children showing some evidence of W+/B− bias (scores of 15–24), and 3% showing some evidence of B+/W− bias (scores 0–9). The sample of 24 Italian children, mean age 5-7, obtained a mean score of 18.7 with 75% showing some evidence of W+/B− bias, and 12.5% showing evidence of B+/W− bias. When mean scores of the two European groups are compared with the American groups from the CMT II standardization study, the French mean (15.7) is found to be higher than the Afro-American mean (14.8) and lower than the Euro-American mean (17.1). The Italian mean (18.7), on the other hand, was appreciably higher than that of the French and the American groups.

Table 3-7 contains a listing of the evaluative adjectives employed in the French and Italian translations together

Table 3-7. Percent of French and Italian Preschoolers Selecting White Animals in Response to Positive Adjectives and Black Animals in Response to Negative Adjectives

POSITIVE ADJECTIVES

English Adjective	French Data Adjective	% Choosing White	Italian Data Adjective	% Choosing White
kind	gentil	71	gentile	79
friendly	amical	51	amichevole	71
nice	aimable	59	brava	67
healthy	robuste	42	sano	83
clean	propre	86	pulito	88
wonderful	extraordinaire	80	meravigliosa	96
helpful	serviable	51	servizievole	71
happy	joyeux	60	felice	79
right	raisonner juste	48	ragiona giusto	75
good	bon	68	buona	88
pretty	jolie	85	carina	83
smart	intelligent	55	in gamba	54

NEGATIVE ADJECTIVES

English Adjective	French Data Adjective	% Choosing Black	Italian Data Adjective	% Choosing Black
ugly	laid	59	brutta	92
wrong	fautif	68	in errore	88
bad	mauvais	78	malvagio	67
sad	triste	41	triste	46
stupid	bête	71	stupida	79
selfish	égoiste	69	egoista	96
sick	maladif	55	malata	83
dirty	sale	81	sporca	79
unfriendly	inamicale	71	scontroso	79
naughty	vilain	75	cattivo	71
cruel	brutal	75	crudele	83
mean	méchant	69	villano	79

with the percent of children who responded to each positive adjective by selecting the white animal and each negative adjective by selecting the black animal. It can be seen that the Italian children were highly consistent in their responses to the adjectives. With only two exceptions, the positive adjectives were associated with the white figures, and the negative adjectives with the black figures, by at least two-thirds of the children. The adjectives most frequently associated with white were "wonderful," "clean," and "good"; while those most frequently associated with black were "selfish," "ugly," and "wrong."

Among the French children, the adjectives for which the white figures were most frequently chosen were "clean," "pretty," and "wonderful"; while those most closely associated with black were "dirty," "bad," "naughty," and "cruel." As one would expect from their lower mean CMT II score, the French children were generally less consistent in their use of the adjectives than the Italian children. While it can be seen in Table 3-7 that the French children responded to a majority of the adjectives in the expected direction, there were several adjectives ("friendly," "helpful," "right") which were associated with the white and black figures with about equal frequency, and there were two adjectives ("healthy" and "sad") which showed some evidence of a reversal from the expected associations.*

In sum, the data in Table 3-7 provide documentation of a pervasive tendency to associate positive evaluation with white and negative evaluation with black in both groups of children. While we must be cautious in making generalizations based on these two small samples of children, the evidence of W+/B− bias among these French and Italian preschoolers is consistent with the findings of Adams and Osgood (1973) that young adults in both France and Italy evaluate white more positively than black.

---

*The more frequent association of *robuste* with the black figure may be due to its connotations of strength. Gordon and Williams (1973) have shown that Euro-American preschoolers associate the adjective strong more frequently with black than with white.

We noted early in this chapter that one of the several possible explanations for the presence of W+/B− bias in preschool children is that they may have a general preference for light things over dark things which develops as a result of aversive early experiences with darkness. If this line of reasoning is correct, we might expect that the degree of the child's W+/B− bias would be related to the strength of his fear of the dark of night, of thunderstorms, etc. This hypothesis was examined by Donna Boswell (Boswell, 1974; Boswell and Williams, 1975) in a study of thirty-nine Euro-American children, with a mean age of 5-7.

After administering CMT II and certain other test procedures, Boswell conducted a structured interview with each child, which included questions concerning his responses to the dark of night and thunderstorms. Subsequently, the child's mother completed a questionnaire which included questions on these same topics. Boswell found that a composite aversion-to-darkness score based on the child's interview responses and the mother's questionnaire responses correlated .40 with CMT II scores; children with high aversion to darkness obtained higher CMT II scores than did children with low aversion to darkness. While we should view this result with some caution since the same person conducted both parts of the investigation, the correlation obtained is consistent with the hypothesis that aversion to darkness is one determinant of W+/B− bias in preschool children.

COLOR MEANINGS AMONG TWO- AND THREE-YEAR-OLDS

The Color Meaning Test, which has proved so useful in studies at the preschool and early school levels, is beyond the test-taking capabilities of some three-year-olds and most two-year-olds. For this reason, Donna Boswell has attempted to develop different techniques for the assessment of responses to the colors black and white among children in these younger age ranges. These techniques have relied on observing the children's free play and choice behavior with regard to black and white toys.

The general approach which Boswell has explored is illustrated by the following study, conducted in 1973, which was the first in which black and white toys were used. This study involved a group of 25 Euro-American children whose ages ranged from 3-2 to 4-1 with a mean age of 3-7. Each child was first administered CMT II by a Euro examiner and was then brought into a room in which there were six pairs of toys (bears, dogs, trucks, airplanes, horses, and elephants) with one toy of each pair colored white, and one colored black. The child was invited to play with the toys while the experimenter "did some other work." The child then played freely with the toys for a period of ten minutes. During this time the child's behavior was observed and recorded. Following this, the experimenter showed each pair of toys to the child, and asked him to select the one which he would like to take home with him if he could. Following this, the child was shown two small rubber panda bears, one white and one black, and asked to select one to keep and take home.

The mean CMT II score in this group of three-year-olds was 15.4, which is almost identical to the mean of 15.3 obtained by the Euro-American three-year-olds in the CMT II standardization study. Thus, evidence of an appreciable degree of W+/B− bias was found at this age level. The data from the study were analyzed further by dividing the children into two groups on the basis of their CMT II scores: a group of 13 children who made scores of 15 and up and who, thus, showed evidence of the W+/B− concept on the test; and a group of 12 children who scored in the 10−14 range and who thus showed no evidence of having learned the W+/B− concept. The children's choice behavior with regard to the black and white toys was found to be related to the CMT II classification: the children who had displayed the W+/B− bias on CMT II tended to select the white animal in preference to the black animal, both in their hypothetical and real take-home choices; the children without the W+/B− bias did not display this tendency. In the free-play situation, the children with the W+/B− bias tended to play more often with the white toys than the black toys, with this tendency being reversed for the other group of children. It was concluded from this study that there was a general correspondence between three-year-old children's performance on CMT II, and their responses to black and white toys.

Boswell conducted a second study of this type in an effort to extend the play-observation procedure downward into the two-year-old age range, where the CMT II picture-story technique is not generally useful. Subjects were 12 Euro-American toddlers ranging in age from 1-8 to 3-6 with a mean age of 2-6. Each child first was observed during ten minutes of free play with the six white and six black toys described above. It was found that seven of the children spent more than half of their time playing with white toys, while the other five children spent more than half of their time playing with black toys. Following the free-play period, the child was presented with one matching pair of the toys, and was asked to indicate which was the good one. This was followed by the presentation of each of the other five pairs, with the child being asked to indicate the one which was bad, pretty, ugly, clean, or dirty. Of the ten toddlers who cooperated in playing this game, five displayed some tendency toward a W+/B− bias, four displayed no consistent choice, and one showed a tendency toward a B+/W− bias. Finally, when each child was asked to choose between a white and a black bear to keep and take home, nine of the children made a choice, with five choosing the white toy, and four choosing the black.

Keeping in mind that only 12 children were studied, the following observations can be made concerning the behavior of these two-year-olds. It was seen that there was a discernible tendency for more children to play with, positively evaluate, and select the white toys in preference to the black toys. On the other hand, this tendency was a very weak one, with many children appearing to be quite indifferent to the color of the toys, and much more interested in whether the toy was an airplane or an elephant. Thus, while we see some tendency toward W+/B − bias among two-year-olds, the evidence is far from dramatic, and leads to the conclusion that the color bias is still developing at this age level. This observation may be related to the fact that two-year-old children are generally more responsive to the form of objects than to their color, while, beginning at the three-year-old level, color tends to dominate form during the remainder of the preschool years (Brian and Goodenough, 1929; Spears, 1964).

COLOR ATTITUDES
IN THE LATER SCHOOL YEARS

In our studies of color meanings at the junior and senior high school levels, we have employed the semantic differential technique described in detail in chapter 2. The differential is a paper-and-pencil rating procedure in which the subject is asked to indicate his feelings about individual color names by checking along a series of seven-point scales. As noted in chapter 2, there are three primary dimensions of "feelings" or affective meanings: *evaluation* (e.g., good-bad), *potency* (e.g., weak-strong), and *activity* (e.g., passive-active). In our studies, most attention has been paid to the dominant dimension of evaluation which is most similar to the general concept of "attitude" as employed by psychologists. The reader should keep in mind that the subjects in these studies were rating the color names in a general, nonracial context and that the results indicate the general affective meanings of the color names rather than any specific racial meanings.

Teenage Euro-Americans

In the first study (Williams and McMurtry, 1970), the semantic differential was used to assess the general affective meanings of ten color names, including white and black, among a group of 106 Euro seventh graders. A group of 99 Euro college students was also studied in order to compare the color meanings in the two groups. The results of the study indicated a high degree of correspondence in the responses of the seventh grade and college groups to the color names. The similarity of response to the color names white and black can be seen in Figure 3-3, which shows the location of the mean scores for the color names white and black along the evaluation, potency, and activity dimensions. Like the college students, the seventh graders rated white as more positive, less potent, and more active than black. It was concluded from this study that the W+/B− tendency seen in young Euro children persists into the teen years, and that the full adult meanings of the color names white and black are well established by the time Euro children reach this age level.

The results of a second, more recent, study of Euro high school students confirms the picture just presented. This 1973 study was conducted by Kenneth Overholt with 200 eleventh and twelfth grade students in Ohio. The mean scores Overholt obtained are presented in Table 3-8 where it can be seen that once again white was found to be more positively evaluated, less potent, and more active than black. An additional feature of Overholt's study was that half of his two hundred Euro subjects were from a school

Figure 3-3. Mean Evaluation, Potency, and Activity Scores in Seventh-Grade and College Groups for the Color Names White (W), Black (BL), Yellow (Y), Brown (BR), and Red (R) (Williams and McMurtry, 1970)

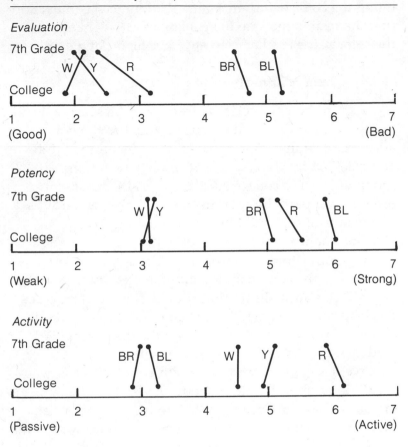

Table 3-8. Mean Semantic Differential Scores for the Color Names White and Black Among Euro-American High School Students in Ohio

	Color Name	
	White	Black
Evaluation	2.10	4.71
Potency	2.85	5.45
Activity	4.88	3.93

system which had been racially desegregated for many years, while the other half were from a racially segregated (all Euro) system. This school experience variable was found to have no appreciable effect on the ratings of the color names. For example, the mean evaluation ratings for the racially desegregated Euro students were *white* = 2.08 and *black* = 4.62; while the comparable means for the racially segregated Euro students were *white* = 2.13 and *black* = 4.80. Apparently, the interracial contact in the integrated school system had little effect on the affective meanings of the color names to these Euro students. This finding will appear even more interesting when we consider the meanings of white and black to the Afro students who were the classmates of the integrated Euro group.

A third study of the general affective meanings of white and black among Euro children in the later school years was conducted in Virginia in 1972 by Morland (1972). In this study, four samples of children corresponding generally to sixth, eighth, tenth, and twelfth graders made evaluative ratings of the color names white, black, red, yellow, and brown. The mean evaluation scores for each grade group are given in Table 3-9. An examination of these data reveals once again the clear tendency toward the positive evaluation of white and neutral to slightly negative evaluation of black among Euro children in the junior-high and high-school age groups. It is also interesting to note the rank order of evaluative meanings for all five of the color names rated. With only one minor exception, the rank order (most positive to least positive) of the five color names in all age groups was white, yellow, red, brown, and black. This is the same general rank order we encountered earlier (chapter 2, pp. 53–56) when considering the cross-cultural meanings of color names in the United States, Europe, and Asia. The fact that these twelve- to eighteen-year-old Euro-American Virginians evaluated the five color names in the same general manner

Table 3-9. Mean Evaluation Scores of the Color Names White, Yellow, Red, Brown, and Black Among Euro-American Children in the Sixth through Twelfth Grades   (Morland, 1972)

| | Color Name Evaluated | | | | |
Age Group	White	Yellow	Red	Brown	Black
Sixth Graders	2.21	2.50	2.63	3.86	4.73
Eighth Graders	2.16	2.58	3.20	3.86	4.33
Tenth Graders	2.25	3.08	3.05	4.01	4.67
Twelfth Graders	2.25	2.98	3.68	4.61	5.16

as young adults in India, Thailand, and the Philippines provides additional evidence both of the generality of these color meanings and of the age at which they are learned.

Teenage Afro-Americans

We will consider here the results of two studies of the affective meanings of color names among Afro-American teenagers, conducted in 1972 and 1973. In chapter 2, we reviewed the studies of Afro college students conducted in the 1960s and saw that they tended to evaluate the color name white more positively than black. This effect was, however, much more prominent in 1963 than in 1969 with the color name white having become "less good" and the color name black "less bad" across this time interval (see chapter 2, figure 2-3). If we assume that these trends continued on into the 1970s, we would expect that black would eventually come to be evaluated more positively than white by Afro persons in the young adult years.

The foregoing expectation has been confirmed in two more recent studies of Afro high school students— Morland's (1972) study of high school seniors in Virginia, and Overholt's 1973 study of high school juniors and seniors in Ohio. On the usual seven-point evaluation scale (where low scores are "good," high scores are "bad," and a score of 4 is neutral), Morland's Afro subjects gave black a mean rating of 2.57 and white a mean rating of 3.40. Less dramatic evidence of the same tendency was seen in Overholt's data where the Afro students gave black a mean rating of 2.89 and white, 3.19. Thus, we see that by 1972–73 Afro high school students were displaying a tendency to rate black somewhat more positively than white, although both color names were still being rated positively in absolute terms, i.e., receiving mean scores on the positive side of the neutral midpoint of 4.

This evidence of change in the evaluative meanings of black and white among Afro young adults in the last few years does not yet have its counterpart at the preschool level. We noted earlier that the tendency for Afro preschoolers to evaluate white positively and black negatively was still clearly evident in the Color Meaning Test II standardization data collected in 1972 and 1973. In this study, half of the Afro preschoolers displayed evidence of a W+/B− tendency while only about 6 percent showed evidence of a B+/W− tendency. The juxtaposition of the preschool and high school findings from the early 1970s suggests that Afro preschoolers have an initial tendency toward the positive evaluation of white and negative evaluation of black which is later reversed by subsequent experiences. Support for this hypothesis is found in some additional findings from the Morland study. When Afro children in the sixth, eighth, tenth, and twelfth grades rated the color names white and black, the mean scores shown in Figure 3-4 were obtained. These mean scores indicated that: the sixth grade students rated the color name white more positively than black; the eighth grade students rated the two nearly equal; and the tenth and twelfth graders rated black more positively than white. This suggests that the shift in color meanings may occur during the junior high school years. Perhaps this is the age at which the rhetoric of the Black Identity

Figure 3-4. Mean Evaluative Ratings of Color Names White and Black by Afro-American Subjects in the Sixth, Eighth, Tenth, and Twelfth Grades (1972) (Morland, 1972)

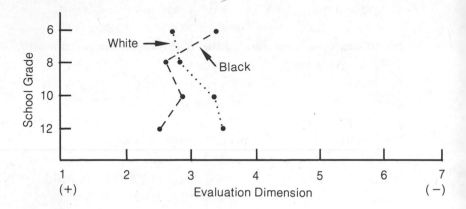

movement has its first meaningful impact upon the young Afro-American. On the other hand, we must be cautious in inferring developmental trends from such cross-sectional data, and longitudinal studies are needed to provide more adequate answers to these questions.

In this chapter we have reviewed the research findings dealing with the attitudes of young children toward the colors white and black. We have seen that such attitudes are evident quite early in life and do not show some of the developmental patterns expected of attitudes which are acquired solely as a result of cultural learning. The theoretical significance of these findings will be discussed in chapter 10. For the moment, let us note that the cross-cultural tendency toward the positive evaluation of white and negative evaluation of black appears to be mirrored in the responses of a majority of the young children who have been studied.

4.
Racial Attitudes

INTRODUCTION: CHILDREN'S RESPONSES TO RACIAL STIMULI

The demonstration that most preschool children have a positive attitude toward the color white relative to the color black has no necessary implications for their responses to light- and dark-skinned persons. In order to understand the manner in which young children respond to persons of different racial groups, one must study this directly. During the preschool years, children become increasingly aware of the many ways in which persons differ from one another in physical appearance and behavior. Among these differences are the physical and behavioral characteristics which adults use to identify the "race" of persons. Thus, most preschool children can be said to demonstrate a "racial awareness," in the general sense that they are capable of discriminating among the stimuli which adults employ in racial classification. We must be cautious, however, in the interpretation which we place on this awareness of racially relevant stimuli. We must not assume, for example, that the young child who responds differently to persons of various skin colors "knows about race" in the sense that adults do. He may be responding to skin color, per se, and have no knowledge of racial concepts or racial classification.

If we are to understand the way children respond to racial differences, we must be careful to let the children speak for themselves, arid be on guard against projecting our adult conceptions of race onto them. The problem is similar to the difficulty encountered when trying to understand sexual behavior in young children. When a child engages in some behavior which would be sexual behavior in an adult, the observer must be careful not to project his adult concepts of sexuality onto the child and assume that the child's behavior has the same meaning to the child as it does to the adult. If we study the responses of young children to stimuli, it is because we do not already understand them; and if we are to develop an understanding, we must attend very carefully to what the children say and do.

Researchers who have studied the responses of young children to racial stimuli have approached the topic in a variety of different ways, which has led to a large and confusing list of terms which are intended to represent different research operations, but which are not employed with consistency. As we discuss the research literature, we will employ a seven-way classification of research operations: *racial attitude, racial acceptance, racial preference, racial self-preference, perceived racial similarity, racial classification,* and *racial self-classification*. The distinctions among these operations and the resulting concepts are illustrated in the following example. Assume that we are testing a preschool child, and that we place before him a picture of two children who differ in skin color and possibly in other racial characteristics. If we first ask the subject to indicate which is the "good" or "bad" child, we would be attempting to assess his evaluative response to the children, hence, his *racial attitude*. If we select one of the two children and ask the subject if he would like to play with this particular child, we are studying *racial acceptance*. If we then ask the subject to choose between the two children as to which he would like to play with, we are assessing his *racial preference*, and if we ask him which child he would "rather be," we are interested in his *racial self-preference*. We might then ask the subject, "Which child do you look like?" taking his answer as an indication of *perceived racial similarity*. We might also ask the subject to indicate the "black child" or the "white child" in order to determine whether he can respond appropriately to common racial labels, i.e., *racial classification*. Finally, we might ask the child whether he is a white child or a black child taking his answer as an indication of *racial self-classification*. Although these seven research operations are reasonably discrete, researchers have sometimes employed several different operations in the same study, without adequately distinguishing among them.

In organizing the material in the following chapters, we have used the seven-fold classification of research operations just described. In the present chapter, we will discuss findings regarding racial attitude, with racial acceptance, preference, and self-preference discussed in chapter 6, and racial similarity, classification, and self-classification reviewed in chapter 7. While this approach destroys the integrity of certain studies in which more than one research operation was employed, it has the advantage of dealing separately with the findings obtained with each type of research operation, and, hopefully, providing some clarification of the relationships among the theoretical constructs defined by them.

Our decision to discuss racial attitudes prior to racial preference and the other racial concepts was not an arbitrary one, but reflects our view that racial attitude is a simpler and perhaps more basic aspect of the child's response to racial figures. For example, it is quite evident that evaluation and preference behavior cannot be equated among adults. An adult's conception of what is good or bad is only one determinant of his behavior in choice situations, and we are all familiar with situations where adults choose "bad" things. While the relationships between evaluation and preference behavior in children are probably simpler than in adults, we must be cautious in assuming that because a child prefers something he necessarily views it as good. For example, we will see that the racial attitudes and racial preferences of Afro-American children are highly similar at the preschool level but show a clear divergence during the early school years.

RACIAL ATTITUDE FINDINGS
FROM MULTICONCEPT PROCEDURES

There have been a number of racial concept studies employing procedures in which some questions would be classified as attitude items, while others would be classified as preference, similarity, or classification items. The prototypes of these multiconcept studies were the classic investigations of Afro-American children conducted by Clark and Clark (1939, 1947) in the late 1930s and early 1940s. In these studies, Afro children were shown dolls intended to represent Afro-Americans and Euro-Americans and were asked to respond to a series of eight requests, each of which required the choice of a doll by the child. Two of the eight items dealt with what we are calling racial attitude: "Give me the nice doll," and "Give me the doll that looks bad." In response to the positive item, 70% of the preschool Afro subjects who made a choice selected the Euro doll while 30% selected the Afro doll; in response to the negative item, 80% selected the Afro doll and only 20% selected the Euro doll. The results thus suggested the presence of a pro-Euro/anti-Afro (E+/A −) bias which was evident as early as three years of age. Clark and Clark also studied early school age Afro children and found the pro-Euro bias to be somewhat reduced, with a 54% Euro choice on the positive item and 76% Afro choice on the negative item.

There have been several more recent studies in which investigators have employed research procedures of the

Table 4-1. Responses of Young Afro-American Children to Attitude Items in Studies Employing a Clark and Clark Type Procedure*

	Preschool Age			Early School Age			Combined Preschool & School†	
	Clark & Clark (1947)	Hraba & Grant (1970)	Greenwald & Oppenheim‡ (1968)	Clark & Clark (1947)	Hraba & Grant (1970)	Gregor & McPherson (1966)	Asher & Allen (1969)	Fox & Jordan (1973)
A. Positive Attitude Item								
% Choosing Afro Doll	30	41	41	46	58	60	23	54
% Choosing Euro Doll	70	59	59	54	42	40	77	46
B. Negative Attitude Item								
% Choosing Afro Doll	80	68	67	76	27	100§	75	41
% Choosing Euro Doll	20	32	33	24	73	0	25	59

*Percentages are based on number of children who responded, excluding nonresponders.
†No age trend was found in these studies.
‡Percentages are based on number of children who chose either Afro or Euro doll, excluding those who chose "mulatto" doll.
§Only 8 of 92 Ss responded to the question.

Clark and Clark type to assess racial concepts in young Afro children. The findings from the racial attitude items in these studies have been extracted and are summarized in Table 4-1. In these studies, the positive attitude item was "nice doll," and the negative attitude item was "looks bad," except in the Greenwald and Oppenheim study where the two items were "good doll" and "bad doll" respectively. An examination of the data in Table 4-1 produces a somewhat confusing picture. Some studies have found support for the age trend reported by Clark and Clark in which pro-Euro bias is found at the preschool level and is reduced and sometimes reversed at the early school level. On the other hand, two of the studies found no evidence of an age trend, and the results of these studies are in disagreement as to whether the general picture is one of strong pro-Euro bias (Asher and Allen, 1969) or slight pro-Afro bias (Fox and Jordan, 1973). The only conclusion to be reached from these data is that Afro children rarely express a strong positive attitude toward the dolls representing Afro persons.

The foregoing picture contrasts with the consistent findings which have been obtained when procedures of the Clark and Clark type have been administered to Euro-American children. Data from the racial attitude items of these studies are summarized in Table 4-2 where it can be seen that Euro preschoolers display a clear tendency toward the selection of the Euro doll on the positive attitude item, and toward the selection of the Afro doll on the negative attitude item, with no appreciable evidence of an age trend from the preschool to early school years.

We can summarize the findings from the racial attitude items of these multiconcept procedures studies by noting that at the preschool age level both Afro and Euro children have usually been found to associate positive evaluation with Euro dolls and negative evaluation with Afro dolls, a conclusion also supported by the work of Porter (1971) who employed a different methodology. In the early school years, this tendency continues among Euro children, while it decreases and sometimes reverses among Afro children. Although the multiconcept studies have been useful in pointing up some major phenomena regarding racial bias in young children, it is clear that a careful assessment of racial attitudes at this level requires a

Table 4-2. Responses of Young Euro-American Children to Attitude Items in Studies Employing a Clark and Clark Type Procedure*

	Preschool Age		Early School Age		Combined Preschool & School†	
	Hraba & Grant (1970)	Greenwald & Oppenheim‡ (1968)	Hraba & Grant (1970)	Gregor & McPherson (1966)	Asher & Allen (1969)	Fox & Jordan (1973)
A. *Positive Attitude Item*						
% Choosing Afro Doll	40	22	26	21	21	29
% Choosing Euro Doll	60	78	74	79	79	71
B. *Negative Attitude Item*						
% Choosing Afro Doll	53	90	69	93	81	68
% Choosing Euro Doll	47	10	31	7	19	32

*Percentages are based on number of children who responded, excluding nonresponders.
†No age trend was found in these studies.
‡Percentages are based on number of children who chose either Euro or Afro doll, excluding those who chose "mulatto" doll.

more refined measurement procedure than that provided by the "two-item tests" included in the studies just reviewed.

STUDIES OF PRESCHOOL CHILDREN EMPLOYING THE PRAM PROCEDURES

In 1966, Williams began a program of studies directed at the development of a method for measuring attitudes in preschool children which would be appropriate to their test-taking skills, and which could be coordinated with the general concept of evaluative attitude as this had been developed through research with older children and adults. The rationale of the method was based on the findings of Charles Osgood and his associates that the evaluation (E) scores from semantic differential* ratings by adults were highly correlated with scores obtained from traditional attitude tests (Osgood et al., 1957, pp. 194–95). Since many of the evaluative adjectives employed with the semantic differential were simple words, found in the vocabulary of the preschool child, we reasoned that a child's tendency to associate evaluative adjectives with certain stimulus characteristics in pictures could provide a useful method of assessing attitudes in preliterate children. The Color Meaning Test described in the preceding chapter represents an application of this method in the assessment of children's attitudes toward the colors white and black, while the Preschool Racial Attitude Measure involves the application of this method in the assessment of racial attitudes.

The Preschool Racial Attitude Measure (PRAM) was developed as a procedure for studying racial attitudes by assessing the child's tendency to choose light-skinned ("Euro-American") or dark-skinned ("Afro-American") figures in response to stories containing positive or negative evaluative adjectives. For example: "Here are

*See chapter 2 (pp. 46–48) for a description of the semantic differential procedure.

two little boys. One of them is a kind little boy. Once he saw a kitten fall into a lake and he picked up the kitten to save it from drowning. Which is the kind little boy?'' Interspersed among the PRAM racial attitude items are sex-role items which serve to make the task more varied for the child, and which also yield a useful control measure of sex-role knowledge. The original version of PRAM—now known as PRAM I—was originally described by Williams and Roberson (1967); the current version, PRAM II, is described in detail by Williams, Best, Boswell, Mattson, and Graves (1975), and also in Appendix B.

The PRAM II procedure consists of 36 color photographs with 36 accompanying stories; 24 are racial attitude items and 12 are sex-role items. The two human figures in each of the 24 racial attitude pictures are identical except for skin color; one has medium brown skin (the "Afro-American" figure) and the other has pinkish-tan skin (the "Euro-American" figure). The figures portray male and female persons in four age groups: young children, teenagers, young adults, and older adults.

The key words in the questions for the 24 racial attitude items are the 12 positive evaluative adjectives and 12 negative evaluative adjectives seen in Table 4-3. The standard scoring of the procedure is to count one point for the selection of the light-skinned figure in response to a story containing a positive adjective; and one point for the selection of the dark-skinned figure in response to a negative adjective. With 24 scoring opportunities, the racial attitude score can range from 0 to 24 with lower scores indicating pro-Afro/anti-Euro (A+/E−) bias, high scores indicating pro-Euro/anti-Afro (E+/A−) bias, and scores in the midrange indicating no racial bias. Statistically speaking, whenever an individual child obtains a score of 17 or above, he is displaying a significant degree of E+/A− bias, while scores of 7 or below are indicative of a significant A+/E− bias.

Table 4-3. Adjectives Used in PRAM Procedures

Positive Evaluative Adjectives (PEA's)	Negative Evaluative Adjectives (NEA's)
clean	bad
good	dirty
kind	mean
nice	naughty
pretty	stupid
smart	ugly
friendly	cruel
happy	sad
healthy	selfish
helpful	sick
right	unfriendly
wonderful	wrong

Note: All 24 adjectives are used in PRAM II procedure. Adjectives above dotted line were also used in PRAM I. The same adjectives are employed in the CMT procedures described in chapter 3.

The principal difference between PRAM II and its predecessor, PRAM I, is that in the earlier procedure there were only twelve racial attitude items—the six positive and six negative adjectives in the upper half of Table 4-3. With this shorter procedure, the range of possible scores is 0–12, with high scores indicating a pro-Euro/anti-Afro attitude (E+/A−), low scores indicating a pro-Afro/anti-Euro attitude (A+/E−), and scores in the midrange, around 6, indicating no racial bias. Statistically speaking, whenever a child obtains a score of 9 or up, he is showing evidence of a significant E+/A− bias, while scores of 3 and down are indicative of a significant A+/E− bias. PRAM I contains the same twelve sex-role items as PRAM II. In both procedures, the sex-role items are scored so that high scores are indicative of a high knowledge of sex-typed behaviors in our culture (women baking pies, men fixing cars, etc.).

Before beginning our discussion of the research using the PRAM procedures, we repeat our caution concerning the interpretation of forced-choice scores. PRAM is a forced-choice procedure which requires the child to make a response to each of the picture-story presentations. If the story contains a positive adjective, the child must choose one of the two human figures; if the story contains a negative adjective, the child must again choose. Under these conditions, the child's responses indicate his *relative* evaluation of the light- and dark-skinned figures, not his absolute evaluation of them. Thus, when a child makes a very high PRAM score it does not follow that he has a very negative attitude to dark-skinned persons. It merely means that he views light-skinned persons more positively than dark-skinned persons. A more detailed discussion of this methodological issue is given in Appendix A.

Racial Attitudes Among Euro-American Preschoolers

In discussing racial attitudes among Euro-American preschoolers, we will first describe those studies which have employed PRAM I, followed by the more recent studies which have used PRAM II. As an aid in integrating the findings from the two forms of the procedure, the reader may find it useful to remember that if PRAM I scores are doubled they are generally equivalent to PRAM II scores.

The first study to employ PRAM I was conducted in North Carolina in 1966 (Williams and Roberson, 1967). The subjects were 111 Euro preschoolers, mean age five years, four months (5-4), tested by Euro examiners. The mean PRAM I racial attitude score in this group was 10.3, with 86% of the children showing E+/A− bias (scores 9 to 12), 14% scoring in the unbiased range (4 to 8), and 0% showing A+/E− bias (scores 0 to 3). It was thus clear that the great majority of these preschool Euro-American children showed evidence of a bias toward the positive evaluation of light-skinned persons relative to dark-skinned persons.

The foregoing results were obtained in 1966 from

middle-class children in the mid-South, and questions naturally arose concerning the generality of these findings. Do Euro children from other regions of the country score similarly? Can the E+/A− bias be shown with even younger children? Did the degree of E+/A− bias decrease in the years following 1966? While there are not sufficient data to answer all of these questions definitively, the results of additional PRAM I studies by other investigators provide some general information regarding them.

Table 4-4 summarizes the findings of several studies in which PRAM I has been used to study the racial attitudes of Euro preschoolers, who were tested by Euro examiners. For each study, the table lists the average age of the children, the state and year in which the study was conducted, and the mean racial attitude score which was obtained. An examination of the mean scores obtained in various sections of the country provides no evidence of regional variation; mean scores obtained in New York, Connecticut, and Ohio are highly similar to those obtained in North Carolina and Texas. Apparently, the determinants of the E+/A − bias are not associated, to any appreciable degree, with regional variations in patterns of interracial attitudes and interactions. Regarding the presence of the E+/A − bias in younger children, the group of California children tested by Thompson indicates that an appreciable degree of bias can be found in children as young as three years. Concerning the question of changes in the degree of E+/A − bias after 1966, the mean score of 10.0 from Tse's group tested in 1971 is virtually the same as the mean score of 9.8 from the similarly aged group from the Williams and Roberson study, tested in 1966.

The initial standardization study on PRAM II (Williams, Best, Boswell, Mattson, and Graves, 1975) was completed in 1972. The general design of this study was to administer PRAM II and the Peabody Picture Vocabulary Test (PPVT)

Table 4-4. Mean Racial Attitude (RA) Scores of Euro-American Children in Various Studies Employing PRAM I

Investigators	N	Av. Age	State-Year	Mean RA Score
Williams and Roberson (1967)	111	5–4	N.C. ('66)	10.3
Williams and Edwards (1969)	84	5–6	N.C. ('67)	9.6
Thompson, K.*	27	3–8	Calif. ('68)	9.1
Bridges, M. A.*	31	4–8	Tex. ('69)	9.7
Bridges, M. A. *	24	6–11	Tex. ('69)	11.5
Firestone, C. & Feinstein, C.*	16	4–11	Conn. ('69)	10.0
Keller, K. S.*	24	5–9	Ohio ('70)	9.8
Tse, M.*	30	4–4	N.Y. ('71)	10.0
Walker (1971)	40	5–4	Ky. ('71)	10.9

*Throughout the book, studies without a formal citation are previously unpublished studies conducted under the sponsorship of the authors.

to Euro and Afro preschool children, using female Euro and Afro examiners with both subject groups. The subjects for the study were 272 preschool children from the Winston-Salem, N.C., area. The children ranged in age from 3-1 to 7-1 with a mean age of 5-4. Half of the children were Euro, and half were Afro, with each race group composed of equal numbers of males and females. Half of each race-sex group was tested by Euro examiners, and half by Afro examiners. The joint variation in race of subject and race of examiner produced four major groups in the standardization study: Euro children tested by Euro examiners; Euro children with Afro examiners; Afro children with Euro examiners; and Afro children with Afro examiners. We will consider here the PRAM II scores of the two groups of Euro subjects, and consider the scores of the Afro subjects in the next section of this chapter.

The frequency distributions of PRAM II scores in the two Euro-American groups are shown in Figure 4-1. An examination of the scores seen in this figure leads to

Figure 4-1. Frequency Distributions of Racial Attitude Scores of Euro-American Preschoolers in the PRAM II Standardization Study (Williams, Best, Boswell, Mattson, and Graves, 1975)

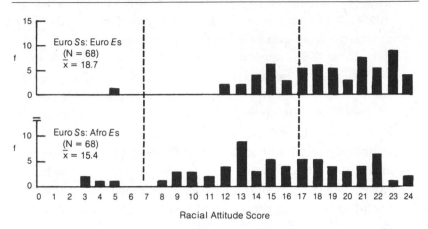

several interesting observations. Bearing in mind that a PRAM II score of 12 represents a nonbiased performance, we note that the scores in both groups are generally distributed toward the upper or E+/A— end of the score range. Second, we note that the distribution of scores is influenced by the race of the examiner, with higher (more E+/A—) scores obtained when the examiner was Euro than when she was Afro. This is reflected in the mean score of 18.7 for the Euro examiner condition and 15.4 for the Afro examiner condition.*

Because of the two-choice nature of the PRAM procedure, the binomial distribution provides a convenient way to determine when an individual child was responding in a manner which would be unlikely on a chance basis. With 24 response opportunities, the probability of an unbiased child obtaining a score of 17 or up was only .033; the same probability existed for scores of 7 or down. Thus, scores in the former category (17 up) were taken as evidence of a "definite" pro-Euro/anti-Afro bias (E+/A—), while scores in the latter category (7 down)

*Race of examiner effects are not always found with PRAM II at the preschool level; see Appendix B for summary of study by Deborah Best (1972) which fails to demonstrate the effect.

reflected a "definite" pro-Afro/anti-Euro bias (A+/E−).
Likewise, scores of 15 and 16, and 8 and 9, were taken as
evidence of "probable" bias, while scores in the 10–14
midrange were characterized as "unbiased."

In Table 4-5 is shown the percent of Euro children in
the two race of examiner groups who obtained scores in
each of the foregoing classes. Perhaps the most dramatic
evidence seen in Table 4-5 is the high degree of "definite"
E+/A− bias (17 up) in both subject groups, being found in
approximately 7 out of 10 children with Euro examiners
and 4 out of 10 children with Afro examiners. At the other
extreme, evidence of definite A+/E− bias (7 down) was
found in only 5 of the 136 children tested. If we pool the
data for the probable and definite bias categories for all
subjects, 73% of the children showed some evidence of
E+/A− bias while only 7% showed evidence of A+/E−
bias.

PRAM II has been employed in several additional
studies of Euro-American preschoolers who have been
tested by Euro-American examiners. In these studies,
which are summarized in Table 4-6, the mean PRAM II
scores ranged from 17.0 to 19.2 and were thus indicative
of a high degree of E+/A− bias in all groups tested.

Has the general level of E+/A− bias among Euro
preschoolers changed in the past few years? Apparently
very little. If we refer back to Table 4-4, we see that these
PRAM I studies were conducted in the years 1966–71. If

Table 4-5. Percent of PRAM II Scores of Euro-American Preschool Children Tested by
Euro and Afro Examiners Falling into Each of Five Categories
(Williams, Best, Boswell, Mattson, and Graves, 1975)

Score Range	Category	Euro Examiner (N = 68) (Mean Age = 5–4)		Afro Examiner (N = 68) (Mean Age = 5–4)		Chance Expectancy
		N	%	N	%	%
0–7	Definite A+/E− bias	1	1.4	4	5.9	3.3
8–9	Probable A+/E− bias	0	0.0	4	5.9	12.1
10–14	No bias	8	11.8	21	30.9	69.2
15–16	Probable E+/A− bias	10	14.7	9	13.2	12.1
17–24	Definite E+/A− bias	49	72.1	30	44.1	3.3

Table 4-6. Mean PRAM II Racial Attitude (RA) Scores of Euro-American Preschool Children Tested by Euro-American Examiners in Various Studies

Investigator(s)	N	Av. Age	State-Year	Mean RA Score
Williams, Best, Boswell, Mattson, and Graves (1975)	68	5–4	N.C. ('72)	18.7
Collins (1972)	60	5–0	Tenn. ('72)	19.2
Graves, D. J.*	60	5–8	N.C. ('72)	18.1
Boswell (1974)	50	5–7	N.C. ('73)	18.1
Smith, S. C.*	35	5–4	N.C. ('73)	18.2
Traynham (1974)	20	5–6	Ark. ('73)	18.7
Young, B.*	23	4–6	Ontario, Can. ('73)	17.0
Carter, P. C.*	14	5–7	Ky. ('74)	18.3
Wade, W.*	80	5–8	Wis. ('74)	17.9

*Unpublished studies.

we average the mean racial attitude scores of the eight preschool groups in this table we obtain a mean of 9.9. On the other hand, the mean of the means for the nine PRAM II groups in Table 4-6, tested in 1972–74, is 18.24—half of which is 9.12. Thus, at the most, there is evidence of only a slight decline in E+/A− bias among Euro-American preschool children in recent years.

In sum, the findings from the PRAM II studies of Euro children confirm the general picture seen in the PRAM I findings: a large majority of Euro preschoolers show evidence of a pro-Euro/anti-Afro bias. In addition, the PRAM II studies indicate that the expression of this bias can sometimes be influenced to a degree by the race of the examiner, with less bias being expressed when the examiner is Afro. Having observed these effects among Euro children, we will now consider studies in which the PRAM procedures have been employed to assess racial attitudes in preschool Afro children.

PRAM I has been used in several studies designed to assess racial attitudes in Afro-American children. The first study to be described was conducted by Jacqueline Vocke in South Carolina in 1970 (Vocke, 1971). In this study, 90 Afro children, mean age 5-5, were administered PRAM I. Half of the children were given the procedure by an Afro examiner and were found to have a mean score of 8.6, with 56% of the group showing evidence of E+/A − bias (scores 9–12), 40% scoring in the unbiased range (scores 4–8), and 4% showing evidence of A+/E − bias (scores 0–3). The other half of the children were administered PRAM I by a Euro examiner and had a mean of 9.2, with 71% of the group showing E+/A − bias, 25% unbiased, and 4% showing A+/E − bias. These findings indicated that E+/A − bias was evident in a majority of the children in both examiner groups, but was somewhat more evident in the Euro examiner group. On the other hand, A+/E − bias was found in only a small percent of the children tested and did not seem to be affected by the race of the examiner.

The two means from the Vocke study are listed in Table 4-7 in which also are summarized the findings from several other PRAM I studies of Afro preschoolers. While there is some variability in the mean scores which may be attributable to differences in race of examiner or age, there is clear evidence of a tendency toward E+/A − bias in all groups tested.

The E+/A − bias found in Harriette McAdoo's Mississippi group is of particular interest. This group consisted of children from Mound Bayou, Mississippi, a virtually all-Afro community founded in 1877 by former slaves, and which has been Afro-controlled since that time. In this unique community, the higher status business and professional positions, as well as the more ordinary and menial positions, are occupied by Afro-American persons.

Table 4-7. Mean PRAM I Racial Attitude (RA) Scores of Afro-American Preschool Children in Various Studies

Investigator	N	Av. Age	Race of Examiner	State-Year	Mean RA Score
Vocke (1971)	45	5–5	Afro	S.C. ('70)	8.6
Vocke (1971)	45	5–5	Euro	S.C. ('70)	9.2
Walker (1971)	20	5–4	Euro	Ky. ('71)	10.0
McAdoo, J. (1970)	65	4–6	Afro	Mich. ('69)	7.8
McAdoo, H. (1970)	35	5–2	Afro	Mich. ('69)	8.7
McAdoo, H. (1970)	43	5–6	Afro	Miss. ('69)	8.9
McAdoo, H. (1973)	68	5–0	Afro	D.C. ('72)	8.6
McAdoo, H. (1973)	59	5–0	Afro	D.C. ('73)	8.4

The evidence of an E+/A − bias in the Mound Bayou children suggests that close personal contact with Euro persons is not a necessary condition for the development of E+/A − bias in young Afro children. It suggests also that the opportunity to identify with high status Afro models is not sufficient to override the other determinants of the E+/A − bias. In addition, McAdoo found that the racial attitude scores of the subjects in her groups were not correlated with IQ, as estimated by the Peabody Picture Vocabulary Test.

What can we conclude from the foregoing review of studies in which PRAM I has been used to assess the racial attitudes of preschool Afro-American children? The major conclusion is that most Afro children, like most Euro children, display an E+/A − bias; they tend to associate positive evaluation with light-skinned figures and negative evaluation with dark-skinned figures. Regarding the E+/A − bias, it can also be concluded that: the bias among Afro children is not as strong as among comparably aged Euro children; the degree of bias expressed is affected only slightly by the race of the examiner; and the bias seems equally evident among Afro children reared in quite different regional and racial environments.

We will now consider findings concerning the racial attitudes of Afro children as assessed by the PRAM II procedure where the scores may range from 0 to 24 with a neutral or unbiased midpoint of 12. One hundred thirty-six Afro preschoolers were administered PRAM II as part of the initial standardization study completed in 1972 (Williams, Best, Boswell, Mattson, and Graves, 1975). One half of the children were administered the procedure by Afro examiners, and one half by Euro examiners. The frequency distributions of PRAM II scores in these two subject groups are shown in Figure 4-2 where it can be seen that both distributions show a displacement toward the high (E+/A −) end of the scale. This is reflected in the mean scores for the two groups, both of which are significantly higher than the chance mean of 12.

Table 4-8 displays the scores of the children classified as to type and degree of bias. It can be seen that in both subject groups approximately one-third of the scores fall in the unbiased score range. Beyond this, it is interesting to note that the percent of children displaying E+/A − bias is noticeably greater than the percent displaying A+/E − bias. Perhaps most dramatic are the findings in the Afro examiner condition. Under this condition, 48.5% of the children expressed some degree of E+/A − bias while only 16.2% expressed some degree of A+/E − bias. Thus, even when being given the test by a dark-skinned examiner, the PRAM II performance of the Afro children reveals a tendency toward the positive evaluation of light-skinned figures. These PRAM II findings are in general agreement with the PRAM I findings and indicate that E+/A − bias is much more prevalent than A+/E − bias among Afro children.

The PRAM studies yield conflicting evidence as to whether the general level of E+/A − bias among Afro preschoolers has declined in the past few years. Earlier we noted that when PRAM I was administered to Afro children by Afro examiners in 1970, Vocke obtained a mean of 8.6, while Harriette McAdoo's two 1969 groups had means of 8.7 and 8.9. McAdoo's Washington groups,

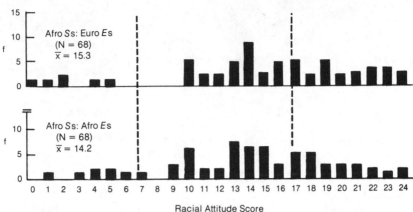

Figure 4-2. Frequency Distributions of Racial Attitude Scores of Afro-American Preschoolers in the PRAM II Standardization Study (Williams, Best, Boswell, Mattson, and Graves, 1975)

Table 4-8. Percent of PRAM II Scores of Afro-American Preschool Children Tested by Euro and Afro Examiners Falling into Each of Five Categories (Williams, Best, Boswell, Mattson, and Graves, 1975)

Score Range	Category	Euro Examiner (N = 68) (Mean Age = 5–4)		Afro Examiner (N = 68) (Mean Age = 5–4)		Chance Expectancy
		N	%	N	%	
0–7	Definite A+/E− bias	6	8.8	8	11.8	3.3
8–9	Probable A+/E− bias	0	0.0	3	4.4	12.1
10–14	No bias	24	35.3	24	35.3	69.2
15–16	Probable E+/A− bias	8	11.8	9	13.2	12.1
17–24	Definite E+/A− bias	30	44.1	24	35.3	3.3

tested in 1972 and 1973, obtained means of 8.6 and 8.4 suggesting that the degree of bias had not changed. On the other hand, the Afro examiner group in the PRAM II standardization study, completed in 1972, yielded a mean of 14.2—half of which is 7.1. While this figure is less than those obtained by Vocke and McAdoo, the fact that different forms of PRAM were employed makes interpretation uncertain. Therefore, the evidence is mixed and provides little firm support for the idea that E+/A − bias declined among Afro children during the years mentioned.

Racial Attitudes Among Preschoolers from Other Cultural Groups

In 1974, Wendy Wade collected PRAM II data from 51 American Indian children, aged 4-6 to 6-6, who were enrolled in one of three different preschool programs in Wisconsin. The 10 children who lived off the reservation and attended a public school in which they were in a minority had a mean score of 18.1. The 23 children who lived on the reservation and attended a parochial school taught by Euro-American nuns had a mean of 12.2. The 18 children who attended a public school on the reservation and were taught by Indian-Americans obtained a mean of 9.2. Since the PRAM II procedure involves no mention of the race of the persons depicted, it is possible that these children may have identified the darker-skinned figures as Indian-American. If so, the pattern of means would seem consistent with Wade's observation that in both reservation schools there was a concerted effort to emphasize Indian values, culture, identity, and pride. Unfortunately, the practical constraints of Wade's study prevented her from determining how the children identified the darker figures and, thus, we cannot draw any firm conclusions from this interesting set of data.

In the investigation cited in chapter 3 (Best, Naylor, and Williams, 1975), Cindy Naylor employed translated versions of PRAM II, as well as CMT II, in her study of preschool children in France and Italy. The French and Italian adjectives employed in the translated PRAM II procedure were the same as those used for the CMT II translation (see Table 3-7). When administered PRAM II by Euro-American examiners, the 65 French children (mean age 5-11) obtained a mean score of 15.9, with 63% of the children showing some evidence of E+/A− bias (scores 15 and up), and 5% showing evidence of A+/E− bias (scores 9 and down). The 24 Italian children obtained

a mean score of 16.5, with 83% showing evidence of
E+/A− bias, and 0% showing evidence of A+/E− bias.
Holding race of examiner constant (i.e., Euro-American),
these French and Italian means are found to fall between
the Afro-American mean of 15.3 and the Euro-American
mean of 18.7, being somewhat closer to the former than
the latter. While the European children were perhaps
slightly more biased than the Afro-American children,
they were noticeably less biased than the Euro-American
children.

The finding of pro-light-skinned/anti-dark-skinned bias
among these European preschoolers has important
implications. Descriptions of the preschool populations
involved indicate that these children had had virtually no
personal contact with dark-skinned persons. Further, in
France and Italy there is neither the general preoccupation
with race and racial classification nor the degree of racial
discrimination and prejudice which may be encountered
in the United States. In other words, these European
preschoolers display a positive attitude toward light-
skinned persons which cannot be considered a racial
attitude, in the usual sense.* Their bias could be due to a
general tendency to view light things more positively than
dark things, or it could be that the light-skinned persons
are positively evaluated because they are more familiar to
the child, or because he perceives them as more similar to
himself. We will consider this matter further in our
discussion of theory in chapter 10.

*Other Findings Concerning PRAM II Scores
at the Preschool Level*

One of the principal advantages of PRAM II over
PRAM I and earlier procedures is that the 24-item
PRAM II procedure provides the opportunity for a more

*This argument may be more persuasive for the Italian children than for the
French, since it is possible that the latter may have had some contact with
negative attitudes toward dark-skinned Algerians.

careful assessment of individual differences in racial attitude. We shall comment on the reliability of the PRAM II scores, on the correlations which have been found with other subject variables such as age, sex, and IQ, and on the relationship between the racial attitudes of children and their mothers. We also wish to consider the question of the degree to which the PRAM II findings are dependent on the particular skin colors of the stimulus figures.

Reliability / The effectiveness of an attitude measurement procedure in identifying individual differences in attitude is assessed by the reliability of the scores obtained by the procedure. The reliability of the PRAM II racial attitude scores has been studied in two ways: in terms of the *internal consistency* of the measure at a given point in time; and in terms of the *stability* of the measure from one time to another (Williams, Best, Boswell, Mattson, and Graves, 1975). One index of internal consistency is the correlation between the part-scores which children make on the two halves of PRAM II—Series A and Series B. In employing this index we are asking, in effect, whether the child who reveals a particular type of bias on one half of the test reveals a similar bias on the other half. The answer to this question is in the affirmative: in the preschool standardization study the two part-scores from PRAM II were found to correlate .71. This result leads to an estimated internal consistency coefficient of .83 for the whole 24-item test. This degree of internal consistency would be considered acceptable in most attitude assessment situations and is particularly impressive in view of the fact that we are dealing here with the test performance of preschool children.*

*The correlation between scores on Series A and Series B, and the fact that the two series generate comparable means and standard deviations, have led to the conclusion that the two series may be considered as equivalent short forms of the PRAM II procedure. The existence of equivalent forms is particularly useful for "pre-post" studies of attitude change such as those reported in chapter 5.

The second type of reliability involves the stability of PRAM II scores over time. The question here is whether those children who demonstrate a particular bias at one point in time will demonstrate a similar bias at a subsequent retesting. One such study involved 38 Euro five-year-olds who were administered PRAM II twice with a four-month interval between testings. The correlation of scores between the two administrations yielded a coefficient of .46. More impressive were the results of a study by Linda Mattson who readministered the PRAM II procedure to a group of 57 five-year-old Euro and Afro children who had taken the test approximately one year earlier as four-year-olds. The first and second administrations were conducted by different examiners who were of the same race. When Mattson compared the test and retest scores she obtained a correlation coefficient of .55 which indicated an appreciable similarity in the rank-order of scores across the one year time interval; children who showed a strong E+/A − bias at four years also tended to show a similar bias at five years. It was found that 40% of the children had score changes of 2 points or less, 65% had changes of 4 points or less, and only 35% had score changes of 5 points or more. Considering the possible score range of 24 points and the actual score range of 20 points (4–24) at the first testing, these score changes appear relatively small and provide additional evidence of the stability of the PRAM II scores across this time interval.

While even greater reliability in PRAM scores would be desirable, we conclude that PRAM II scores have sufficient internal consistency to make us confident that true individual differences are being measured, and that PRAM II scores have sufficient stability to make us confident that these individual differences tend to persist over time. Perhaps the reader has been taking all this for granted, but we cannot afford to do so. Researchers spend a sizable proportion of their time proving the obvious, and the history of science is replete with instances where the obvious has been found to be unprovable.

Correlates of PRAM II Scores at the Preschool Level / Having just seen that PRAM II scores reflect moderately stable individual differences in children's racial attitudes, we will now consider the available evidence regarding the relationship of PRAM II scores to other variables of interest. We have already considered one such characteristic—the race of the child—and have seen that Afro children make consistently lower scores on the PRAM procedures than do Euro children. While the first inclination is to attribute this to racial membership, we must consider the possibility that the observed difference might be due to some other variable which is confounded with the racial classification. For example, the PRAM II procedure requires a child to be familiar with the meanings of certain evaluative words such as good, bad, helpful, unfriendly, etc. If the Afro children, as a group, are less familiar with some of these words, then their lower average score might be simply a reflection of the fact that some of the test items are not comprehensible to them. We will return to an examination of this question later in this section after we have reviewed the evidence regarding the relationship of PRAM II scores to general vocabulary level.

In conducting psychological research with children it is important to examine the data for possible sex differences. When such an examination is made for PRAM II scores, one finds a consistent tendency for boys to score slightly higher than girls. For example, some evidence of this effect was found in all four of the race of subject/race of examiner groups in the preschool standardization study. When all of the subjects from this study are combined and subdivided by sex, the 136 boys obtained a mean score of 16.45 while the 136 girls obtained a mean score of 15.30. While this difference is not large in magnitude (and is not statistically significant) it would still seem wise to maintain equal ratios of boys to girls in future research studies of racial attitude at the preschool level.

Let us consider the relationship of PRAM II scores to the variables of chronological age and vocabulary-IQ, as assessed by the Peabody Picture Vocabulary Test. For comparative purposes we will also examine the control sex-role scores which were obtained during the administration of PRAM II. These latter scores reflect the child's awareness of conventional sex-stereotyped behaviors, such as men fixing cars and building barns, and women buying dresses and baking pies. These scores range from 0 to 12 with high scores indicative of high sex-role awareness and midrange scores (around 6) indicative of little awareness. Low scores, which would indicate a reversal of conventional sex-roles, are rarely found (additional details concerning the sex-role measure may be found in Appendix B).

Table 4-9 summarizes product-moment correlations from the PRAM II standardization study among the subject variables of racial attitude (RA), sex-role (SR), chronological age (CA), and Peabody Picture Vocabulary Test IQ. It will be observed that the racial attitude and sex-role scores from the PRAM II procedure showed only a weak positive correlation (.16) with one another, indicating that the two PRAM II scores are essentially independent of one another.

Note first the correlations of the sex-role scores with age and IQ. In both instances, substantial positive associations are found. As preschool children increase in age, their knowledge of sex-role behaviors increases and, at any given age, the brighter children show more such knowledge than do the duller children. This finding is consistent with the idea that the preschool child is acquiring his knowledge of sex-roles from his contact with the surrounding culture—as he grows older he learns more and, if he is brighter, he learns more rapidly.

Table 4-9. Intercorrelations of Racial Attitude (RA) Scores, and Sex-Role (SR) Scores with Chronological Age (CA), and Peabody Picture Vocabulary Test (PPVT) IQs (N = 268) (Williams, Best, Boswell, Mattson, and Graves, 1975)

	SR	CA	IQ
RA	.16	.08	.15
SR	—	.41*	.33*

*p < .01

Compare these sex-role findings with the findings for the racial attitude scores in the table. In this case, we find only weak positive associations between the racial attitude scores and the age and IQ variables—statistically, neither of the correlations reaches the 1% level of significance. These findings indicate that there is little or no tendency for racial attitude scores to increase with age within the age range studied (3-1 to 7-1); nor is there any appreciable tendency for the brighter children to obtain scores different from those of the duller children. These conclusions, in turn, are not consistent with the idea that preschool children learn their racial bias solely on the basis of contact with the dominant, pro-Euro, American culture. If they did, we would expect to see their racial attitude scores increase appreciably with age and correlate appreciably with IQ—and they do not.

Returning to the earlier question regarding the mean differences in racial attitude scores between Afro and Euro preschoolers, if we propose that Afro children score lower on PRAM II because they are less familiar with the words used in the test items, then we are proposing in effect that children's performance on the test is related to their level of vocabulary development. However, we have just seen that this is not so—the racial attitude scores of children are not related to their vocabulary IQ's. Hence, the evidence seems to speak against the notion that the mean difference in the scores of Afro and Euro children is due to vocabulary differences, and we conclude that the difference probably is due to the racial membership variable.

Other possible correlates of PRAM II scores were explored by Donna Boswell (1974) in a study of five-year-old Euro-American children. In this investigation, each child was administered PRAM II and CMT II and the child's mother completed a questionnaire, which included a measure of attitude toward Afro-Americans and measures of the personality traits of manifest anxiety and authoritarianism. As described in chapter 3, Boswell also measured the child's aversion to the dark of night and thunderstorms by means of a composite score based on an interview with the child and the mother's responses to certain questionnaire items. Boswell intercorrelated her various measures and found several interesting relationships. PRAM II and CMT II were found to have a significant positive correlation ($r = .71$), confirming the finding of several other studies which will be reviewed in chapter 8. The children's PRAM II scores were found to correlate significantly and in the expected direction with mother's racial attitude ($r = .28$), while CMT II scores did not ($r = -.10$). On the other hand, CMT II scores correlated significantly with the aversion to darkness scores ($r = .40$) while PRAM II scores did not ($r = .16$). Neither PRAM II nor CMT II scores were found to correlate with the two maternal personality variables, but Boswell noted that the evidence of defensiveness of many of the mothers in taking these procedures makes this finding inconclusive. Since both the CMT II scores and mother's racial attitude scores correlated with the PRAM II scores, but not with one another, they were combined as independent predictors to yield a multiple correlation of .79 with PRAM II scores. This indicated that the degree of racial bias in these preschool children could be predicted quite well by a joint consideration of the child's white-black color bias, and his mother's attitude toward Afro-American persons.

While the existing evidence regarding correlates of PRAM II scores is useful, the picture is an incomplete one with many variables remaining to be investigated. For example, there are no data relating PRAM II scores to the child's socioeconomic background, a variable which Porter (1971) found to be related to the racial attitudes of the preschool children whom she studied.

Color of Stimulus Figures: The Baugher Study

To what degree is the evidence of E+/A− bias obtained with the PRAM II procedure dependent upon the particular skin colors employed in the stimulus figures, i.e., the pinkish-tan color used to represent Euro-Americans and the medium-brown color used to represent Afro-Americans? Robert Baugher (1973) has conducted an investigation bearing on this question. This study, done in California in 1972, involved 43 Euro and 40 Afro preschoolers who ranged in age from 3-1 to 5-11, with a mean age of 4-5. Baugher employed stimulus figures (doll cutouts) of three different skin colors: a pink-tan color; a light-brown color; and a dark-brown color. The dolls were presented in pairs to the children, sometimes with the pink-tan doll paired with the light-brown, sometimes with the pink-tan paired with the dark-brown, and sometimes with the light-brown paired with the dark-brown. Other than this variation in stimulus figures, Baugher's procedure was modeled after PRAM II and involved the presentation of a given pair of stimulus figures, the telling of a story containing a positive or negative evaluative adjective, and the recording of the child's choice of figure as the one described.

Baugher's data indicate that the same finding was obtained with all three pairs of stimulus figures; namely, the lighter figure of the two was positively evaluated relative to the darker figure. What we have been calling E+/A− bias was equally evident when the pink-tan figure was paired with the light-brown figure, and when it was paired with the dark-brown figure. Baugher's most striking finding concerned the difference in the children's responses to the light-brown figure depending on the figure with which it was paired. As shown in Table 4-10, when the light-brown figure was paired with dark-brown, it tended to be positively evaluated; when paired with pink-tan, it tended to be negatively evaluated. We also see that this effect was evident among both Euro and Afro children, but was not as pronounced among the latter.

Baugher concluded that his findings suggested the operation of a light-dark gradient in the responses of young children to persons differing in skin color, i.e., that children tend to evaluate lighter persons more positively than darker persons regardless of the particular skin colors involved. This conclusion is of considerable theoretical importance.

Baugher used all 24 of the PRAM II adjectives and computed a PRAM-like total score by counting one point each time the lighter figure was selected for a positive adjective, and one point each time the darker figure was selected for a negative adjective. Scored in this way, Baugher obtained mean scores of 17.6 for his Euro subjects and 15.0 for his Afro subjects. Since a Euro examiner was used in the Baugher study, the foregoing means can be compared with the Euro examiner means from the PRAM II standardization study which were 18.7 for Euro preschoolers and 15.2 for Afro preschoolers. From this

Table 4-10. Percent Frequency of Positive Evaluation of the Light-Brown Figure   (Baugher, 1973)

	Light Brown w/Dark Brown	Light Brown w/Pink-Tan
Euro Ss	71	25
Afro Ss	59	31
All Ss	65	28

comparison, we see that the degree of light/dark skin-color bias shown by Euro and Afro children on Baugher's procedure is highly similar to the degree of E+/A − bias which Euro and Afro children display on PRAM II.

STUDIES OF RACIAL ATTITUDES IN THE EARLY SCHOOL YEARS

Although the PRAM II technique was developed to provide a measure of racial bias at the preschool level, the procedure has also been found to be useful in studies of children in the early school years (Williams, Best, and Boswell, 1975). In the fall of 1972, a large-scale PRAM II study was conducted in a single, interracial, public, elementary school in Winston-Salem, North Carolina. The racial composition of the children in all classrooms in the school approximated 70% Euro-American and 30% Afro-American, and the racial composition of the school faculty was approximately the same. In this study all first and third graders, and samples of second and fourth graders, were administered PRAM II and the Peabody Picture Vocabulary Test by female college student examiners. The basic design of the study was similar to that of the preschool standardization study for PRAM II, with approximately half of the children in each race of subject group being administered the procedure by Euro examiners, and the others being tested by Afro examiners. This joint variation in race of subject and race of examiner led again to four major research groups: Euro children/Euro examiner; Euro children/Afro examiner; Afro children/Euro examiner; Afro children/Afro examiner. Each subject group was composed of approximately the same number of boys and girls. After the random elimination of some subjects to equalize the numbers of children tested by Euro and Afro examiners, mean PRAM II scores were computed for each of the four research groups at each of the four school grade levels. These are shown in Table 4-11.

An examination of the means on the right margin of Table 4-11 indicates that, at each grade level, the Euro-American children scored higher than the Afro-American children, and this observation was confirmed by statistical tests. Thus, the tendency toward a higher degree of E+/A− bias in Euro children, seen earlier at the preschool level, was also evident in the early school years. The evidence regarding race of examiner effects was less clear. While there was some indication in grades one, two, and three of a tendency for children to obtain higher scores with Euro examiners than with Afro examiners, the difference was statistically significant only at the third grade level.

Since race of examiner was not a major influence on the scores obtained, the two race of examiner groups at each grade level were pooled in order to examine the developmental trends in more detail. Also employed for reference purposes were the mean scores obtained by Euro and Afro preschoolers in the PRAM II standardization study. For the Euro-American children, the respective mean scores for the five age groups (preschool through fourth grade) were 17.0, 18.3, 19.0, 16.4, and 15.6. Statistical analyses revealed that the degree of E+/A− bias in the Euro group increased significantly from the preschool to the second grade level, and decreased significantly from the second to the third. At the third and fourth grade levels, the Euro-American children were displaying significantly less bias than at the first grade level, an effect congruent with Traynham's (1974) finding that the PRAM II scores of his third graders indicated less E+/A− bias than did those of his kindergarten subjects. For the five age groups of Afro-American children, the respective means were 14.7, 14.3, 13.2, 12.6, and 13.5. The suggestion of a trend toward a diminution in E+/A− bias from the preschool level through the early school years was not confirmed by the statistical analysis.

Table 4-11. Mean PRAM II Racial Attitude Scores for Children in Grades One through Four Classified by Race of Subject and Race of Examiner   (Williams, Best, and Boswell, 1975)

Race of Subject	Race of Examiner		
	Euro	Afro	Total
A. *Grade One*			
Euro	19.0 (N = 49)	17.6 (N = 49)	18.3 (N = 98)
Afro	15.3 (N = 27)	13.3 (N = 27)	14.3 (N = 54)
Total	17.7 (N = 76)	16.1 (N = 76)	16.9 (N = 152)
B. *Grade Two*			
Euro	19.4 (N = 19)	18.6 (N = 19)	19.0 (N = 38)
Afro	14.4 (N = 21)	11.9 (N = 21)	13.2 (N = 42)
Total	16.8 (N = 40)	15.1 (N = 40)	15.9 (N = 80)
C. *Grade Three*			
Euro	18.3 (N = 56)	14.5 (N = 56)	16.4 (N = 112)
Afro	13.3 (N = 23)	11.9 (N = 23)	12.6 (N = 46)
Total	16.8 (N = 79)	13.7 (N = 79)	15.3 (N = 158)
D. *Grade Four*			
Euro	16.2 (N = 18)	15.1 (N = 18)	15.6 (N = 36)
Afro	13.3 (N = 16)	13.6 (N = 16)	13.5 (N = 32)
Total	14.9 (N = 34)	14.4 (N = 34)	14.6 (N = 68)

The school-age data were also examined by computing the percent of Euro and Afro children at each grade level who obtained racial attitude scores falling in the following score categories: A+/E− bias (scores of 0–9); no bias (scores of 10–14); and E+/A− bias (scores of 15–24). The percents of children at the five grade levels scoring in each of these three categories are shown in Figure 4-3. It can be seen that approximately three-quarters of the Euro preschool through second grade children show E+/A− bias, with a sharp reduction in grades three and four to only slightly more than one-half. There also appears to be a related increase in the proportion of Euro children in the No Bias category, from approximately one-fifth of the preschool through second graders to approximately one-third of the third and fourth graders.

Figure 4-3. Percent of Children in Five School Grades (Preschool through Fourth) Displaying Pro-Afro/Anti-Euro (A+/E−) Bias, No Bias, or Pro-Euro/Anti-Afro (E+/A−) Bias (Williams, Best, and Boswell, 1975)

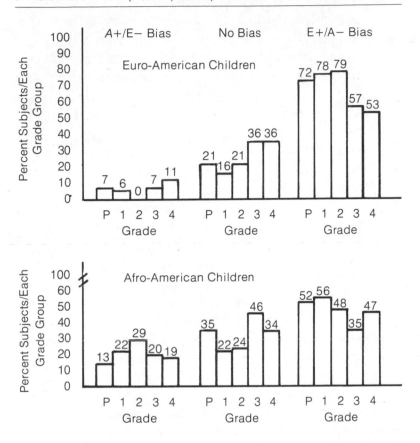

The data of the Afro children seen in Figure 4-3 show little evidence of consistent age trends. While the proportion of Afro children showing E+/A− bias appears to drop between the first and third grade levels, it appears to rise again at the fourth grade level. Likewise, the proportion of children in the No Bias category appears to rise from the second grade to third grade levels but to fall again at the fourth grade level. Of particular interest is the absence of any simple age trend in A+/E− bias which appears to increase from preschool to second grade, and to fall again at the third and fourth grade levels. It can also be observed that, at each grade level studied, the proportion of Afro children displaying E+/A− bias was considerably higher than the proportion displaying A+/E− bias.

As noted earlier, the school-age data which we have been discussing were obtained from children in a single school in Winston-Salem, North Carolina. How representative are these data? A comparative study of racial attitude scores in several groups of second grade children from different geographical locations was conducted during 1972–73 by Alex Mabe, Kinny Mack, Ken Reckenbeil, and Wayne Hodges. The examiners for all of these groups were Euro-American, and the two comparable second grade groups from the Winston-Salem study were included for reference purposes. The mean scores for these groups are presented in Table 4-12.

Six groups of Euro-American children were tested: three from interracial public schools in North Carolina; one from an interracial public school in South Carolina; one from a private all-Euro school in South Carolina; and one from a public all-Euro school in New York State. As can be seen in the table, the mean scores for all of these groups fell toward the upper end of the PRAM II score range and, thus, were all indicative of relatively strong E+/A− bias. The fact that the highest mean score was obtained in the group from the all-Euro school in South Carolina (21.0) and the lowest mean score was obtained in the all-Euro school in New York (18.5) is suggestive of a slight regional variation in scores. On the other hand, the pattern of means provides no indication that the racial composition of the school affects the racial attitudes of Euro second graders. The relatively small size of the four groups of Afro second graders reported in Table 4-12 makes us cautious about drawing conclusions, and we note only that the mean scores in three groups were indicative of a

Table 4-12. Mean PRAM II Racial Attitude Scores of Second Grade Children Tested by Euro-American Examiners (Williams, Best, and Boswell, 1975)

	Race of Subjects	
	Euro-American	*Afro-American*
Winston-Salem, N.C.		
Public, Interracial School	19.2 (N = 34)*	14.2 (N = 23)*
Mooresville, N.C.		
Public, Interracial School	19.9 (N = 44)	11.6 (N = 14)
Greenville, N.C.		
Public, Interracial School	19.0 (N = 32)	14.6 (N = 20)
Beaufort, S.C.		
Public, Interracial School	20.5 (N = 18)	14.2 (N = 18)
Beaufort, S.C.		
Private, All-Euro School	21.0 (N = 36)	———
Albertson, N.Y.		
Public, All-Euro School	18.5 (N = 73)	———

*The numbers of subjects reported here are the total numbers tested by Euro examiners before the random exclusion of subjects for statistical analyses (see Table 4-11).

moderate degree of E+/A− bias, while in the other group there was no indication of racial bias. Regarding the question of the representative nature of the Winston-Salem groups, we see that the Euro children's mean score of 19.2, and the Afro children's mean score of 14.2, were neither unusually high nor unusually low when compared with the other groups tested. While this evidence of typicality at the second grade level is useful, we cannot, of course, conclude that the score trends across the primary grades would be exactly the same in other localities.

Returning to the data from the major Winston-Salem study, it was found that the PRAM II scores of children in the first four school grades revealed a high degree of reliability, as assessed by internal consistency. For example, the correlations between the part-scores obtained for the two halves of the PRAM II procedure ranged from .64 to .78, which enables us to estimate the reliability of the total scores as falling between .78 and .88.

When the PRAM II total scores were examined in relation to IQ scores from the Peabody Picture Vocabulary Test, negligible correlation coefficients were obtained. Thus, the school-age data are consistent with the preschool data, both indicating that the reliable individual differences in racial attitude scores are not appreciably correlated with individual differences in intelligence, as assessed by vocabulary level. Another similarity between the preschool and school-age levels was the absence of any significant relationship between children's sex and their racial attitudes.

Our interpretation of the findings of the developmental study must be tempered by the usual cautionary statements concerning cross-sectional research designs. The assessment of developmental trends via such designs requires the assumption that there are no major factors influencing the research data other than those normally associated with increases in chronological age. In effect, we must assume that our first graders are subject to the same influences which our fourth graders were three years earlier when they were first graders. In view of many significant changes relating to race in recent years, this assumption is more difficult to meet in the study of racial bias than in other areas of developmental research.

With the foregoing caution in mind, we can note that the pro-Euro/anti-Afro bias of preschool children appears to be carried forward into the early school grades. Among Euro-American children, pro-Euro bias appears to increase to the second grade level and then to decline. Afro-American children, in general, appear to maintain a moderate degree of pro-Euro bias through the early school years, with no appreciable evidence of any age trends. Likewise, no evidence was found of any systematic increase in pro-Afro bias among the minority of Afro-American children displaying such bias.

A question naturally arises concerning the development of racial attitudes during the later school years. While it is beyond the scope of this book to attempt a systematic review of all research studies of racial attitudes at the junior high school and high school levels, the results of one of our recent studies can be used to point up some of the trends which may be developing at this age level. In the study, conducted in Virginia in 1972 (Morland, 1972), Euro and Afro students from the sixth, eighth, tenth, and twelfth grades rated a variety of race and color concepts on the semantic differential. Among the concepts rated were "White American," "Black American," and "American." The Evaluation (E) scores of the differential were used as an indication of attitude toward these concepts, with low E scores indicative of more favorable attitudes and high E scores indicative of less favorable attitudes. The mean E scores obtained for the concepts "White American" and "Black American" are shown in Figure 4-4. It can be seen that among the Euro-American students the sixth graders rated "White American" more positively than "Black American" and that this same finding was obtained throughout the junior and senior high school years. Among the Afro-American students the picture was quite different. At the sixth-grade level, the Afro students rated "White American" somewhat more positively than "Black American," but this picture changed. Starting in the eighth grade, the Afro students rated "Black American" more positively and this effect continued through the high school years. While such cross-sectional findings must be interpreted with caution, these results suggest that the early junior high school years may be the period during which young Afro-Americans first come to feel more positively about

Figure 4-4. Mean Evaluation Scores (Low = Positive) for the Concepts "White American" and "Black American" Rated by Euro- and Afro-American Students in Grades 6 through 12   (Morland, 1972)

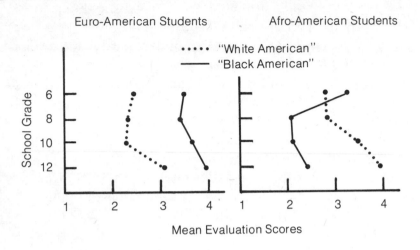

their own racial group than they do about the majority group. It is interesting to note also the ratings which the students assigned to the concept "American." In general, the evaluative ratings of this concept were quite similar to the ratings which each racial group gave to the concept "White American." Thus, the Afro sixth and eighth graders rated "American" positively, with the ratings moving in a negative direction among tenth and twelfth graders. One could infer from this that the older Afro students did not identify their own racial group with the concept "American."

Our review of the research evidence regarding the development of racial attitudes in young children has shown that preschool children—both Euro and Afro—display a bias favoring light-skinned (Euro) persons over dark-skinned (Afro) persons, with the degree of this bias being somewhat less among Afro children. This E+/A− bias appears to continue into the early school grades and, while seeming to have diminished somewhat by the fourth grade, is still evident in studies at the sixth grade level. Thus, we have seen that, throughout the period of childhood, both Euro and Afro children share a bias toward the positive evaluation of light-skinned human figures.

5.
Modification of Color and Racial Attitudes

The studies reviewed in the two previous chapters have dealt with the natural development of race and color attitudes in young children. We might refer to these as "measurement" studies to reflect the fact that the researchers' interest was in measuring the children's attitudes without intending in any way to influence them. We will now review a group of "modification" studies, in each of which there has been a deliberate attempt to produce a systematic change in children's attitudes toward color and/or race. It is possible that our earlier discussions may have led to a tacit assumption that, once such attitudes develop, it would be difficult to change them. We shall see that this assumption is incorrect, and that the evaluative responses of preschool and early school-age children to the colors black and white, and to dark- and light-skinned human figures, can be modified under proper learning conditions. We shall also see that the process of attitude change in children of this age has not yet been fully researched and is not well understood. One reason for this has been the lack of well-articulated theory regarding the development and maintenance of these attitudes in young children.

Research conducted without adequate theoretical guidance tends to yield a fragmentary picture of the phenomena under investigation—and such is the present case. A second reason for the incomplete picture is the recency of the development of a research interest in this topic—the earliest study which we cite was conducted in 1968—with the result that attitude change has not yet received proper time and attention. For example, we know that attitudinal responses can be changed in a laboratory learning situation, but we know little about the persistence of these effects across time or the generalization of these effects to behaviors in nontest situations. These important questions are not, of course, peculiar to attitude modification research but are encountered whenever one attempts a systematic modification of human behavior. For example, are the behavior changes brought about in the school classroom or the psychotherapist's office specific only to that time and place? Or do they tend to persist and generalize to other behavioral situations? While these questions must ultimately be answered regarding attitude modification, they should not deter us from a consideration of the prior question concerning the original conditions under which children's attitudes can be changed. Virtually all of the research we review has been focused on this latter question.

We saw in chapter 4 that many preschool children, both Euro- and Afro-American, display a tendency toward the positive evaluation of light-skinned persons relative to dark-skinned persons, and we will now review studies in which there has been an attempt to weaken this E+/A− bias. All these studies have employed some version of the Preschool Racial Attitude Measure (PRAM) which is described in chapter 4 and Appendix B.

RACIAL ATTITUDE CHANGE VIA DIRECT
BEHAVIOR MODIFICATION TECHNIQUES

We will describe three studies in which an effort was made to change the E+/A− bias of preschool children by laboratory learning procedures. These procedures make use of the principle that responses which are followed by positive consequences ("reinforcers") tend to increase in frequency, while responses followed by negative consequences ("punishers") tend to decrease in frequency. The reinforcers and punishers employed have been relatively innocuous, consisting of verbal comments such as "that's right" or "that's wrong," the giving or taking away of coins or candy, and so forth.

The first two studies were conducted by Drew Edwards in 1968 (Edwards and Williams, 1970) and by Allen McMurtry in 1969 (McMurtry and Williams, 1972). In the learning phase of these studies, Euro children were trained individually by Euro experimenters using the racial attitude pictures and three of the evaluative adjectives from PRAM I. Some children were trained on three positive adjectives while others were trained on three negative adjectives. The procedure was designed to provide a "punisher," whenever the child selected a light-skinned figure in response to a "good" word (an E+ response), or selected a dark-skinned figure in response to a "bad" word (an A− response). This was done by giving each child a number of pennies, and telling him that whenever he made a wrong response two of his pennies would be taken away, and that he could keep the pennies he had left at the end of the game. The subject was then given twelve training trials using the PRAM I pictures and stories involving the three evaluative adjectives; each adjective was thus given four times. Whenever a child made an E+ or A− response, two of his pennies were taken away (in the McMurtry study the child was also told, "no, that's wrong"; if the child made an A+ or E−

response, he was told, "yes, that's right"). Under these conditions, the child's tendency to make the "customary" E+ or A− responses rapidly changed, as can be seen in Figure 5-1 which displays the learning phase data from the Edwards study. In this figure, the broken line indicates the performance of the children in the training group who lost pennies when they made E+ or A− responses, while the solid line represents the performance of children in the control group who responded to the stories with no punishment of responses. Both experimental and control groups began the task with a high baseline level of customary E+ and A− responding. Under the impact of the training procedure, the frequency of E+ and A− responses in the experimental group decreased rapidly and, by the end of twelve trials, the children were making only about 15% customary (or 85% noncustomary) responses. The control subjects, on the other hand, continued to make customary responses at the high base rate throughout the twelve trials. The learning data from the McMurtry study were highly similar to that just described, and it was concluded in both studies that the children's initial tendency to evaluate the Euro figures positively and the Afro figures negatively had been reversed by the training procedures. Further, in both studies a control procedure indicated that the change was limited to the child's responses to the racial figures and was not due to the child merely having learned a general tendency to reverse all of his initial response tendencies, i.e., to "say things backwards." While we will not discuss all of the theoretical implications here, the general findings from the second phase of the two studies are of interest. In the Edwards study, it was demonstrated that the children who had been trained to give noncustomary responses to one set of positive or negative adjectives also gave noncustomary responses when subsequently tested on a second set of the same evaluative type to which they had not been previously exposed. For example, children

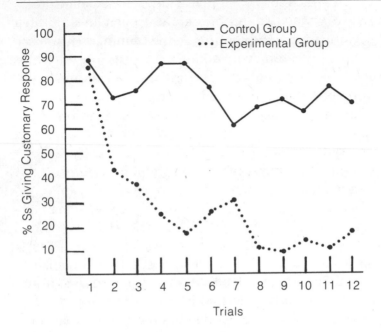

Figure 5-1. Percent of Children in the Training Group and in the Control Group Giving a Customary Racial Attitude Response (Dark-skinned Person to Negative, Light-skinned Person to Positive) on Each of 12 Trials (Edwards and Williams, 1970)

who had been punished for associating *ugly, naughty,* and *mean* with the Afro figure, also showed a reduction in the tendency to associate *dirty, stupid,* and *bad* with this figure. It was evident from this that the training given the children had resulted, not merely in a mechanical reversal of responses to the training words, but in a broader effect, that is, a general reduction in the tendency to associate negative words with Afro figures. In the second phase of the McMurtry study, it was shown that training on one type of evaluative adjective also influenced the children's responses to the other type of adjective. For example, the training of the children to associate the positive adjectives *pretty, good,* and *nice* with the Afro figure resulted in a reduction in their tendency to choose the Afro figure in response to the negative adjectives *ugly, bad,* and *mean.*

Once again we see that the effects of training are not limited to changes in response to the training words but have more general effects on the children's responses to light- and dark-skinned figures. The generalization effects found by McMurtry and Edwards make it possible to think of the behavior modification procedures as resulting in a general change in attitude toward Euro and Afro persons, rather than merely the learning of specific responses.

A third direct behavior modification study was conducted by Suellen Smith in 1973 (Best, Smith, Graves, and Williams, 1975). Because the study has important theoretical and practical implications, we will describe it in some detail. Smith was interested in the efficacy of an audiovisual "teaching machine" procedure for the modification of racial bias. The study was conducted in four stages: a baseline assessment, a modification phase, a postmodification assessment, and a follow-up phase. In the initial assessment phase, 56 five-year-old children were given a modified version of the PRAM II procedure; for each child one-half (e.g., Series A) of the test was administered in standard interview fashion, while the other half (e.g., Series B) was administered by machine. In the latter case, the child stood before a machine which displayed the PRAM II pictures one at a time and which played the appropriate PRAM II story via tape recording. When the child pushed a clear plastic panel to indicate his choice of the two figures displayed, the machine advanced to the next picture, played the next story, and so forth. As the data indicated that the children obtained comparable PRAM II part-scores from the standard and machine-administered procedures, the two part-scores were combined into a single total score for the selection of subjects for participation in the attitude modification phase of the study. Reasoning that it made little sense to talk of modifying racial bias in children who displayed none, Smith selected only those children with total PRAM scores of 14 or higher for the second phase of the study. The group of 39 children chosen in this manner consisted of 29 Euro-American subjects and 10 Afro-American subjects with a mean age of five years, seven months.

The purposes of the modification phase of the study were fourfold: first, to determine if the children would modify their tendency to give E+ and A− responses when the appropriate reinforcements were machine administered; second, to ascertain which of two machine-delivered reinforcement procedures was more effective; third, to determine whether training children to modify their responses to one subset of PRAM II pictures and stories via the machine would result in the modification of their responses to the second subset administered under standard testing conditions; and fourth, to ascertain whether any obtained effects would be found to persist across a one-year follow-up period.

In order to accomplish these objectives, Smith decided to train each child on the PRAM II subset (Series A or Series B) which had been machine administered during the assessment phase, and later to retest him on the subset which had been given in standard fashion during the assessment phase. For example, a child who had received standard Series A and machine Series B during assessment, would be trained on Series B and subsequently retested on Series A. In this instance, the Series A pictures and stories would never be directly associated with the teaching machine or the behavior modification procedure.

We will now describe the two types of reinforcement procedures. For one, the "machine advance" condition, the machine was programmed so that it would not proceed to the next picture and story until the child had made the "correct" (noncustomary) response by pressing the panel above the Afro figure in response to a "good" word, or the panel above the Euro figure in response to a "bad" word. This standard teaching machine procedure relies upon the advancement of the machine to serve as a positive reinforcer. For the second or "token" reinforcement procedure, the machine was programmed to advance on the child's first response, whether it was "correct" (noncustomary) or "incorrect" (customary). In the case of the correct response, however, the machine delivered a coin-like token which the child knew he could exchange for candy at the end of the session.

The 39 subjects were divided between the two reinforcement conditions, with 20 children (15 Euro and 5 Afro) assigned to the machine advance group, and 19 children (14 Euro and 5 Afro) to the token group. A trial consisted of the child responding to each of the 12 picture/stories in the appropriate PRAM II subset. Each subject was given one trial per day for six days. Each day's trial was scored in usual PRAM fashion by counting one point for a conventional (E+ or A−) initial response, on each of the twelve response opportunities.

The progression of learning in the two reinforcement conditions is seen in Figure 5-2. For each group, the first

Figure 5-2. Mean PRAM II Scores on Each Trial of Modification Training for Preschool Children Receiving Machine Advance or Token Reinforcement (Best, Smith, Graves, and Williams, 1975)

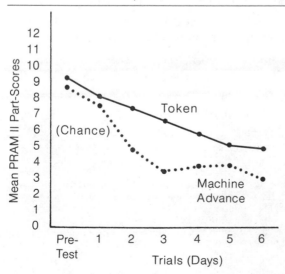

point plotted is the mean machine-administered assessment score obtained during the pretest eight weeks prior to the modification phase. Then follow the mean scores obtained on the six successive training days. The downward slope of the curves indicates that the behavior of the children was being modified by the reinforcement procedures. In the advancement group, where the earlier machine-administered pretest mean was 8.80, the mean for the sixth modification trial was 3.20. In the token group, where the earlier mean was 9.35, the final mean was 4.63. In both groups the modification procedure shifted the children from their initial $E+/A-$ bias to a significant $A+/E-$ bias. The analysis of the data also indicated that the advancement procedure was somewhat more efficacious than the token procedure in bringing about the desired change.*

Having seen that the children's behavior on the training subset could be modified, Smith then tested to see if the learning would generalize to the second PRAM II picture/story subset which had never been associated with the teaching machine. This subset was administered in standard interview fashion one week following the completion of the modification training. The examiners were Euro females who had not been associated with the training. The results of this testing are shown as the posttest means in Table 5-1. The pretest means are those which had been obtained on the same subset two and one-half months earlier. The analyses of these data confirmed the observation that the posttest scores were not significantly different from the chance mean of 6 and,

---

*Some children in the machine-advance condition were remarkably persistent in making incorrect (i.e., customary) responses. In a related study, Samuel Manoogian observed a five-year-old Euro boy who selected the light-skinned figure as the "kind little boy" on the first frame and continued to repeat this response, time after time, occasionally commenting that there must be something wrong with the machine. After response number 650 he was heard to say, "Is it the brown boy? No, it must be the pink one," after which he continued to make the same response. Not until response number 935 did he venture to press the panel over the dark-skinned figure, which made the machine advance to the next item—to his amazement!

hence, that the children now displayed no evidence of racial bias on the nontrained PRAM II subset. Thus, the effects of training were shown to generalize and affect the child's responses to pictures and evaluative adjectives on which he had not been trained. It can also be observed that the relative superiority of the advancement condition seen during training (see Figure 5-2) was not mirrored in a similar superiority on the generalization task where both procedures seemed to have similar effects. There was no untreated control group in the Smith study because of the limited number of subjects available and the well-documented fact that mean PRAM II scores do not decrease from a first to a second administration of the procedure but, if anything, tend to be slightly higher at a second testing (Williams, Best, Boswell, Mattson, and Graves, 1975).

Taken as a whole, the results of the Smith study indicate that the tendency of preschool children to evaluate Euro figures more positively than Afro figures can be systematically weakened by a teaching machine methodology, with effects which generalize to a nontraining test situation. There is also some evidence regarding the persistence of these effects. One year following the completion of the initial study, an effort was made to contact and retest Smith's subjects who were then first graders. Of the original group of 39 children, 30 were retested by Euro female examiners who were experienced in the administration of PRAM II but who had not been

Table 5-1. Mean Pretest and Posttest Scores of Subjects on the PRAM II Subset Not Employed in Training   (Best, Smith, Graves, and Williams, 1975)

	$\bar{X}$ Pretest	$\bar{X}$ Posttest
Advancement Group (N = 20)	9.40	7.20
Token Group (N = 19)	9.00	6.31
Combined Groups (N = 39)	9.21	6.77

involved in the earlier phases of the study. In this testing, the children were first given the same PRAM II subset (A or B) used as the standard-administration pre- and posttests in the original study, and were then given the subset which had been involved in the training on the teaching machine. For the 30 follow-up subjects, the mean standard-administration PRAM II scores were: pre, 9.20; post, 7.17; follow-up, 8.40. The scores were, thus, seen to drop following the training procedure but to increase again during the following year. The follow-up data were also examined by computing the mean scores on the total 24-item PRAM II procedure (standard-administration series plus machine-administration series) at the pre-evaluation and follow-up-evaluation points—18.17 and 16.40, respectively. This evidence of decrease in E+/A− bias is more impressive when it is noted that PRAM II scores usually increase from the kindergarten to first-grade level. From these analyses it was concluded that there was evidence of some persistence in the attitude change which had been accomplished by training on the teaching machine one year earlier.

Having seen that the racial attitudes of young children are amenable to change with direct behavior modification techniques, we will now review several laboratory studies in which an attempt has been made to change racial attitudes by the indirect means of modifying the child's evaluative responses to the colors black and white.

*RACIAL ATTITUDE CHANGE VIA
THE MODIFICATION OF ATTITUDES
TOWARD BLACK AND WHITE*

We saw, in chapter 3, that preschool children—both Euro and Afro—have a tendency toward the positive evaluation of the color white relative to the color black which seems to parallel their tendency to evaluate light-skinned persons more positively than dark-skinned persons. We will see later, in chapter 8, that individual differences in E+/A− racial bias have been found to correlate with individual differences in W+/B− color bias. The experiments reviewed here have been aimed at investigating the possibility of a functional relationship between the color bias and the racial bias.

Theoretically, there are two ways in which W+/B− color bias may be linked to E+/A− racial bias. First, W+/B− bias may be a reflection of a general tendency among young children to respond more positively to light than to darkness, and this tendency may be one determinant of the tendency to view light-skinned persons more positively than dark-skinned persons. Second, the cultural practice of designating light-skinned persons as "white" and dark-skinned persons as "black" establishes an additional link between the color bias and the racial bias and, in effect, invites the child to generalize his feelings about the color names to the racial groups which are so designated. In sum, the theory proposes that the color bias of young children serves as a support for their racial bias. From this, we deduce that the elimination of W+/B− bias should be accompanied by a reduction in E+/A− bias—if a support is removed, then that which is supported should fall. This is the principal idea being tested in this group of studies.

In all of the studies reviewed here, the investigators have used modified versions of the Color Meaning Test (CMT) procedure, which is described in chapter 3 and in Appendix B. In its standard use this picture-story technique involves showing the child a series of drawings, each of which displays a white animal and a black animal. With each picture, the child is told a story in which a positive or negative evaluative adjective is used and is asked to indicate the animal being described. Under standard conditions, most children display a tendency to select the white animals in response to positive adjectives, and the black animals in response to negative adjectives, and hence reveal what is called W+/B− bias. In most of these modification studies, the investigators have employed punishment of the customary W+ and B− responses and/or positive reinforcement of the non-customary W− and B+ responses. Such training procedures would be expected to move the child away from a W+/B− bias in the direction of a B+/W− bias.

The first study dealing with the modification of W+/B− bias in preschool children was conducted in North Carolina in 1968 (Williams and Edwards, 1969). This investigation was concerned with the effects of attempting to weaken and perhaps reverse W+/B− bias by a behavior modification procedure. Euro-American preschoolers were administered a modified version of CMT I in which each of the children's choices between the white and black animals was followed by positive reinforcement or punishment. Punishment was given for making the usual choices of picking white animals in response to "good" adjectives, and also for picking black animals in response to "bad" adjectives. The punishment consisted of saying "no," and taking away two of the pennies which had been given to the child at the start of the procedure. Positive reinforcement was given for making the unconventional responses, i.e., for choosing black with "good" words and white with "bad" words, and consisted of saying "fine" or "all right," and giving the child 3 M & M candies. The findings of the study indicated that the group of 64 children exposed to the 12 trials of this training procedure gradually abandoned their initial W+/B− bias and eventually developed a moderate B+/W− bias. A second (control) group of 20 children, who took the CMT with no reinforcement or punishment of their responses, continued to display the W+/B− bias throughout the procedure. The results of the study also indicated that the effects of the training procedure tended to persist; two weeks after the initial learning session, the trained subjects were still displaying less evidence of the W+/B— concept than were the control subjects. Two weeks following their last training on the white and black stimuli, the children were administered PRAM I and were found to have a mean score of 7.98 which was significantly lower than the mean of 9.60 in the control group. Another way to describe this effect is to note that while 70% of the control subjects displayed a significant degree of E+/A— bias, only 48% of the trained subjects did. It was concluded that the modification of the W+/B— bias had resulted in a reduction in E+/A— bias.

Procedures similar to those in the study just described were employed by John L. McAdoo (1970) in a 1969 Michigan study involving 65 Afro preschoolers who were tested by Afro examiners. McAdoo administered the PRAM I racial attitude measure once before and once after a training procedure aimed at weakening the W+/B— tendency. When the training procedure involved the punishment (loss of pennies) for customary responses to the white and black animals, the racial attitude scores dropped significantly from a pretraining mean of 8.50 to a posttraining mean of 6.30, a greater absolute change than that obtained by Williams and Edwards. On the other hand, when the training procedure involved only the positive reinforcement (receipt of M & M's) of non-customary responses, there was no appreciable difference in the pretraining mean of 7.45 and the posttraining mean of 7.77. McAdoo, thus, found only partial support for the hypothesized link between color attitudes and racial attitudes.

The results of a study conducted in 1971 by Judith Shanahan (1972) at the University of Washington provide further evidence regarding the weakening of the W+/B— concept by behavior modification procedures. Shanahan's subjects were 28 Euro- and 28 Afro-American first graders who were assigned in equal numbers to experimental (trained) and control (nontrained) groups. Shanahan used the CMT II materials and a training procedure involving tokens which were later exchanged for candy in an effort to weaken the W+/B− concept of the children. The training procedure was found to be effective for both Euro and Afro children. Table 5-2 shows the mean CMT II scores obtained for the trained subjects and for comparable groups of nontrained control subjects. From these data, it is evident that the reinforcement schedules were effective in modifying the W+/B− bias. At the end of training, both groups of trained subjects were scoring toward the low or B+/W− side of the neutral midpoint of 12, while both groups of control subjects remained on the high or W+/B− end of the scale. When the subjects were tested subsequently on PRAM II, the subjects in the Euro experimental group obtained a racial attitude mean of 10.14 which was significantly lower than the Euro control group mean of 16.93, thus replicating Williams and Edwards's findings with Euro children. On the other hand, there was no significant difference in the mean racial attitude scores of the two groups of Afro subjects, with neither mean being significantly different from a chance or random mean of 12. This result, which seems at first puzzling, can perhaps be understood by noting the absence of racial bias in the untreated Afro control group. Apparently, there was no appreciable racial bias among these Afro first graders and, hence, there was nothing to be affected when their color bias was reduced.

The most dramatic evidence of change in racial bias through the modification of color attitudes was obtained in a study by Richard Traynham (1974). This study was conducted with 40 five-year-old and 40 eight-year-old Euro-American children in Arkansas. Using randomly selected experimental and control groups at each age level, Traynham employed punishment (loss of pennies) for W+ and B− responses with the experimental subjects and produced a moderate degree of B+/W− bias in both experimental groups. The control subjects responded to

Table 5-2. Mean CMT II Scores in Trained and Nontrained
Subject Groups   (Shanahan, 1972)

	Trained	Nontrained
Euro Children	10.4	18.5
Afro Children	9.1	16.3

the same CMT pictures and stories as the experimental
subjects but with no punishment of responses. Two
weeks after the final training session all subjects were
administered the 24-item PRAM II procedure. The results
of this testing are seen in Figure 5-3 in which the mean
PRAM II scores of the subjects in the experimental and
control groups, at each of the two age levels, are shown.
As the figure suggests, Traynham demonstrated that the
subjects in the two experimental groups where color bias
had been reversed demonstrated an appreciable degree of
pro-Afro bias, while the control groups continued to
display the usual pro-Euro bias.

Another way to examine this effect is to study the
number of children in the experimental and control
groups who displayed an appreciable degree of E+/A−
bias, were unbiased, or who showed an appreciable
degree of A+/E− bias. Such an analysis is shown in
Table 5-3 which displays the percent of pooled experimental subjects and pooled control subjects scoring in
each of three PRAM II score ranges. We observe that
three-fourths of the control subjects displayed E+/A−
bias, with almost one-quarter being unbiased, and only
2.5% (one subject) showing A+/E− bias. Among the
experimental subjects, only 5% showed E+/A− bias,
52.5% were unbiased, and 42.5% showed A+/E− bias.
Thus, we can see that in the Traynham study the
modification of the color bias did not merely reduce the
E+/A− bias, as in the Williams and Edwards study, or
eliminate it, as in McAdoo's study, but produced a
significant degree of pro-Afro bias among the experimental subjects.

Figure 5-3. Mean PRAM II Racial Attitude Scores of Children in Traynham (1974) Study

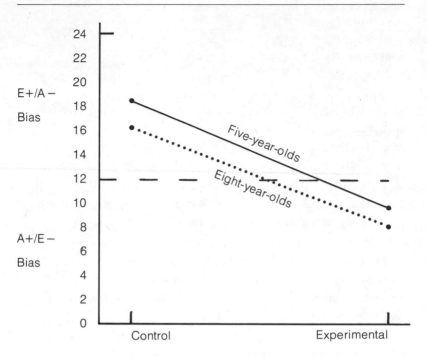

Table 5-3. Percent of Experimental and Control Subjects Scoring in Each of Three PRAM II Score Categories   (Traynham, 1974)

PRAM II Score Range	Control Subjects (N = 40)	Experimental Subjects (N = 40)
E+/A− Bias: 15 up	75.0%	5.0%
No Bias: 10–14	22.5%	52.5%
A+/E− Bias: 9 down	2.5%	42.5%

A fifth study concerned with the use of behavior modification procedures to weaken W+/B− bias was conducted by Margaret Spencer in Kansas in 1970 (Spencer and Horowitz, 1973). In this study, Afro and Euro children, aged 3-3 to 5-11, were positively reinforced for selecting black animals in response to stories containing positive adjectives, and for selecting white animals in response to negative adjectives. Reinforcement was delivered via a mechanical puppet of the "same race" as the child, which nodded and dispensed marbles whenever a B+ or W− response was made. If an "incorrect" (B− or W+) response was made, the experimenter pointed out that the puppet did not give marbles because the subject had not given the correct answer. After two sessions of such training, the initial W+/B− bias of the children was shifted to a clear B+/W− bias. Other children in a control group which had been exposed to all aspects of the procedure except the positive reinforcement and punishment showed no change in their initial W+/B− bias. Additional findings were that the effectiveness of the training procedure was the same for both Afro and Euro children and was not related to the age of the child, i.e., younger and older children appeared to learn equally well.

In the next stage of Spencer's study, the children whose color bias had been reversed were administered a modified PRAM procedure in which the children were asked to select between light- and dark-skinned children as the ones described in stories which contained positive and negative adjectives. The findings indicated that these children displayed no consistent racial bias while children in the control group—where color bias had not been altered—displayed a definite tendency toward E+/A− bias. On this basis, it was concluded that the alteration of the color bias led to the elimination of E+/A− bias among these Euro and Afro preschoolers. The experiment, however, did not stop here. Spencer went on to attempt a further modification of racial bias by using the puppet procedure to train the selection of dark-skinned figures in response to positive words, and the selection of light-skinned figures in response to negative words. Under these conditions, the children shifted from their pre- viously unbiased position and developed a definite tendency toward A+/E− bias while the children in the nonreinforced control group continued to display the E+/A− bias with which they had entered the study. The findings of Spencer and Horowitz, thus, illustrate two types of behavior modification effects: E+/A− bias can be weakened by the changing of the white-black color bias, and can be further modified by direct training procedures.

An interesting theoretical question is whether behavior modification procedures can be used to strengthen further the typical W+/B− bias of the young child and, if so, whether this tends to increase E+/A− bias. This question was explored in a study of Euro and Afro children conducted by Reid Whiteside (1975). The Euro subjects were four-, five-, and six-year-olds enrolled in a private kindergarten. The Afro subjects were enrolled in grades K through 2 in a parochial school, and were thus somewhat older than the Euro subjects. For his experimental subjects, Whiteside used verbal positive reinforcement for conventional CMT responses, i.e., the child was told "that's right" when he selected the white animal figure in response to a "good" word, and when he selected the black animal in response to a "bad" word. The child was also told "that's wrong" whenever a reversed or unconventional response was made. This procedure was continued for 36 trials for each child in the experimental groups. Children in the control groups were administered the CMT procedure with no reinforcement or punishment of responses. The findings of the study indicated that the training procedure was effective in increasing the W+/B− bias in both groups of children. On the last block of 12 training trials, the mean CMT score for the Euro experimental group was 9.75 while that for the Euro control group was 7.35; the mean scores for the Afro experimental and control groups were 9.65 and 7.20, respectively. Subsequently, when PRAM II was administered the children in the experimental group showed more evidence of E+/A− bias than those in the corresponding control groups: Euro experimental group,

19.15; Euro control group, 15.75; Afro experimental group, 16.65; Afro control group, 10.90. Whiteside thus demonstrated that an increase in W+/B− bias was accompanied by an increase in E+/A− bias in both subject groups. Whiteside designed his study with a final stage in which the children were exposed to a special procedure which depicted black in a favorable manner and which was intended to offset the effects of the training which they had received.

In the behavior modification studies discussed above, the training procedures have been based on the principles of operant conditioning, i.e., the modification of the child's bias by having his responses followed by positive or negative consequences. By contrast, there have been studies based on the principles of classical conditioning in which there has been an effort to modify W+/B− bias by the association of white and black with words which are high in affective meaning. Jeffrey Collins (1973) was interested in determining whether the degree of E+/A− bias expressed by Euro preschoolers would be increased by their listening to a tape-recorded story in which white animals were described with a number of positive adjectives and black animals were described with a number of negative adjectives. For example, one group of children heard a story about a pretty white kitten, who lived in a clean white house, who met a naughty black rabbit and an unfriendly black bear, etc. Another group of children heard a similar story in which there was no reference to evaluative adjectives or to the colors black and white. Collins found that the exposure to these stories had no effect on the children's subsequent scores on CMT II or PRAM II. Since the experimental procedure was not effective in modifying the children's W+/B− bias, Collins was unable to make a satisfactory test of his hypothesis that an increase in W+/B− bias would be accompanied by an increase in E+/A− bias.

Two studies conducted by Thomas Parish (Parish, 1972;

Parish and Fleetwood, 1975) indicate that the tendency toward the negative evaluation of black by Euro kindergarten children may be modified by classical conditioning procedures. In a study conducted in Illinois, Parish first had kindergarten children judge a variety of words to determine which they considered to be "good" words. He then exposed his subjects to a classical conditioning procedure in which the color black was regularly associated with such good words as cake, Christmas, and friend. (In the classical conditioning paradigm, the color black was considered the conditioned stimulus, the good word the unconditioned stimulus, and the positive meaning of the good word the unconditioned response.) Parish's expectation was that the association of black with the good words would weaken its negative meaning to the children. The effectiveness of this procedure was subsequently assessed by a variation of the CMT technique in which black animals were presented singly with the child being asked, "Is this a smart dog or a stupid dog?" Using this method, Parish was able to demonstrate a reduction in the children's tendency to associate negative adjectives with the black animals. On the other hand, Parish found no evidence that the training procedure had an effect on the children's attitudes toward Afro persons, as subsequently assessed by a variation of the PRAM II procedure in which the child is presented with single dark-skinned figures, and asked to choose between positive and negative adjectives ("Is this a good boy or a bad boy?"). Reasoning that a more extended training period might produce effects which would generalize to Afro persons, Parish and Fleetwood (1975) conducted a study with Euro-American kindergarten children in Oklahoma in which some children received one training session, other children four sessions, and other children eight. In each training session, the children were seated in a group and viewed the projection of the colors black, orange, blue, and green on a wall. Each color was presented singly a total of 36 times in each training session. On each of the 36 presentations of the color black, the experimenter spoke a positive word (see above) which the children repeated aloud. Following the completion of the requisite number of training sessions, the children were tested individually on Series A of PRAM II or on Parish's 12-item nonforced-choice procedure. The results of the study are shown in Table 5-4 where the PRAM II scores indicate that E+/A− bias diminished regularly with increased amounts of training, finally reaching an unbiased position in the eight-session training group. The scores for the 12-item Parish procedure—one point for each negative adjective selected—also show a systematic reduction in the tendency to associate negative adjectives with dark-skinned figures. Parish concluded from his second study that his classical conditioning procedure had been effective in modifying the attitudes of Euro-American children toward Afro-American persons.

In spite of some inconsistency in the findings of the studies reviewed in this section, the bulk of the evidence supports the idea of a functional relationship between black-white color meanings and racial attitudes. While all of the necessary conditions are not yet fully understood, it appears that laboratory procedures which strengthen or weaken the evaluative meanings associated with the

Table 5-4. Mean Racial Attitude Scores Obtained by Children Receiving Varying Degrees of Training Involving the Association of Positive Words with the Color Black   (Parish and Fleetwood, 1975)

Racial Attitude Measure	Number of Training Sessions			
	0	1	4	8
PRAM II Series A	10.14	8.10	6.80	6.00
Parish Procedure	7.67	4.22	3.67	2.89

colors black and white can lead to changes in pro-Euro/ anti-Afro bias among young children.

RACIAL ATTITUDE CHANGE VIA SPECIAL CURRICULA

Having seen that laboratory learning procedures can effect significant changes in racial attitudes, let us consider four studies in which special classroom curriculum programs have been employed with the same objective. The first study to be described was conducted by Patricia Walker (1971) in Kentucky. Subjects were four classes of kindergarten children: two classes of Euro-American children and two classes of Afro-American children. Walker's primary interest was in determining whether the reading of a special selection of books involving Afro persons would result in a reduction in the children's pro-Euro/anti-Afro bias. The books included in the program contained illustrated stories which portrayed Afros in a favorable manner and/or portrayed Afros and Euros playing or working together in a mutually satisfying way. The experimental program, administered to one Euro class and one Afro class, consisted of a story period of 15 to 20 minutes conducted daily for a period of 6 weeks by the child's regular kindergarten teacher. While the teachers attempted to answer any questions raised by the children, they did not encourage discussion of the stories and pictures. The Euro class and Afro class which served as controls received a daily story period in which books dealing with animals or various informational topics were read.

PRAM I scores were obtained from the children in all classes prior to, and following, the special curricula. The mean scores for the children in each class are given in Table 5-5. Since scores in the upper portion of the 0–12 score range indicate E+/A− bias, it is evident from the

Table 5-5. Mean PRAM I Scores of Four Kindergarten Classes Before and After Special Reading Programs (Walker, 1971)

	Before	After
Afro-American Children		
Experimental Class	10.0	9.9
Control Class	9.9	9.1
Euro-American Children		
Experimental Class	10.5	10.5
Control Class	11.4	11.7

"before" scores that there was a relatively high initial level of such bias in all classes, both Euro and Afro. It is equally evident that there was no appreciable change in PRAM I scores as a result of the special curriculum received by the two experimental classes. This does not mean that the stories had no impact at all on the children. It is possible that Walker's procedure did bring about some degree of positive change in the children's view of Afro persons but, if so, it apparently was not sufficient to compete with the children's strong positive view of Euro persons.

Another investigation in which an effort was made to modify E+/A− bias by a special curriculum was John McAdoo's (1970) Michigan study. In addition to the laboratory learning groups noted earlier, McAdoo also had a group of Afro preschoolers who participated in a "Black consciousness" curriculum conducted by Afro-American men and women who were active in Afro student groups at the University of Michigan. The curriculum consisted of three one-hour sessions each week, for a period of six weeks. McAdoo has described his curriculum as follows:

The curriculum consisted of songs about famous Black heroes, stories about famous Blacks who contributed to the growth of the country, other books that depicted Black men and Black women in a positive light, art activities and revised traditional games. The subjects were also taken for walks around the community to see and discuss all the different kinds of Black people. Each week for six weeks, the subjects reviewed what they had learned the previous week and a new song,

Modification of Color and Racial Attitudes / 157

story, game, coloring project, was taught to the subjects by the teaching aides (TA). The major emphasis in the project was to give the subjects a positive experience in learning about their own ethnic group and to help them develop a positive self image. The TAs followed the same curriculum and each group used identical instructional materials (McAdoo, J. L., 1970, pp. 24–25).

PRAM I was administered to the children by Afro examiners before and after the special curriculum. The mean score obtained before was 7.48; the mean score obtained after was 8.48. While the change in mean scores was not statistically significant, it can be observed that the change was in the unexpected direction, i.e., the subjects displayed slightly *more* E+/A− bias at the conclusion of the special curriculum. This finding is more dramatic when it is recalled that, in the same study, McAdoo was successful in reducing E+/A− bias in another subject group in which the affective meanings of the colors black and white had been altered by the punishment of W+ and B− responses.

We share McAdoo's puzzlement about the lack of effectiveness of the special curriculum. Could it be that the principal impact of the curriculum was to sensitize the children to the issues of race and color meanings without altering the tendency toward negative associations with dark-skinned persons? This "cut-and-fit" hypothesis is consistent with the relatively low initial level of E+/A− bias in this group of subjects (mean = 7.48) and the apparent increase in bias following the special program. McAdoo's finding may also be related, in at least a general way, to the findings of J. A. Floyd, Jr., who conducted a study of Afro preschoolers in which the racial preference of the child was related to the strength of the parent's belief in Black identity and activism. Floyd summarized his findings as follows: ". . . the stronger the parent support of 'Black Power,' 'Black Pride,' and the 'Black Revolution' in general, the more the child wants to be white" (Floyd, 1969, pp. 48–49). If the rhetoric of the Black Identity movement contains the dual messages that Euro-Americans have been viewed more positively than Afro-Americans, and that this idea is wrong and must be changed, it may be that preschool children are more susceptible to learning the first message than the second. In any event, it appears that there are some complex effects at work in this area which are not yet well understood.

Another study in which a curriculum procedure was used in an attempt to modify racial attitudes was conducted by Deborah Graves in North Carolina in 1973 (Best, Smith, Graves, and Williams, 1975). The subjects in the study were 60 Euro-American five-year-olds, and Graves was interested in the effect of two variables on their racial attitudes: a special race- and color-related curriculum block; and the race of the teachers who conducted the curriculum. The study was conducted in three phases: the pretest assessment consisting of Series A of PRAM II, administered in November; the eight-week curriculum period in February and March; the posttest administration of Series B of PRAM II, conducted in April. During the curriculum period, half the children (N = 30) participated in a race- and color-related curriculum block, while the other half (N = 30) took part in a control curriculum block. In each block, there were two 45-minute sessions per week for the eight-week period, making a total of sixteen sessions and approximately twelve contact hours. The race-related curriculum block was patterned after that employed by Yancey (1972) and included a variety of activities intended to present the colors black and brown and dark-skinned persons in a favorable manner. Activities included stories, games, songs, and art activities. The control curriculum block included similar types of activities that avoided any reference to dark colors or dark-skinned persons. The teachers of the special curriculum blocks were Euro and Afro undergraduate women who had had previous experience in working with kindergarten children, but who had had no formal teacher training. The children receiving each of the two curriculum blocks were subdivided into three groups of ten children each, one group having two Euro teachers, one two Afro teachers, and the third with one Afro and one Euro teacher. The pre- and post-evaluations were conducted by other Euro women who were not associated with the teaching of the curriculum.

The results of the Graves study are presented in Table 5-6 in which the mean pretest and posttest PRAM II part-scores are displayed for each of the groups in the study. It will be recalled that PRAM II part-scores can range from 0 to 12, with high scores indicative of E+/A− bias. As is suggested by an inspection of the table, the analyses of these data provided no evidence of an effect of either the curriculum variable or the race of teacher variable. Regarding the former, twelve instructional hours dealing positively with dark colors and dark-skinned persons had no measurable effect on the E+/A− bias of these Euro children. Regarding the latter, it had been expected that contact with the Afro teachers in the context of an interesting special curriculum block might itself lead to a reduction in E+/A− bias, but such was not the case. The means for the twenty children with two Afro teachers were: pretest, 9.4; posttest, 9.4. The means for the twenty children with two Euro teachers were: pretest, 9.9; posttest, 9.9.

While the results of the Walker, McAdoo, and Graves studies indicate that racial attitudes are not easily modified by curriculum procedures, the findings of a study by Anna Yancey (1972) support the belief that it can be done. Yancey conducted her study in Pennsylvania in 1972. This was an "all Euro" study in which a Euro teacher attempted to reduce E+/A− bias in her first grade Euro pupils by means of a special instructional program. Yancey's curriculum involved a multifaceted "total push"

Table 5-6. Mean Pretest and Posttest PRAM II Part-Scores for Two Curriculum Conditions and Three Races of Teacher Conditions (Best, Smith, Graves, and Williams, 1975)

	Pretest	Posttest
Color- and Race-Related Curriculum		
Two Euro Teachers (N = 10)	9.7	10.2
Two Afro Teachers (N = 10)	9.4	9.6
One Euro and One Afro Teacher	9.1	8.8
(N = 10)		
Total (N = 30)	9.4	9.5
Control Curriculum		
Two Euro Teachers (N = 10)	10.2	9.6
Two Afro Teachers (N = 10)	9.4	9.2
One Euro and One Afro Teacher	9.4	9.3
(N = 10)		
Total (N = 30)	9.7	9.4

approach aimed toward developing positive associations to the color black and to dark-skinned persons. The basic program consisted of a half-hour session daily for 30 consecutive school days, with an additional weekly session of 15 minutes for art activities. Yancey has described the experimental program as follows:

Each day a biography of a famous American Negro was presented to the experimental group followed by a short discussion and the reading of one or two (dependent on length) library books about black children. . . . The stories either showed clear illustrations of black children or adults as central characters or else they showed multiracial situations with Blacks and Whites as central characters. The stories selected also portrayed Blacks in a positive manner without negative stereotypes. . . . [The children] were allowed to make short comments about the story as it was presented, but discussion was withheld until the completion of the story. . . . On Friday of each week the children became involved in special art activities using either black or brown as the predominant color. During a 10–15 minute free time period existing immediately after lunch, the children were encouraged to individually express their own creative notions concerning the color black or black people. Rainy afternoons offered an opportunity to show filmstrips or movies in place of a scheduled recess. . . . All of these films depicted black people and/or the color black in a favorable perspective.

Another facet of the study was scheduled each day for 2:00 P.M. when the experimental group returned from math classes. This involved the selection of a slip of paper from either a black or white box. . . . The white box contained slips of paper with messages, 75% of which were neutral and 25% of which were positive. In the black box were messages, 75% of which were positive and 25% of which were neutral. No negative messages were contained in either box. An example of a neutral message was "George Washington was the first president of the U.S." or "Mrs. Hughes is our school librarian." Positive messages included such things as an extra 10 or 15 minute free time period, or a treat such as two black jelly beans, a piece of black licorice, four M & M's, or a candy kiss. The choice of boxes was determined by a majority vote" (Yancey, 1972, pp. 24–26).

In order to have an untreated comparison group, Yancey selected another first grade class in the same school. During the period while the experimental class was participating in the special curriculum just described, the control class was involved in typical homeroom activities.

The racial attitudes of all children in the experimental and control classes were assessed before and after the one-month period during which the special curriculum was given. In making this assessment, Yancey took advantage of the fact that the two halves of the PRAM II procedure can be used as equivalent short forms, Series A and Series B, each of which yields scores on a 0–12 scale, with 6 as a neutral midpoint and higher scores indicative of E+/A− bias. All testing was done by a teaching aide who was not associated with the instruction of the children in the study.

The mean racial scores obtained at the "before" and "after" points for the experimental and control classes are displayed in Figure 5-4. In the figure it can be seen that both classes displayed a reasonably high degree of E+/A− bias prior to the special curriculum period. As a result of

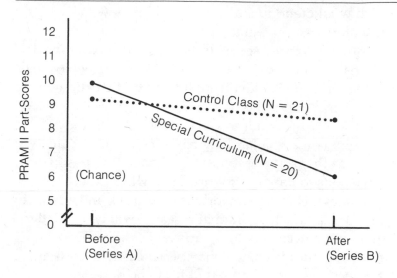

Figure 5-4. The Yancey Study: Mean Pretest and Posttest PRAM II Part-Scores in Special Curriculum and Control Classes (Yancey, 1972)

their participation in the special curriculum, the mean score of the subjects in the experimental class dropped from 9.80 to 6.15. In other words, prior to the special curriculum, these children had associated "good" words with light-skinned figures and "bad" words with dark-skinned figures approximately 10 times out of 12; following the special curriculum the children were associating good and bad words equally often with both types of figures. The mean scores for the control class also showed a slight decline from the "before" to the "after" point. Although this change was statistically non-significant, Yancey points out that children in the control class had some contact with children in the experimental class in the course of the regular first grade curriculum and may have had some exposure to bulletin boards, etc., used in the special curriculum. Thus, a slight decline in the control group scores was not unexpected.

Why was Yancey's curriculum study successful in reducing racial bias while those of Walker, McAdoo, and Graves were not? While the answer to this question is not clear, we have some speculative impressions. First, Ms. Yancey was the children's regular classroom teacher, which would tend to make the children view the curriculum as an integral part of their school work. Second, Ms. Yancey seems to have had a very strong personal commitment to the project which may have led to a higher degree of involvement and participation on the part of her children. Third, we note the "massed practice" aspect where the children were involved with the curriculum on a regular daily basis for a month. Finally, there was the heavy emphasis on developing positive associations to dark colors through a wide variety of techniques including art work and the black and white box game. While much additional research will be needed to pinpoint the necessary and sufficient conditions for successful attitude change via special curricula, it is at least encouraging to know that it can be done.

Concerning efforts to modify color and racial attitudes in young children, we have seen that direct behavior modification procedures are effective in altering the typical child's tendency to evaluate light-skinned figures more positively than dark-skinned figures. With appropriate training procedures, this bias can be extinguished or even reversed. Further, these changes can be accomplished not only in an interpersonal, interview-type situation, but also via a teaching machine procedure. We observed that the effects of the direct behavior modification were not confined to the training situation per se but generalized to a testing situation involving stimulus materials not employed in the training situation. There is evidence that modification effects can be observed one year following the original training. Thus, direct behavior modification procedures can bring about a general and somewhat persisting change in racial attitude in young children.

Regarding black-white color bias, we conclude that the tendency of young children to evaluate the color white positively relative to the color black can be systematically altered by direct behavior modification procedures. When the W+/B− tendency is modified in this manner, there is usually a change in pro-Euro/anti-Afro bias (E+/A−). While we know that W+/B− bias and E+/A− bias are not identical phenomena, the fact that modification of the former frequently produces a change in the latter indicates that an important relationship exists between the two.

Finally, on the basis of these studies, we must conclude that attitude modification via classroom curriculum procedures is, at best, very difficult to accomplish. Of four well-designed and well-executed studies, only one revealed evidence of significant attitude change—and we cannot pinpoint the critical differences between this study and the others. However, we offer the following general hypothesis for future research: curriculum procedures will prove to be effective only when they approximate the conditions of the behavior modification situation by insuring the involvement of all of the children, by requiring them to respond actively to race and color stimuli, and by providing clear and consistent training in the direction of the desired attitude change.

6.
Racial Acceptance and Preference

In the preceding chapters we summarized research findings concerning children's racial attitudes when assessed in a direct manner by determining the child's evaluative responses to light- and dark-skinned human figures. We shall now survey findings relating to other measures of racial response which also appear to depend heavily on the child's feelings about racial figures, but in a somewhat less direct way. Thus, when we inquire concerning racial acceptance and preference, the children's responses would seem to be governed primarily by how they feel about racial figures rather than how they think about them, i.e., by affective rather than cognitive factors. The research relating to more cognitive measures, such as perception of racial similarity and racial classification, will be reviewed in chapter 7.

MORLAND PICTURE INTERVIEW (MPI)

The preponderance of the research findings in this chapter and the next have been obtained with the Morland Picture Interview (MPI), described in detail in Appendix B. As its name implies, the MPI involves the use of color photographs about which questions are asked. When the MPI is administered to a young child, the first picture shown is of six children, three boys and three girls, of the subject's own race and approximate age. The second picture is highly similar to the first, taken in exactly the same setting, but the children pictured are of another race. The third picture shows six men, three of one race and three of the other, and the fourth picture shows six women, three of each of the two races. The fifth picture is of six girls, three of each of the two races, and the final picture is of six boys, three of one race and three of the other. The pictures were made by professional photographers, and nonracial characteristics of the models, such as dress and facial expressions, were kept as similar as possible. There are two versions of the MPI, one with Afro- and Euro-American models and the other with Chinese and European models. In the American version, Afro-American models include those of light, medium, and dark shades of skin color and of different hair styles, and Euro-American models include blonds and brunettes. A comparable variety of models is also found in the Chinese-European version.

In the standard MPI administration, the child is first asked questions relating to racial acceptance, preference, similarity, and self-preference, in that order. Following these questions, race is mentioned for the first time as the child is asked questions to determine his ability to classify other persons and himself using common racial designations.

RACIAL ACCEPTANCE

As we have indicated, racial acceptance refers to the willingness of children to play with children of their own or of another race when no choice is involved. In order to measure acceptance on the MPI, subjects are given three chances to say whether they would like to play with children of their own race and three chances to say if they would like to play with children of the other race. They are asked about groups and individuals of both sexes. For pictures 1 and 2 (groups), picture 5 (girls), and picture 6 (boys), the question is asked, "Would you like to play with these children (or with this child)?" followed by "Why?" or "Why not?" No mention of race or color is made as the pictures are shown and the questions asked. On the basis of their responses to these questions, the subject is classified as displaying "acceptance," "non-acceptance," or "rejection." Acceptance is indicated when the child's most frequent response to the questions is "yes," indicating a majority of times a willingness to play with those of the race in question. When the child's most frequent response to the questions is "no," this is taken as indicating Nonacceptance if race is not mentioned by the child, and Rejection if the child says he would not like to play with those depicted for racial reasons. For example, a reply to "Why not?" scored as Nonacceptance would be, "Because I don't know them." A reply scored as Rejection would be, "Because I don't like white children," or "Because they're black."

It should be noted that whenever we refer to "children of their own race" in this and in other chapters, we are referring to the societal designation of race. A given child may or may not know to which race he belongs or be aware of the racial classification of the persons in the MPI pictures. As was seen in chapter 1, the social-legal definition of races is not along strict biological lines, for indeed there are no clear-cut biological lines present. Persons classified as Afro-American vary considerably in skin color, hair form, nasal index, and other physical characteristics by which races are distinguished. Euro-Americans vary less widely in skin color than Afro-Americans but perhaps more widely in hair form and hair color. Learning to classify persons according to race is not an easy task for young children, and even adults have problems in determining the racial membership of some persons. In the next chapter we shall look at studies of the ability of children to recognize racial categories by applying racial designations. In this chapter, race refers to the societal designation of the subject and of the persons depicted in the MPI pictures.

Acceptance of Playmates of Same Race

The frequency with which children accept other children of their own race as playmates provides a baseline against which to evaluate their acceptance of children of the other race.

Acceptance of Afro-American Children by Afro-American Subjects / Table 6-1 summarizes the results of ten studies in which the MPI has been used to assess the acceptance of children of their own race by Afro-American children. These data indicate that a great majority of Afro children, an average of almost 90%, indicated a willingness to play with the Afro-American children in the photographs, with only 1% rejecting them for racial reasons. The minor variation in degree of acceptance observed in these studies was not statistically significant, and thus provided no evidence of change across the time interval 1955–73, or as a result of school level (which also means age), or geographic locality.

Acceptance of Euro-American Children by Euro-American Subjects / The willingness of Euro-American subjects to play with children of their own racial category can be seen in Table 6-2 which summarizes the findings from several MPI studies. Again, the overwhelming majority of subjects accepted members of their own race, and there was no rejection because of race. No statistically significant differences among the studies were found, indicating that the date of testing, school level, age of subjects, and place of study did not affect the results.

By comparing the summaries of all the data from Tables

Table 6-1. MPI Studies: Acceptance of Afro-American Children by Afro-American Subjects

Investigator(s)	Year of Study	Place of Study	School Level of Subjects*	Number of Subjects	Acceptance (Percent)	Non-acceptance (Percent)	Rejection (Percent)
Cowan & Leslie (1959)	1955–58	Va.	Preschool	144	93	6	2
Morland (1966)	1961	Mass.	"	41	85	15	0
Allen, Crosby, Garrison (1964)	1964	Va.	"	40	98	2	0
Morland†	1965	Conn.	"	35	80	20	0
Viele†	1965	Va.	"	80	86	14	0
Hagan & Watson (1968)	1968	Va.	"	52	81	15	4
Floyd (1969)	1969	Penna.	"	35	84	16	0
Morland (1972)	1972	Va.	"	58	90	5	5
	Summary for Preschool			485	88	10	1
Morland (1972)	1972	Va.	Inschool	50	92	6	2
Floyd (1973)	1973	N.Y.	"	40	92	8	0
	Summary for Inschool			90	92	7	1

*Preschool includes ages 3 through 6, with comparatively few 6-year-olds; inschool in Morland study includes ages 6 through 9; in Floyd study, ages 8 through 9.
†Previously unreported data.

Table 6-2. MPI Studies: Acceptance of Euro-American Children by Euro-American Subjects

Investigator(s)	Year of Study	Place of Study	School Level of Subjects*	Number of Subjects	Acceptance (Percent)	Non-acceptance (Percent)	Rejection (Percent)
Cowan & Leslie (1959)	1955–58	Va.	Preschool	393	93	7	0
Morland (1966)	1961	Mass.	"	41	93	7	0
Morland†	1965	Conn.	"	44	95	5	0
Morland (1972)	1972	Va.	"	55	96	4	0
	Summary for Preschool			533	94	6	0
Morland (1972)	1972	Va.	Inschool	103	90	10	0

*Preschool includes ages 3 through 6, with comparatively few 6-year-olds; inschool includes ages 6 through 9 (kindergarten through third grade).
†Previously unreported data.

6-1 and 6-2 we can learn whether the Afro-American subjects were any more or less willing than the Euro-Americans to accept members of their race. This comparison is shown in Table 6-3 and reveals that there is a small difference in the willingness of Afro-American and Euro-American subjects to play with children of their own racial grouping, with Euro-American subjects being more likely than Afro-American subjects to accept members of their race. At the same time, it can be noted that the level

Table 6-3. MPI Studies:* Acceptance of Same Race by Afro-American and Euro-American Subjects

Race of Subject	Acceptance of Own Race (Percent)	Nonacceptance of Own Race (Percent)	Rejection of Own Race (Percent)
Afro-American (N = 575)	89	10	1
Euro-American (N = 636)	93	7	0

*Derived from Tables 6-1 and 6-2.

of acceptance is quite high in both groups and that rejection almost never occurred.

Acceptance of Playmates of Other Race

Acceptance of Euro-American Children by Afro-American Subjects / Having established baselines of own-race acceptance, we will consider the degree to which young Afro- and Euro-American children are willing to play with each other, according to studies made with the MPI. As before, Acceptance, Nonacceptance, and Rejection were based on the child's most frequent reply to questions concerning whether or not he or she was willing to play with a group of children of the other race, with a girl of the other race, and with a boy of the other race.

The results of ten studies of the willingness of Afro-American subjects to accept Euro-American children are summarized in Table 6-4. Eight of the studies were carried out with preschool children and two with inschool children. In all studies, the Afro subjects showed a high degree of acceptance of the Euro children in the photographs. It can be noted, however, that there was comparatively greater acceptance of Euro-Americans by preschool than by inschool Afro-American subjects, 95% versus 86%, a statistically significant difference. There is, then, a decrease in the acceptability of Euro-American playmates to Afro-American children following

Table 6-4. MPI Studies: Acceptance of Euro-American Children by Afro-American Subjects

Investigator(s)	Year of Study	Place of Study	School Level of Subjects*	Number of Subjects	Acceptance (Percent)	Non-acceptance (Percent)	Rejection (Percent)
Morland (1962)	1957–61	Va.	Preschool	126	97	3	0
Morland (1966)	1961	Mass.	"	41	95	5	0
Allen, Crosby, Garrison (1964)	1964	Va.	"	40	98	2	0
Morland†	1965	Conn.	"	35	91	9	0
Viele†	1965	Va.	"	80	96	3	1
Hagan & Watson (1968)	1968	Va.	"	52	92	8	0
Floyd (1969)	1969	Penna.	"	35	86	13	1
Morland (1972)	1972	Va.	"	58	97	2	2
	Summary for Preschool			467	95	5	‡
Morland (1972)	1972	Va.	Inschool	50	86	8	6
Floyd (1973)	1973	N.Y.	"	40	85	15	0
	Summary for Inschool			90	86	11	4

*Preschool includes ages 3 through 6, with comparatively few 6-year-olds; inschool in Morland study includes ages 6 through 9; in Floyd study, ages 8 through 9.
†Previously unreported data.
‡Less than one-half of 1%.

Table 6-5. MPI Studies: Acceptance of Afro-American Children by Euro-American Subjects

Investigator(s)	Year of Study	Place of Study	School Level of Subjects*	Number of Subjects	Acceptance (Percent)	Non-acceptance (Percent)	Rejection (Percent)
Morland (1962)	1957–61	Va.	Preschool	281	80	16	4
Morland (1966)	1961	Mass.	"	41	88	12	0
Morland †	1965	Conn.	"	44	84	14	2
Bartholomew, Livingston, Strickland (1968)	1968	Va.	"	74	86	9	5
Morland (1972)	1972	Va.	"	55	76	15	9
	Summary for Preschool			495	82	14	4
Morland (1972)	1972	Va.	Inschool	103	66	16	18

*Preschool includes ages 3 through 6, with comparatively few 6-year-olds; inschool includes ages 6 through 9 (kindergarten through third grade).
†Previously unreported data.

their entry into the interracial school situation. This preschool-inschool difference is one that we shall note in other MPI measures to be reviewed later. On the other hand, it is clear that there is still a high degree of acceptance of Euro-American playmates even among the inschool groups.

*Acceptance of Afro-American Children by Euro-
American Subjects* / Studies of Euro-American acceptance
of Afro-Americans are summarized in Table 6-5, which
shows that the great majority of Euro subjects accepted
Afro children. The findings of the five studies of preschool
Euro-American subjects do not differ significantly from
one another, but all of the preschool subjects taken
together do differ significantly from the group of inschool
subjects, with the latter less likely to accept Afro-
Americans. Again we see evidence of a decline in
acceptance of children of the other racial group among
inschool children. On the other hand, acceptance of Afro-
American playmates remains the rule for most Euro-
American children.

Are preschool Euro- and Afro-American children
equally accepting of one another? This question can be
answered by reference to Table 6-6, which summarizes
data from the two preceding tables. Here it can be seen
that there is a greater likelihood for Afro subjects to accept
Euro children than for Euro subjects to accept Afro
children. This finding can be interpreted as indicating a
bias for Euro-Americans among preschool children,
although it is to be noted again that the great majority of
both racial groupings accepted members of the other
grouping.

Before proceeding further with our discussion of racial
acceptance, we should point up a methodological matter
which may contribute to the high levels of racial
acceptance we have noted. We refer here to the "yea-
saying" response set of young children which leads them
to say "yes" more often than "no" when asked questions
about ambiguous situations (see Appendix A, pp. 292–94).
Thus, when subjects are asked, "Would you like to play
with these children?" some of the "yes" responses may be
attributable to this response set and not be indicative of
true acceptance. Because of this possibility, we note that
the apparent levels of racial acceptance may be somewhat

Table 6-6. MPI Studies:* Acceptance of Children of the Other Race by Preschool Afro-American and Euro-American Subjects

Race of Subject	Acceptance of Other Race (Percent)	Nonacceptance of Other Race (Percent)	Rejection of Other Race (Percent)
Afro-American (N = 467)	95	5	†
Euro-American (N = 495)	82	14	4

*Summarized from Tables 6-4 and 6-5.
†Less than one-half of 1%.

inflated and may suggest a greater degree of cross-race acceptance than in fact exists. A similar caution can be noted with regard to the possible operation of a cultural norm which calls on children to "be nice" to other children.

Acceptance of Chinese by Afro- and Euro-Americans

Two studies of preschool American children have been made using the American and the Chinese-European versions of the MPI in such a way that scores for the acceptance of each of the three races could be compared. Both studies were carried out in 1968 in Lynchburg, Virginia, one with Afro-American children and the other with Euro children.

Table 6-7 gives the results of the study with the Afro subjects. Although the acceptance scores for Afro models are lower than for the other two racial categories, the differences are not statistically significant and the extent of acceptance of all three is very high. By contrast, the responses of Euro-American subjects to pictures of Afro-Americans, Chinese, and Euro-Americans, shown in Table 6-8, revealed that the Euro children were

Table 6-7. Acceptance by 52 Preschool Afro-American Subjects of Afro-American, Chinese, and Euro-American Children   (Hagan and Watson, 1968)

Racial Category Responded To	Responses of Afro-American Subjects		
	Acceptance (Percent)	Nonacceptance (Percent)	Rejection (Percent)
Afro-American	81	15	4
Chinese	90	10	0
Euro-American	92	8	0

Table 6-8. Acceptance by 74 Preschool Euro-American Subjects of Afro-American, Chinese, and Euro-American Children   (Bartholomew, Livingston, and Strickland, 1968)

Racial Category Responded To	Responses of Euro-American Subjects		
	Acceptance (Percent)	Nonacceptance (Percent)	Rejection (Percent)
Afro-American	86	9	5
Chinese	68	32	0
Euro-American	94	6	0

significantly less accepting of the Chinese than either the Afro- or the Euro-American models. There was, however, no expressed rejection of the Chinese for racial reasons.

The differential acceptance of the Chinese children by the Euro and Afro subjects is interesting and we will have occasion to look at the responses of Afro- and Euro-American subjects to the photographs of Chinese children in our analyses of other racial measures, both in this and in the next chapter. The view of this racial group by American children who have very little, if any, direct contact with Chinese persons may give us additional perspective on the development of racial concepts in young children.

On the MPI racial acceptance measure we have just reviewed, the children were free to express acceptance of playmates of both races—and most of them did. We shall now look at the responses of young children who are asked to express a preference between playmates of different races, a relative measure which may be more sensitive to racial bias. Racial preference has been measured in several different ways. We shall first consider the findings obtained from the use of the MPI, since this is the technique with which we have just been dealing. Then we shall report the racial preference results obtained in studies employing other kinds of instruments.

Racial Preference Findings from Studies Using the MPI

On the MPI, questions about racial preference immediately follow the ones about racial acceptance. After the subjects are asked if they would like to play with the children in the first two pictures, they are then shown both pictures at the same time and asked, "Would you rather play with these children (the ones in Picture 1), or with these (the ones in Picture 2)?" Following this, the subjects are asked which of the girls in the fifth picture and which of the boys in the sixth picture they would rather play with. Again, race or color is not mentioned. With three choices between races to be made, answers to the Afro-American–Euro-American version of the MPI are classified as "Prefer Afro-American," or "Prefer Euro-American," depending on the most frequent response. Children who fail to show a preference are classified as "Preference Not Clear."

Racial Preference of Afro-American Children / Table 6-9 summarizes the racial preferences of Afro-American subjects in eleven studies conducted over the past sixteen

Table 6-9. MPI Studies: Racial Preference of Afro-American Subjects

Investigator(s)	Year of Study	Place of Study	School Level of Subjects*	Number of Subjects	Prefer Afro-American (Percent)	Prefer Euro-American (Percent)	Preference Not Clear (Percent)
Morland (1962)	1957–61	Va.	Preschool	126	17	58	25
Morland (1966)	1961	Mass.	"	41	46	44	10
Allen, Crosby, Garrison (1964)	1964	Va.	"	40	20	70	10
Morland†	1965	Conn.	"	40	13	70	17
Viele†	1965	Va.	"	80	33	55	13
Floyd (1969)	1969	Penna.	"	35	26	74	0
Westie & Morland (1971)	1969–70	Va.	"	80	30	59	11
Lipscomb (1971)	1971	N.C.	"	59	51	48	1
Morland (1972)	1972	Va.	"	58	41	55	3
		Summary for Preschool		559	30	58	12
Morland (1972)	1972	Va.	Inschool	50	54	26	20
Floyd (1973)	1973	N.Y.	"	40	63	14	23
		Summary for Inschool		90	58	21	21

*Preschool includes ages 3 through 6, with comparatively few 6-year-olds; inschool in Morland study includes ages 6 through 9; in Floyd study, ages 8 through 9.
†Previously unreported data.

years in six different states. It can be seen that, on the average, about six out of ten of the preschool Afro subjects expressed a preference for the Euro children, while only about three out of ten expressed a preference for the Afro children, indicating once more a pro-Euro bias. In the nine studies of preschool children there was a wide range of variation in the percentage preferring Euro-Americans, from a high of 74% to a low of 44%. There was far less variation in the two studies of inschool Afro subjects, with no statistically significant difference between them being found. It can also be noted that a majority of the inschool Afro subjects, unlike the preschool Afro subjects, expressed a preference for the Afro-American children in the photographs. This shift in preference from pro-Euro to pro-Afro following entry into the interracial school situation parallels the reduction in acceptance of Euro playmates noted in the previous section. We will return to discuss the possible dynamics of these changes in chapters 9 and 10.

Racial Preference of Euro-American Children /

Table 6-10. MPI Studies: Racial Preference of Euro-American Subjects

Investigator(s)	Year of Study	Place of Study	School Level of Subjects*	Number of Subjects	Prefer Afro-American (Percent)	Prefer Euro-American (Percent)	Preference Not Clear (Percent)
Morland (1962)	1957–61	Va.	Preschool	281	10	73	17
Morland (1966)	1961	Mass.	"	50	28	70	2
Morland†	1965	Conn.	"	44	11	86	2
Westie &	1969–						
Morland (1971)	70	Va.	"	281	15	71	15
Morland (1972)	1972	Va.	"	55	7	87	5
		Summary for Preschool		711	13	74	14
Morland (1972)	1972	Va.	Inschool	103	7	79	15

*Preschool includes ages 3 through 6; inschool includes ages 6 through 9.
†Previously unreported data.

When Euro-American subjects are given the MPI, they express a clear preference for the Euro rather than for the Afro children in the photographs. As can be seen in Table 6-10, almost three-fourths preferred the Euro-Americans as playmates, while only about one out of eight preferred the Afro-Americans. The responses of the Euro subjects show considerable consistency over the fifteen-year time span covered, at both preschool and inschool levels, and in the three states in which the testing took place.

When the findings of Tables 6-9 and 6-10 are compared, it is evident that there are important differences in the development of racial preference in Afro and Euro children. At the preschool level, there is a much greater likelihood for the Euro subjects to prefer Euro models than for the Afro subjects to prefer Afro models. In fact, in all but two of the nine preschool studies of Afro subjects, more Afro children preferred Euro than Afro models. Another way to state this is to note that preschoolers of both races display a pro-Euro bias, but that the bias is not as strong among Afro children as among Euro children. Put this way, we see that the preschool racial preference findings parallel the racial attitude findings discussed in chapter 4. At the same time, the juxtaposition of the racial preference and racial acceptance findings indicates that the preference for Euro playmates cannot be taken as indicating an active rejection of Afro playmates, an interpretation that has sometimes been made. The racial acceptance findings make it clear that large majorities of both Afro and Euro subjects indicated a willingness to play with the Afro models when no choice was involved. In reference to this finding, Westie (1964) has made the apt analogy that a child may choose a banana split over plain ice cream but this does not mean that he will reject the ice cream when it alone is offered.

The other important difference found in the data of Tables 6-9 and 6-10 is seen in the comparison by school level. While Euro children display a similar pro-Euro bias at both school levels, the pro-Euro bias of the Afro child shifts to pro-Afro following entry into the interracial school situation. There is thus an important asymmetry in the process of racial preference development for Afro and Euro children.

Racial Preference in Three-Way Choice / Further evidence of pro-Euro bias in racial preference is seen in the two studies previously mentioned in which photographs of Chinese, along with those of Afro- and Euro-Americans, were used. The Afro and Euro preschool subjects were given a three-way choice. They were shown photographs of groups of Afro-American, Chinese, and Euro-American models and asked with which of the three they would most like to play. Similar questions were asked about girls of the three races and about boys of the three races. Table 6-11 gives the results of this three-way choice. It will be noted that Euro-Americans in the photographs were most frequently chosen by both Afro and Euro subjects. Also, both Afro and Euro preferred Chinese to a greater degree than they preferred Afro-Americans. The rather startling finding that these Afro preschoolers preferred the Chinese to the Afro models may be related to the skin color of the models. We note that the Afro subjects, like the Euro subjects, displayed the greatest preference for the relatively light-skinned

Table 6-11. Racial Preference of Preschool Afro-American and Euro-American Subjects in Three-Way Choice among Afro-American, Chinese, and Euro-American Children (Hagan and Watson, 1968; Bartholomew, Livingston, and Strickland, 1968)

Race of Subjects	Prefer Afro-American (Percent)	Prefer Chinese (Percent)	Prefer Euro-American (Percent)	Preference Not Clear (Percent)
Afro-American (N = 52)	12	21	44	23
Euro-American (N = 74)	4	12	68	16

Euro models, the next greatest preference for the somewhat darker-skinned Chinese models, and the least preference for the darkest-skinned Afro models. Viewed in this way, these findings are consistent with those of Baugher (1973), who demonstrated that Afro (and Euro) preschool children tend to evaluate lighter-skinned human figures more positively than darker-skinned figures, regardless of the particular skin colors involved. This suggests that the preschoolers in the three-way choice studies may have been responding primarily to skin color rather than "race," hence, the greater preference for Chinese over Afro-American playmates.

The Relationship of MPI Racial Preference to Other Variables

The only variables we have considered thus far in our discussion of racial preference are race of subject and level of school. We shall now look briefly at findings regarding the relationship of four other variables to racial preference; namely, sex, age, socioeconomic level, and race of interviewer.

Sex / The question posed here is whether young boys differ from young girls in their responses regarding racial preference. The answer to this question from every study of racial preference using the MPI is "no." Indeed, no statistically significant difference by sex has been reported for any of the measures obtained with the MPI.

Age / In the preceding discussion we made a distinction between preschool and inschool subjects in analyses of racial preference. We found a significant difference by school level among Afro but not among Euro subjects. In one sense, school level represents a difference in age, although there is some overlap between the oldest preschool children and the youngest inschool children. It appears that both school level and increased age are involved in the shift of Afro-American subjects from a pro-Euro to a pro-Afro bias. Within the preschool grouping and within the inschool grouping there have usually been no significant differences in racial preference by age for either Afro or Euro subjects in MPI studies, although there are some exceptions (e.g., Morland, 1962). Among both Afro and Euro children, subjects of ages three through six in nursery schools have responded in a generally similar way to questions about racial preference. Tables 6-12 and 6-13 present data obtained in 1970 which are representative of MPI findings among preschool children. In Table 6-12, we note that the degree of pro-Euro bias among Afro three-year-olds is quite similar to that among Afro six-year-olds, with no evidence of a systematic age trend. Although we see evidence of an age trend toward greater pro-Euro bias with increasing age among Euro preschoolers, the difference by age is not statistically significant. It seems clear from findings such as these that age is not a variable of major importance in the determination of racial preference in preschool children. This conclusion is similar to that reached in chapter 4 with regard to racial attitude responses of preschool children. The limited data on children in the early school grades likewise show little difference by age in each of the racial categories. For example, Table 6-9

Table 6-12. Racial Preference of Preschool Afro-American Subjects, by Age   (Westie and Morland, 1971)

Age Category	Prefer Afro-American (Percent)	Prefer Euro-American (Percent)	Preference Not Clear (Percent)
3 Years of Age (N = 19)	26	58	16
4 Years of Age (N = 31)	32	61	7
5 Years of Age (N = 20)	30	60	10
6 Years of Age (N = 10)	30	50	20

Table 6-13. Racial Preference of Preschool Euro-American Subjects, by Age   (Westie and Morland, 1971)

Age Category	Prefer Afro-American (Percent)	Prefer Euro-American (Percent)	Preference Not Clear (Percent)
3 Years of Age (N = 77)	20	64	16
4 Years of Age (N = 101)	15	71	14
5 Years of Age (N = 79)	11	71	18
6 Years of Age (N = 24)	8	88	4

shows that the inschool Afro children of ages six through nine studied by Morland (1972) did not differ significantly from the inschool Afro children of ages eight through nine studied by Floyd (1973). A similar finding can be seen in Table 6-4 in regard to racial acceptance scores. This lack of age differences within the preschool and inschool groupings will be discussed later when we attempt to interpret the research findings.

Socioeconomic Status / Socioeconomic status is a

construct arrived at in a number of different ways, and it is essential to know how the term is being defined operationally before it can be used in comparative analysis. Frequently this is not made clear, and consequently comparisons by socioeconomic status or social class can be misleading. In MPI studies employing the concept of socioeconomic status (e.g., Morland, 1958, 1962, 1969), subjects were divided into "upper status" and "lower status" groupings, primarily on the basis of parental occupation, using the Revised Scale for Rating Occupation devised by Warner, Meeker, and Eels (1949, pp. 140–41), and by place of residence in the city. In these studies, no significant difference in racial preference by socioeconomic status has been reported for Afro-American subjects. In fact, no statistically significant difference by socioeconomic status has been reported for Afro-American children on any MPI measure. On the other hand, Euro-American children have been found to differ in racial preference scores by status, with lower-status subjects more likely than upper-status subjects to prefer Euro- to Afro-Americans. At the same time, lower-status Euro subjects were found to be more likely to accept Afro-American children as playmates than were upper-status Euro-Americans. Thus, socioeconomic status does not appear to be clearly or consistently related to racial preference in the MPI studies. However, it should be noted that in a study by Judith Porter (1971), in which the variables of racial contact, age, sex, and shade of skin color were controlled, socioeconomic differences did have an effect on racial preference in an attitude index.

Race of Interviewer / There is a widespread assumption and some empirical support for the idea that the race of the examiner affects the way children respond to test procedures involving racial stimuli. The assumption seems to be that the respondent will "slant" answers in such a way as to make them more favorable, or at least less unfavorable, to the race of the interviewer, and some evidence of such an effect was seen with regard to the racial attitude findings reviewed in chapter 4. The hypothesized race of examiner effect has been tested in two studies of the MPI.

One study was done in 1967–68 (Jones, 1968) in a nursery school attended only by Afro-American children. The 60 subjects were randomly divided into two groups, one of which was tested by an Afro-American examiner and the other by a Euro-American examiner, both using the same version of the MPI. No significant difference was found either in racial acceptance or in racial preference scores. The second study, done in 1968–69 (Gurkin, 1969), involved 20 Euro-American children who attended a single nursery school and were divided by the school into two age groups of ten children each. The groups occupied separate rooms and were supervised by different teachers. In November, the Afro examiner interviewed one group and the Euro examiner interviewed the other. Three months later, the examiners exchanged groups, with an alternate form of the MPI being used for the second administration. When the racial acceptance and preference scores made by the 20 children with the Afro examiner were compared with the scores made by the same 20 children with the Euro examiner, it was found that the scores were not significantly different. In fact, the scores made with one interviewer were almost exactly the same as those made with the other interviewer, testifying to the reliability of the MPI procedure. Admittedly, these two studies are limited, but they do question the presence of a significant race of examiner effect with the MPI.

Racial Preference in Studies Using the Clark and Clark Doll Test (CDT)

The Clark and Clark Doll Test (CDT) was described, in part, in chapter 4 when findings concerning racial attitudes were discussed. The one question on the test that constitutes a measure of racial preference, as we have defined it, is, "Give me the doll that you like to play with." The subject would then choose between a doll that represented an Afro-American and one that represented a Euro-American. Some studies employing the CDT have not reported the responses to this particular question. Rather, they have combined the first four questions (which include: "Give me the doll that you like to play with; . . . that is nice; . . . that looks bad; . . . that is a nice color") into an index of "racial preference" (e.g., Simon, 1973). Although the Clarks themselves labeled these four questions measures of "racial preference," combining them into a single index confuses racial attitude, racial preference, and color attitude. For this reason we summarize here only those studies that report responses to the one question separately.

Seven studies which have reported the responses of Afro-American children to the racial preference question on the CDT are summarized in Table 6-14. This table shows that in five of the seven studies more than one-half of the Afro children chose the "white" over the "brown" doll. On the average, 54% preferred the white doll and thus revealed a pro-Euro bias similar to that found in the MPI studies. It was not possible to differentiate the preschool from the inschool children in several of the studies, for the responses were not reported separately for school level or by age category. In those studies where such separation could be made, a statistically significant difference was found by school level, with the inschool children less likely than the preschool children to prefer the doll representing Euro-Americans. In the other studies in which responses to the preference question were not given by school level or by age, the authors stated that with an increase in age, there was a decrease in the proportion of Afro children choosing the "white" doll.

In five of the studies listed in Table 6-14, Euro-American children were also tested and the results of these studies

Table 6-14. CDT Studies: Responses of Afro-American Subjects to the Request, "Give me the doll that you like to play with."

Investigator(s)	Year of Study	Place of Study	Age of Subjects	School Level of Subjects*	Number of Subjects†	Chose Brown Doll (Percent)	Chose White Doll (Percent)
Clark & Clark (1947)	1939–40	Ark. & Mass.	3–7	Both	252	33	67
Gregor & McPherson (1966)	Not Given	"Deep South"	6–7	Inschool	92	49	51
Greenwald & Oppenheim (1968)	1961	N.Y.	3–5	Preschool	33‡	26	74
Asher & Allen (1969)	1967	N.J.	3–8	Both	184	30	70
Hraba & Grant (1970)	1969	Neb.	4–8	Both	89	70	30
J. McAdoo (1970)	1969	Mich.	3–5	Preschool	65	46	54
Fox & Jordan (1973)	Not Given	N.Y.	5–7	Inschool	359	60	40
				Totals	1,071	46	54

*"Both" means "Both Preschool and Inschool."
†Does not include the very few in some of the studies who gave no response.
‡Does not include 5 subjects who chose a "mulatto" doll.

Table 6-15. CDT Studies: Responses of Euro-American Subjects to the Request, "Give me the doll that you like to play with."

Investigator(s)	Year of Study	Place of Study	Age of Subjects	School Level of Subjects*	Number of Subjects†	Chose Brown Doll (Percent)	Chose White Doll (Percent)
Gregor & McPherson (1966)	Not Given	"Deep South"	6–7	Inschool	80	5	95
Greenwald & Oppenheim (1968)	1961	N.Y.	3–5	Preschool	31‡	33	67
Asher & Allen (1969)	1967	N.J.	3–8	Both	150	23	77
Hraba & Grant (1970)	1969	Neb.	4–8	Both	70	16	84
Fox & Jordan (1973)	Not Given	N.Y.	5–7	Inschool	349	23	77
				Totals	680	20	80

*"Both" means "Both Preschool and Inschool."
†Does not include the very few in some of the studies who give no response.
‡Does not include one subject who chose a "mulatto" doll.

are presented in Table 6-15. In each of the studies a large majority of the Euro subjects chose the white doll over the brown doll, with an average of 80% choosing the white doll, a figure comparable to that found with the MPI studies. As was also true of the MPI studies, the CDT studies showed no significant variation by school level or by age of the Euro children. Once again we see evidence of a difference in the developmental pattern of racial preference among Euro- and Afro-American children.

While studies of racial preference using the CDT have usually revealed a pro-Euro-American bias among both the Euro and Afro children, we are reminded that such a preference for the white doll should not be interpreted as meaning a rejection of the brown doll, as is asserted by Clark and Clark (1947). In the absence of a racial acceptance measure, it is risky to make such a generalization. If the question, "Would you like to play with this doll?" were asked about each of the dolls, an acceptance score could be obtained with the CDT. Then the matter of rejection could be checked directly.

It is of interest from a methodological point of view to note that, in spite of differences in research techniques, the MPI and CDT yield similar results, namely pro-Euro bias and greater variation by school level among Afro than among Euro children. At the same time, there is a risk in basing a judgment of racial preference on a single response, as is true of the CDT. On the MPI with its three preference questions, it was found in a number of cases that the same subject would choose Afro models in one photograph and Euro models in another, thus indicating that racial preference is not an all-or-nothing matter. This and other related methodological problems are discussed in Appendix A.

Racial Preference from Other Studies

Studies employing techniques other than the MPI and CDT have also measured racial preference. In one of these studies, Mary Ellen Goodman (1964) conducted research during the 1940s in Boston and its vicinity with nursery school children of ages four and five. Of the 103 subjects, 57 were Afro- and 46 Euro-American. Goodman used a number of devices to determine various aspects of race awareness: nonparticipant observation in nursery schools, jigsaw puzzles, toys and doll houses, pictures, and dolls. By studying each child with all of these techniques, she determined whether the child had an "In-group Preference" or an "Out-group Preference." Among the Afro subjects, she found that 26% showed an in-group preference, i.e., a preference for Afro-Americans, while 74% showed an out-group or Euro-American preference. For the Euro subjects, 92% showed an in-group and 8% an out-group preference. Goodman's findings are in accord with others which show a pro-Euro bias. However, it would be exceedingly difficult, if not impossible, to replicate Goodman's study because of the use of multiple techniques which were scored and combined in a manner which is not carefully specified.

Stevenson and Stewart (1958) studied 220 children,* 125 Euro and 95 Afro, in nursery and elementary schools in Austin, Texas. The subjects ranged in age from three through seven years, and the actual date of data-collection was not given. The investigators used four different techniques to determine the development of racial attitudes and awareness. One of these was very similar to that used in the CDT. Four dolls, two Afro-American (one of each sex), and two Euro-American (one of each sex), were shown to the subject who was asked, "Which two dolls would you rather play with?" The authors found that approximately 68% of the Euro subjects made choices of own-race dolls, while 46% of the Afro subjects made choices of own-race dolls.

Renninger and Williams (1966) studied 129 Euro children of ages three, four, and five in North Carolina in 1965. They used two doll-like cut-out figures of the child's own sex, figures that differed only in skin and hair color. The subject was asked, "Which of these little girls (boys) would you like to go play with?" Eighty-two percent of

*The authors state that there were 225 subjects. However, they also say there were 25 Euro subjects in each of 5 age categories (a total of 125), and that there were a total of 95 Afro subjects in the 5 age categories. The grand total, then, appears to be 220.

the subjects expressed a preference for the light-skinned figures, and there was no significant variation by age. Once again, we have evidence of a strong pro-Euro bias among Euro preschoolers and a similarity in this bias regardless of age.

Judith Porter (1971) studied 184 Afro and 175 Euro children in ten nursery schools in the greater Boston area during 1965. She devised a TV-story game in which subjects were asked to make choices between Afro and Euro dolls. From the questions asked, six preference items were constructed into an overall attitude index. Controlling for sex, social class, and age, she found that more Euro than Afro children preferred dolls of their own race on the attitude index.

Alex Mabe (1974) used a sociometric procedure to determine racial preference among 52 second grade children in an interracial public school in North Carolina. The children were asked to indicate which of their classmates they would like to sit beside, to work with, and to play with. It was found that out of a total of 9 choices, Euro-American children selected Euro associates an average of 7.34 times, while Afro children selected Afro associates an average of 5.30 times. Thus, while both groups of children chose their own race most frequently, the choice for children of the other race was greater among Afro children than among Euro children—just as in the MPI studies of inschool children noted above.

RACIAL SELF-PREFERENCE

Only the MPI provides a measure of what we term "racial self-preference." The procedure for determining this is as follows. In the photograph of six children of the subject's sex, three of each race, questions were asked the subject for each racial pair depicted, "Which one would you rather be?" The subject was then asked, "Of all the children in the picture, which one would you most rather be?" It is the subject's response to this latter question which has been used as the measure of racial self-preference. It might be added that this has sometimes been called a measure of racial self-identification. However, we prefer the more descriptive term, self-preference, for the term racial self-identification seems to imply a conscious and deliberate alignment with a particular race, and we know that children who seem oblivious to race can still express this type of preference.

Responses of Afro-American subjects to the question asking which one they would most rather be are presented in Table 6-16. In most of these studies a majority of the preschool Afro subjects indicated that they would rather be one of the Euro models in the pictures, with an average of 57% giving this response. However, in both of the inschool studies, a clear majority of the Afro subjects responded that they would rather be one of the Afro children in the photographs. Once again, the difference between the preschool and inschool Afro subjects is statistically significant.

Six studies which have reported racial self-preference responses of Euro-American children are summarized in Table 6-17. The strong Euro bias is seen once more, for a large majority in each of the studies indicated they would rather be one of the Euro models. Although there is some variation in the percentages of Euro subjects indicating a Euro self-preference, in each of the studies over two-thirds of the subjects made such an indication. And, again, in contrast to the findings with the Afro subjects, the preschool Euro subjects did not differ appreciably from the inschool Euro subjects in their pro-Euro bias. Within each of the studies there were no significant variatiors by age, for the youngest subjects were as likely as the oldest to show they would rather be one of the Euro models.

In this review of research regarding racial acceptance,

Table 6-16. MPI Studies: Responses of Afro-American Subjects to the Question, "Which one would you most rather be?"

Investigator(s)	Year of Study	Place of Study	School Level of Subjects*	Number of Subjects	Rather Be Afro-American (Percent)	Rather Be Euro-American (Percent)	Answer Not Clear (Percent)
Morland (1963)	1957–61	Va.	Preschool	126	29	66	6
Morland (1966)	1961	Mass.	"	41	56	39	5
Allen, Crosby, Garrison (1964)	1964	Va.	"	40	20	75	5
Morland†	1965	Conn.	"	39	21	72	8
Viele†	1965	Va.	"	80	38	51	11
Floyd (1969)	1969	Penna.	"	35	40	57	3
Westie & Morland (1971)	1969–70	Va.	"	80	40	53	8
Lipscomb (1972)	1971	N.C.	"	59	58	42	0
Morland (1972)	1972	Va.	"	58	35	59	7
Summary for Preschool				558	37	57	6
Morland (1972)	1972	Va.	Inschool	50	64	32	4
Floyd (1973)	1973	N.Y.	"	40	67	28	5
Summary for Inschool				90	66	30	4

*Preschool includes ages 3 through 6, with comparatively few 6-year-olds; inschool in Morland study includes ages 6 through 9; in Floyd study, ages 8 through 9.
†Previously unreported data.

Table 6-17. MPI Studies: Responses of Euro-American Subjects to the Question, "Which one would you most rather be?"

Investigator(s)	Year of Study	Place of Study	School Level of Subjects*	Number of Subjects	Rather Be Euro-American (Percent)	Rather Be Afro-American (Percent)	Answer Not Clear (Percent)
Morland (1963)	1957–61	Va.	Preschool	281	68	18	14
Morland (1966)	1961	Mass.	"	50	70	26	4
Morland†	1965	Conn.	"	44	84	2	14
Westie & Morland (1971)	1969–70	Va.	"	281	68	19	13
Morland (1972)	1972	Va.	"	55	87	11	2
Summary for Preschool				711	70	18	12
Morland (1972)	1972	Va.	Inschool	103	79	13	9

*Preschool includes ages 3 through 6, with comparatively few 6-year-olds; inschool includes ages 6 through 9 (kindergarten through third grade).
†Previously unreported data.

preference, and self-preference, we have noted several consistent findings. We saw that both Afro and Euro subjects readily accepted children of their own and of the other race, rarely rejecting anyone for racial reasons. It can be said, then, that there was little evidence of racial prejudice in terms of outright rejection of children of another race. Nor was there much evidence of racial self-rejection; rather, the picture was one of racial self-acceptance. However, there was a greater likelihood for Afro subjects to accept Euro children than for Euro subjects to accept Afro children, a finding that indicates the presence of a pro-Euro bias in both subject groups. At the same time, a considerable majority of both races accepted as playmates children of the other race.

A pro-Euro bias was clearly manifested in racial preference and self-preference responses. Euro subjects were far more likely to prefer the Euro-American models than Afro subjects were to prefer Afro models. In fact, in most of the studies of preschool Afro subjects, a majority expressed a preference for Euro playmates and said they would rather be one of the Euro-Americans in the photographs.

For all three measures—acceptance, preference, and self-preference—the pro-Euro bias of preschool Afro children was seen to shift to a pro-Afro bias among inschool Afro children. On the other hand, the pro-Euro bias of Euro children continued largely unchanged into the school years.

7.
Perception of Racial Similarity and Classification

Having reviewed research findings on racial attitude, acceptance, and preference, all of which seem to depend heavily on the child's feelings about racial figures, we shall now review the findings on racial similarity and racial classification responses— behaviors which appear to be more dependent on the child's knowledge and perceptions than on his feelings. Racial similarity responses are obtained by showing the child sets of racial figures and asking him which one he looks most like and which ones look most like his parents. Racial classification ability is determined by the child's ability to choose appropriate figures when asked, for example, to indicate the "white" children or the "black" children in photographs. Finally, for the subject who demonstrates a general knowledge of racial classification terms, racial self-classification is studied by asking the question, "Are you black or are you white?" While all three of these measures appear to ask for "objective" judgments by the child, we will see that none of them is completely independent of affective factors.

RACIAL SIMILARITY

Three different measures relating to the perception of racial similarity have been employed in studies of young children. The measure most widely used has been obtained by asking subjects which of the dolls (or drawings or photographs) of different races they look most like. The other two measures are obtained by asking subjects which of several men of different races looks most like their father, and which of several women of different races looks most like their mother. Often, items of this type have been termed measures of racial self-identification. To us, this term seems to carry too much surplus meaning and we prefer the more precise and descriptive term racial similarity.

Similarity to Self

When the Clark Doll Test (CDT) (see chapters 4 and 6) is employed to study racial responses in young children, the final request is, "Give me the doll that looks like you." A summary of studies reporting the choices of Afro-American subjects is given in Table 7-1. These studies show that, on the average, the preschool Afro subjects chose the "white" dolls with about the same frequency as the "brown" dolls, while the inschool Afro subjects were much more likely to choose the "brown" than the "white" dolls.

Four studies with the CDT have reported responses of Euro-American children to the question of which doll they thought they looked like. Table 7-2 presents the results of these studies which show that a large majority of the preschool Euro subjects chose the "white" doll and that this percentage increased even further among inschool Euro subjects. When the studies of the Afro and Euro children in Tables 7-1 and 7-2 are compared, it is found that preschool Euro children are much more likely to

Table 7-1. CDT Studies: Responses of Afro-American Subjects to the Request, "Give me the doll that looks like you."

Investigator(s)	Year of Study	Place of Study	School Level of Subjects*	Number of Subjects	Chose Brown Doll (Percent)	Chose White Doll (Percent)	Made No Choice (Percent)
Clark & Clark (1947)	1939–40	Mass. & Ark.	Preschool	106	49	49	2
Ellsworth & Kane (1957)	1957	Va.	"	36	36	56	8
Greenwald & Oppenheim (1968)	1961	N.Y.	"	24†	67	21	3
	Summary for Preschool			166	49	46	5
Clark & Clark (1947)	1939–40	Mass. & Ark.	Inschool‡	147	78	22	0
Gregor & McPherson (1968)	Not Given	"Deep South"	Inschool	92	95	5	0
Fox & Jordan (1973)	Not Given	N.Y.	"	397	79	18	3
	Summary for Inschool			636	81	17	2

*Preschool level includes ages 3 through 5.
†Does not include 15 who chose the "mulatto" doll.
‡Ages 6 and 7 presumed to be in school.

Table 7-2. CDT Studies: Responses of Euro-American Subjects to the Request, "Give me the doll that looks like you."

Investigator(s)	Year of Study	Place of Study	School Level of Subjects*	Number of Subjects	Chose Brown Doll (Percent)	Chose White Doll (Percent)	Made No Choice (Percent)
Ellsworth & Kane (1957)	1957	Va.	Preschool	38	16	61	24
Greenwald & Oppenheim (1968)	1961	N.Y.	"	27†	26	63	11
	Summary for Preschool			65	20	62	18
Gregor & McPherson (1968)	Not Given	"Deep South"	Inschool	83	0	100	0
Fox & Jordan (1973)	Not Given	N.Y.	"	360	7	84	9
	Summary for Inschool			443	6	87	7

*Preschool level includes ages 3 through 5; the inschool children in the Gregor & McPherson study include ages 6 and 7; in the Fox & Jordan study, ages 5 through 7.
†Does not include 9 who chose the "mulatto" doll.

choose the doll representing their race than Afro children are to choose the doll representing their race. Similar results have been reported by Porter (1971) in a study in which she gave preschool subjects in Boston three chances to choose from Afro and Euro dolls "the one that looks just like you." She found that significantly fewer Afro than Euro subjects chose dolls representing their race. This difference held when the variables of sex, social class, and age were controlled. These findings provide still another indication of asymmetry in the racial responses of young Euro and Afro children.

The Morland Picture Interview (MPI) measure comparable to the CDT measure just discussed involves showing the subject the photograph of the six children of their own sex, three of each race, and asking about each racial pair, "Which one do you look more like?" The subject is then asked of all six children in the photograph, "Which one do you look most like?" The answer to this latter question is used for the MPI measure of racial self-similarity. The results from a number of different MPI studies of Afro-American subjects are presented in Table 7-3, where it can be seen once again that roughly half of the preschool Afro children selected Afro figures and half selected Euro figures. In these studies somewhat more of the preschool Afro subjects indicated they looked like the Euro than the Afro models in spite of the fact that subjects have a much wider choice of models on the MPI than on the CDT, for on the MPI subjects can choose among Afro models of light, medium, and dark skin. As was the case with the CDT findings, the MPI results with inschool Afro subjects showed that a large majority said they looked like Afro rather than Euro models. This significant shift in self-similarity responses from the preschool to inschool levels parallels the shift from pro-Euro preference to pro-Afro preference which we noted in the previous chapter.

The racial self-similarity responses from six MPI studies of Euro-American children are summarized in Table 7-4. Here we observe that the great majority of the Euro children at both school levels perceive a similarity between themselves and the Euro models. When the preschool Euro data are compared with the preschool Afro data, we note that the Euro subjects were much more

Table 7-3. MPI Studies: Responses of Afro-American Subjects to the Question, "Which one do you look most like?"

Investigator(s)	Year of Study	Place of Study	School Level of Subjects*	Number of Subjects	Most Like Afro-American (Percent)	Most Like Euro-American (Percent)	Answer Not Clear (Percent)
Morland (1963)	1957–61	Va.	Preschool	126	41	54	5
Morland (1966)	1961	Mass.	"	41	51	37	12
Allen, Crosby, Garrison (1964)	1964	Va.	"	40	28	65	8
Morland†	1965	Conn.	"	40	15	55	30
Vielet†	1965	Va.	"	80	44	46	10
Floyd (1969)	1969	Penna.	"	35	46	40	14
Westie & Morland (1972)	1969–70	Va.	"	80	44	51	5
Lipscomb (1972)	1971	N.C.	"	59	41	20	39
Morland (1972)	1972	Va.	"	58	48	48	4
		Summary for Preschool		559	41	47	12
Morland (1972)	1972	Va.	Inschool	50	82	12	6
Floyd (1973)	1973	N.Y.	"	40	70	8	22
		Summary for Inschool		90	77	10	13

*Preschool level includes ages 3 through 6, with comparatively few 6-year-olds;. inschool level in Morland study includes ages 6 through 9; in the Floyd study, ages 8 through 9.
†Previously unreported data.

Table 7-4. MPI Studies: Responses of Euro-American Subjects to the Question, "Which one do you look most like?"

Investigator(s)	Year of Study	Place of Study	School Level of Subjects*	Number of Subjects	Most Like Afro-American (Percent)	Most Like Euro-American (Percent)	Answer Not Clear (Percent)
Morland (1963)	1957–61	Va.	Preschool	281	14	72	14
Morland (1966)	1961	Mass.	"	50	16	74	10
Morland†	1965	Conn.	"	44	7	80	14
Westie & Morland (1971)	1969–70	Va.	"	281	13	74	13
Morland (1972)	1972	Va.	"	55	6	91	4
		Summary for Preschool		711	13	75	13
Morland (1972)	1972	Va.	Inschool	103	7	79	15

*Preschool includes ages 3 through 6, with comparatively few 6-year-olds. Inschool subjects include ages 6 through 9.
†Previously unreported data.

likely than the preschool Afro subjects to say they looked like models representing their race. That Afro preschoolers choose Euro and Afro models with about equal frequency but Euro preschoolers do not is subject to several possible interpretations, which we shall consider in subsequent chapters. For the present, we note only that socially accurate judgments of racial similarity appear to develop earlier among Euro children than among Afro children.

Similarity to Father

The general pattern of the racial self-similarity results is repeated in the findings regarding racial similarity to father. In the MPI photograph showing six men, three Afro and three Euro, the subject is asked for each of the three racial pairs, "Which one looks more like your father?" and then in regard to all six, "Which one looks most like your father?" Responses of Afro children to the last question are shown in Table 7-5, where it can be seen that at the preschool level only slightly more children chose Afro than Euro models, while at the inschool level a large majority chose the Afro models.

In the five MPI studies that have reported responses of Euro-American subjects to the question concerning racial similarity to father, approximately three-fourths of the subjects indicated that their fathers looked most like one of the Euro models. Table 7-6 gives these data and shows that preschool and inschool Euro subjects responded in much the same way, although the inschool subjects appeared to be somewhat more likely than the preschool subjects to identify their fathers with the Euro models. When the inschool data in Tables 7-5 and 7-6 are compared, it can be seen that, while a majority of both Euro and Afro children selected models of their own race, the percent of Afro children who made this response was appreciably lower than the percent of Euro children—70% and 85%, respectively.

Similarity to Mother

The last measure of the perception of racial similarity we shall consider concerns the race of the models with which subjects identified their mothers. This measure has been obtained in more MPI studies than the similarity-to-father measure; hence, the findings are based on a larger number of subjects. The procedure for determining this identification was similar to that for the father, with the photograph of six women, three of each race,

Table 7-5. MPI Studies: Responses of Afro-American Subjects to the Question, "Which one looks most like your father?"

Investigator(s)	Year of Study	Place of Study	School Level of Subjects*	Number of Subjects	Most Like Afro-American (Percent)	Most Like Euro-American (Percent)	Answer Not Clear (Percent)
Morland (1966)	1961	Mass.	Preschool	41	46	37	17
Morland†	1965	Conn.	"	39	33	44	23
Vielet	1965	Va.	"	80	35	46	19
Westie & Morland (1971)	1969–70	Va.	"	80	48	40	12
Floyd (1969)	1969	Penna.	"	35	43	31	26
Lipscomb (1972)	1971	N.C.	"	59	68	32	0
Morland (1972)	1972	Va.	"	58	47	40	14
	Summary for Preschool			392	46	39	15
Morland (1972)	1972	Va.	Inschool	50	76	14	10
Floyd (1973)	1973	N.Y.	"	40	63	11	26
	Summary for Inschool			90	70	13	17

*Preschool level includes ages 3 through 6, with comparatively few 6-year-olds. Morland inschool study includes ages 6 through 9; Floyd inschool study includes ages 8 through 9.
†Previously unreported data.

Table 7-6. MPI Studies: Responses of Euro-American Subjects to the Question, "Which one looks most like your father?"

Investigator(s)	Year of Study	Place of Study	School Level of Subjects*	Number of Subjects	Most Like Afro-American (Percent)	Most Like Euro-American (Percent)	Answer Not Clear (Percent)
Morland (1966)	1961	Mass.	Preschool	50	2	96	2
Morland†	1965	Conn.	"	44	7	77	16
Westie & Morland (1971)	1969–70	Va.	"	281	12	71	17
Morland (1972)	1972	Va.	"	55	15	82	3
	Summary for Preschool			430	11	76	13
Morland (1972)	1972	Va.	Inschool	103	3	85	12

*Preschool level includes mostly ages 3, 4, and 5, with a few 6-year-olds. Morland inschool study includes ages 6 through 9.
†Previously unreported data.

being used. For each racial pair the subject was asked which one looked more like his mother and then which of the six looked most like his mother. Responses to the last question by Afro-American subjects in ten studies are reported in Table 7-7. It will be noted that more of the preschool Afro subjects chose Euro than Afro models as looking most like their mothers. In contrast, and following previous patterns, the great majority of inschool Afro subjects said that their mothers looked most like one of the Afro models. One intriguing finding which comes

Table 7-7. MPI Studies: Responses of Afro-American Subjects to the Question, "Which one looks most like your mother?"

Investigator(s)	Year of Study	Place of Study	School Level of Subjects*	Number of Subjects	Most Like Afro-American (Percent)	Most Like Euro-American (Percent)	Answer Not Clear (Percent)
Morland (1963)	1957–61	Va.	Preschool	126	34	61	6
Morland (1966)	1961	Mass.	"	41	46	34	20
Morland†	1965	Conn.	"	39	33	41	26
Viele†	1965	Va.	"	80	26	63	11
Floyd (1969)	1969	Penna.	"	35	34	49	17
Westie & Morland (1971)	1969–70	Va.	"	80	30	60	10
Lipscomb (1972)	1971	N.C.	"	59	72	28	0
Morland (1972)	1972	Va.	"	58	50	36	14
		Summary for Preschool		518	39	50	11
Morland (1972)	1972	Va.	Inschool	50	78	16	6
Floyd (1973)	1973	N.Y.	"	40	67	5	28
		Summary for Inschool		90	73	11	16

*Preschool level includes ages 3 through 6, with comparatively few 6-year-olds. Morland inschool study includes ages 6 through 9; Floyd inschool study includes ages 8 and 9.
†Previously unreported data.

from comparing the data from Tables 7-5 and 7-7 is that the preschool Afro subjects are significantly less likely to identify their mothers with Afro models than they are their fathers. Assuming that most children at this young age have more contact with their mothers than with their fathers, it might be expected that children would be more accurate in perceiving the racial similarity of their mothers. Of course, one of the problems in checking the validity of this measure of racial self-identification is that we do not know what the parents of these children actually look like, and, we must add, it was not determined if the subjects knew who their fathers and mothers were. On the other hand, it is to be recalled that the MPI Afro models in the photographs show considerable variation in skin color, thereby offering the respondent some choice in deciding which one looks most like his parent. It would be profitable for the understanding of how young children acquire racial concepts to pursue the questions raised by this finding through additional research.

MPI studies reporting perception of racial similarity of

Table 7-8. MPI Studies: Responses of Euro-American Subjects to the Question, "Which one looks most like your mother?"

Investigator(s)	Year of Study	Place of Study	School Level of Subjects*	Number of Subjects	Most Like Afro-American (Percent)	Most Like Euro-American (Percent)	Answer Not Clear (Percent)
Morland (1963)	1957–61	Va.	Preschool	281	9	82	9
Morland (1966)	1961	Mass.	"	50	20	76	4
Morland†	1965	Conn.	"	44	11	77	11
Westie & Morland (1971)	1969–70	Va.	"	281	9	83	8
Morland (1972)	1972	Va.	"	55	0	100	0
	Summary for Preschool			711	9	83	8
Morland (1972)	1972	Va.	Inschool	103	3	86	11

*Preschool level includes mostly ages 3, 4, and 5, with a few 6-year-olds. Inschool includes ages 6 through 9.
†Previously unreported data.

mother by Euro-American subjects are summarized in Table 7-8. In each of these studies the great majority of Euro subjects said their mothers looked most like a Euro rather than an Afro model. The response was not significantly different for the preschool and the inschool subjects, nor for subjects of different ages and sex within each of these two school levels, indicating considerable consistency for the Euro children. When the responses of the Euro-American subjects are compared with the responses of Afro-Americans, it is found that at both the preschool and inschool levels the Euro subjects were significantly more likely than the Afro to state their mothers looked most like the race of the subject. The familiar pattern is again repeated, namely, a stronger perception of similarity to their own race among Euro- than among Afro-American children.

When the findings of Table 7-6 are compared with those of 7-8, it is seen that the preschool Euro subjects were significantly more likely to say their mothers were like the Euro models than they were to say their fathers were like the Euro models, an effect opposite to that found among Afro preschoolers. While it appears logical to expect that children would be able to judge with greater accuracy the racial similarity of their mothers, there is some risk in assuming we know how logic operates in the development of racial concepts.

Racial Similarity in Three-Way Choice

The studies of Afro-American children by Hagan and Watson (1968) and of Euro-American children by Bartholomew, Livingston, and Strickland (1968) in which there was a three-way choice among Afro-American, Euro-American, and Chinese models, were described in chapter 6 in regard to racial preference. Racial similarity measures were also obtained in these studies and they are presented in Table 7-9. The data indicate a consistent pattern of response for both Euro and Afro children on all three racial similarity measures; Euro models were chosen most frequently, Chinese models next most frequently, and Afro models least frequently. Put another way, a clear majority of the Euro-American subjects said they and their parents looked most like models of their own race, while the Afro-American subjects were least likely to indicate that they and their parents looked most like models of their own race. That these findings parallel the racial preference findings in these studies discussed in chapter 6 suggests that for young children the judgment of racial similarity is not a purely cognitive exercise but one influenced by such affective factors as their tendency to evaluate lighter-skinned persons more positively than darker-skinned persons (Baugher, 1973).

Several conclusions emerge from the foregoing review of the research on racial similarity. Afro-American subjects at both the preschool and inschool levels were far less likely than Euro-American subjects to say they and their parents looked like models of their own race. However, the perceived similarity to Afro models was found to increase from the preschool to the inschool level for Afro subjects, although when school level was controlled, the

Table 7-9. Perception of Racial Similarity of Preschool Afro-American and Euro-American Subjects in Three-Way Choice Among Afro-American, Euro-American, and Chinese Models (Hagan and Watson, 1968; Bartholomew, Livingston, and Strickland, 1968)

Type of Racial Similarity	Responses (in Percent) of Afro-American Subjects (N = 52)				Responses (in Percent) of Euro-American Subjects (N = 74)			
	Afro	Chinese	Euro	Not Clear	Afro	Chinese	Euro	Not Clear
Subject looks most like:	17	35	42	6	6	14	62	18
Father looks most like:	21	27	40	12	5	26	59	10
Mother looks most like:	11	29	50	10	5	13	69	13

Afro subjects did not vary in perception of racial similarity by age. Finally, preschool Euro children did not differ significantly from inschool Euro children in racial similarity responses, for at both school levels the great majority saw themselves and their parents as most like the Euro models.

RACIAL CLASSIFICATION

We turn now to a consideration of the ability of young children to classify persons in a racially "correct" manner, i.e., to apply racial labels in the way adults in our society do. In this group of measures, we deal for the first time with the child's responses to questions which involve race in an explicit manner. The measures of racial similarity, preference, attitude, etc., which we considered earlier do not involve any mention of the race of the persons depicted, and these measures are "racial" only in the sense that the persons or figures depicted would be classified by adults as belonging to one or another racial group. For example, it is possible that a young child who is oblivious to the societal concept of race may express a "pro-Euro bias" simply because he prefers lighter-skinned to darker-skinned persons. The racial classification findings bear directly on the question of the degree to which young children are aware of the way persons in our society are grouped into racial categories. In chapter 8 we shall consider the degree to which such awareness influences the child's responses to the other measures which we have studied.

Learning to differentiate races and to place oneself in the "correct" racial category is probably not an easy matter for children in American society. There are numerous differences which children observe in the persons around them, and finding out which characteristics are significant and which are not is a complicated matter. Some differences are physical, like height, weight, and skin color. Other differences are in style of hair, type of clothing, and pattern of speech. The task is to learn which differences are considered important enough to require special categorization and differential treatment. For example, if we agree that skin color is the most salient feature by which races are distinguished in America (and the use of color names to distinguish races reinforces the importance of this feature), we can appreciate how sorting people out by race is quite difficult for the young child. The color of skin varies considerably within each racial category in America. Those in the "white" category range from a light pinkish to a dark tannish color, while those categorized as "black" vary from light tan to dark brown in skin color. In fact, some "whites" are darker in skin color than some "blacks." In addition to skin color, hair styles and certain facial features can give clues to the child about racial classification, but neat categorization, even by adults, is not easy from observation alone. This difficulty is understandable from what was stated in chapter 1 concerning the rather arbitrary basis for categorizing races found in social traditions and census definitions.

Racial Classification Ability

Racial classification ability is the capacity of the child to apply current racial terms to persons in the manner in which adults do. One of the problems of measurement of this capacity is to determine which racial designations are currently in widest use. So far as the term used to identify Euro-Americans is concerned, the problem has been minimal, for "white" has been consistently employed through the years. "Caucasian" has occasionally been used, but primarily in technical treatments rather than in everyday speech. However, there have been changes in the popularity of terms used for designating Afro-Americans, and such changes pose difficulties regarding just which term to employ in testing racial classification ability. When the Clarks tested in the late 1930s and early 1940s they reported that "colored" was the designation most familiar to their subjects from Massachusetts and Arkansas (Clark and Clark, 1947). Morland (1958) found the same to be true in Virginia in the mid-1950s. But then the term "Negro" gained wider usage in the 1960s, followed by "black" toward the end of the 1960s. Today, "black" is the designation that seems to dominate, not only to denote the racial category but also to connote a philosophical and political position of considerable significance for many Afro-Americans. Of course, there is no reason why all of these terms cannot be tested for in order to ascertain how able the subjects are to use them.

In studies employing the Clark Doll Test (CDT), racial classification ability is determined by responses to two questions. Subjects are told, "Give me the doll that looks like a black (or colored or Negro) child," and "Give me the doll that looks like a white child." Thus, ability to use racial classification terms is based on a single response for each of the two races. Studies with the CDT have shown that ability to apply racial terms correctly appears early and increases with age. The findings by Clark and Clark (1947) in Table 7-10 show clearly this steady increase in ability by age; by seven years of age all of their subjects used "white" and "colored" correctly. Other CDT studies, e.g., Hraba and Grant (1970), have reported that their findings on racial classification ability were "similar" to those of the Clarks, but these studies have not presented their results by age. Fox and Jordan (1973) have given their findings on the ability to use racial terms for inschool children of ages five, six, and seven. For the most part they reported an increase by age similar to that found by the Clarks, with seven-year-old Afro and Euro children giving the highest percentage of correct answers. Porter (1971), in a modification of the CDT, found that five-year-olds could identify the "Negro," "colored," and "white" dolls more accurately than the three- and four-year-olds. Porter also found that the five-year-olds had a greater ability than her younger subjects to match correctly dolls of the same color, although over 70% of the younger children made correct matching.

The sensitivity of the CDT as a measure of racial classification ability is open to question, for subjects have a fifty-fifty chance of choosing the correct doll if they are merely guessing. Other measures of racial classification ability which have been more stringent than that of the CDT have reported lower percentages of children who could use racial terms correctly. At the same time, these other studies have found the same significant increase in ability by age as the CDT studies. For example, Stevenson and Stewart (1958) gave their subjects eight chances to discriminate drawings of Afro- and Euro-Americans. They found that three-year-olds had great difficulty in recognizing racial differences and that it was not until the age of seven that their subjects could distinguish between the races with ease. Renninger and Williams (1966) used

Table 7-10. Racial Classification Ability of Afro-American Children from Massachusetts and Arkansas, by Age   (Clark and Clark, 1947)

| | Percent of Subjects Responding Correctly to the Question, "Give me the doll that looks like a . . . | |
Age of Subjects	Colored Child	White Child
3-year-olds (N = 31)	77	77
4-year-olds (N = 29)	83	86
5-year-olds (N = 46)	94	94
6-year-olds (N = 72)	96	97
7-year-olds (N = 75)	100	100

doll-like cut-out figures of pinkish-tan and medium-brown skin color. They asked 129 Euro children of ages three, four, and five to pick out "Negro," "colored," and "white" persons, with each label being used twice. A child had to pick out two white figures correctly and either two Negro or two colored figures to be scored as "aware" of racial labels. The researchers found that 19% of the three-year-olds, 53% of the four-year-olds, and 79% of the five-year-olds were "aware" of the use of the terms. In another study Williams and Roberson (1967) employed the PRAM I stimulus figures and gave 111 Euro children four opportunities to point out a "white person," four opportunities to point out a "colored person," and four to point out a "Negro person." A subject was categorized as "aware" if he got all four "white persons" correct and either four "colored" or four "Negro" correct. The authors found a statistically significant increase in the percentage "aware" by age. Those scoring aware included 46% of the four-year-olds, 81% of the five-year-olds, and 97% of the six-year-olds.

Findings on racial classification ability with the MPI are more similar to those of Stevenson and Stewart, Renninger and Williams, and Williams and Roberson than to those with the CDT, probably because the MPI utilizes a multiple-item procedure. For each of the six pictures, subjects are asked if they see a "white" person, if they see a "black" (or "colored" or "Negro") person, and, if so, to point to that person. With twelve questions being asked, subjects who are correct at least ten times out of twelve are scored "high" on racial classification ability, while those who are correct nine times or less are scored "low." The use of this stringent criterion means that there is less than one chance in one hundred of a child being classified as "high" when he is, in fact, not aware of racial classification and, hence, responding by chance.

A principal finding in the MPI studies of preschool children is that racial classification ability increases regularly with age, as can be seen in Table 7-11 in which the data from a number of studies have been combined and displayed by the age of the subjects. For both Euro and Afro children the percent "high" in classification ability increases with age, with a particularly sharp increase from age three to age four in both racial categories.

A second result that stands out in Table 7-11 is the difference by race. Starting at age four, Euro subjects are significantly higher in classification ability at every age level than are Afro subjects. These findings are in general agreement with those of Stevenson and Stewart (1958) who found that their Euro-American subjects learned to discriminate between the races at an earlier age than their Afro-American subjects. However, there might be a regional difference operating, for one study has shown that Euro-Americans in the South learn to use racial terms at an earlier age than Euro-Americans in the North (Morland, 1966). The majority of Euro subjects in the pooled MPI data of Table 7-11 were from the South, and the children studied by Stevenson and Stewart were also from the South.

The results just discussed were obtained from interviews with preschool children. One study has used the MPI to test racial classification ability of inschool children

Table 7-11. MPI Studies:* Racial Classification Ability of Preschool Afro-American and Euro-American Children, by Age

| | Classification Ability Scores | | | |
| | Afro Subjects (N = 332) | | Euro Subjects (N = 430) | |
Age of Subjects	High (Percent)	Low (Percent)	High (Percent)	Low (Percent)
3-year-olds	16	84	23	77
4-year-olds	45	55	71	29
5-year-olds	59	41	87	13
6-year-olds	79	21	95	5

*Studies of Afro subjects include Viele (previously unreported data, 1965); Morland (previously unreported data, 1965); Jones (1968); Westie & Morland (1971); Morland (1972).
Studies of Euro subjects include Morland (previously unreported data, 1965); Morland (1966); Westie & Morland (1971); Morland (1972).

Table 7-12. Racial Classification Ability of a Random Sample of Lynchburg, Virginia, Public School Children of Ages 6 Through 9 in 1972, by Race   (Morland, 1972)

| | Percent Scoring "High" on Ability to Use the Following Terms | | | | |
Race of Subject	"Black"	"White"	"Colored"	"Negro"	"Caucasian"
Afro-American (N = 50)	100	100	88	76	24
Euro-American (N = 103)	100	100	87	71	6

(Morland, 1972). A random sample of Lynchburg, Virginia, public school children of ages six through nine was tested in the spring of 1972 for the ability to employ five racial terms: "black," "white," "colored," "Negro," and "Caucasian." The findings of this study are given in Table 7-12 where it can be seen that the terms "black" and "white" were the terms best known to the children. It can also be noted that the term "colored" was better known than "Negro" by children in both racial groups. It is interesting that "colored" continues to be known as a racial designation (probably more in the South than elsewhere), but it may be that its actual use is restricted to older persons and that children's knowledge of it will decline in the future. While the term "Caucasian" was known by comparatively few of the subjects, it is of interest that more Afro than Euro subjects were aware of its use as a designation for light-skinned persons.

Racial Self-Classification

Learning to apply racial terms correctly to other persons is obviously related to, but not the same as, learning to make a correct racial self-classification. One can imagine a child who has learned to designate other persons as "white" or "black" but has not yet learned to apply such a term to himself. Conversely, a child may have learned in rote fashion that he is a "black child" but not yet have learned to apply racial terms to other persons. This lack of identity between the child's ability to classify himself and to classify others is supported by research findings.

How does a child learn to classify himself racially? Apparently there is very little direct teaching of preschool children as to which race they belong, except by parents for whom race has unusual importance, for example, black militants and white supremacists. This can be contrasted with the learning situation regarding sexual identity where the typical child has his sex indicated to him with great regularity through parental comments such as "That's a good boy," or "You're a nice girl." Furthermore, the learning of sexual identity is greatly facilitated by the presence of persons of the opposite sex in the same household which permits the child to have direct experience with both positive and negative instances, e.g., "Brock, you are a boy like your brother Tom; but your sisters Kim and Jeannette are not boys—they are girls." It is the rare child of either race who has the opportunity to learn his racial identity through such clear, firsthand experiences. Rather, racial self-classification appears to result from a variety of indirect influences including the casual comments of parents, playmates, and teachers, interracial television programs and reading materials, etc. Much more research is required if we are to understand the way in which young American children learn to apply to themselves the racial designation which society says is correct.

The available evidence concerning racial self-classification comes from studies employing the MPI. After the general racial classification questions have been answered, the child is asked, "Are you white, or are you black (or whatever racial term was current at the time of the study)?" The answer to this question serves as the measure of racial self-classification. In the MPI studies, it has been customary to report racial self-classification responses only among subjects scoring high in general racial classification ability, for it cannot be assumed that subjects scoring low know the meaning of racial terms used in the questions that measure racial self-classification. The responses of those scoring high are reported in Table 7-13, where it can be seen that Euro-American subjects were appreciably more likely to say they were "white" than the Afro-American subjects were to say they were "black." Fifteen percent of the Afro subjects, all of whom had demonstrated that they knew the general meaning of the racial terms, said that they were "white" and another 9% indicated they were not sure. In contrast, none of the Euro subjects said they were "black" (or "Negro" or "colored") and only 2% were not sure. In addition, examiners report that it is not uncommon for Afro-American children to show dis-comfort and reluctance to reply when asked the racial self-identification question. A few even reverse their initial answer. For example, when asked if she were a Negro or if she were a white, a four-year-old Afro-American

Table 7-13. MPI Studies:* Racial Self-Classification of Preschool Afro-American and Euro-American Subjects Scoring "High" on Racial Recognition Ability, in Response to the Question "Are you black,† or are you white?"

| | Racial Self-Classification | | |
| | | | |
Race of Subject	Said They Were "White" (Percent)	Said They Were "Black" (Percent)	Were Not Sure (Percent)
Afro-American (N = 169)	15	76	9
Euro-American (N = 288)	98	0	2

*See Table 7-11 for a listing of these studies.
†In studies prior to 1970, the terms "Negro" and "colored" were used.

girl in Hartford, Connecticut, in 1965 first replied that she was a Negro. But then she changed her answer and said defiantly, "No, I'm white. I want to be somebody big!" Such a dramatic reversal is rare, but it perhaps provides a clue as to the reasons why almost one-fourth of the Afro subjects did not give a correct racial self-classification. This suggests that for some Afro children the racial self-classification task is not strictly cognitive in nature but also is influenced by their feelings and desires.

Earlier in this chapter we saw that all of the 153 Euro and Afro children randomly selected from kindergarten and the first three grades in the Lynchburg, Virginia, public schools in 1972 (Morland, 1972) could use the racial terms "white" and "black" correctly. When these subjects were asked, "Are you black, or are you white?" 147 or 96% replied correctly. Only one Afro-American said he was white, and one Euro-American said he was black. Three Afro-American subjects said they were not sure, and one Euro-American said he was not sure. Thus, it was evident that these inschool children were quite aware of the racial categories to which their society had assigned them.

Several conclusions emerge from our review of the studies of racial classification ability and racial self-classification. First, racial classification ability was found to increase with increasing age during the preschool years. This finding supports our earlier contention that such ability is largely a cognitive matter, for it is evidently one of the concepts that young children learn in the process of growing up in American society. This increase in classification ability by age stands in contrast to the development of racial attitudes, preference, and similarity, which, it will be recalled, changed only slightly if at all with increasing age during the preschool years.

Second, the findings of most studies show that pre-school Euro children tend to learn racial classification terms earlier than preschool Afro children. However, the findings are not all consistent, and they appear to characterize children in the South more than children in other regions. Is it possible that there is a relationship between classification ability and the degree of bias seen in racial attitudes and preferences? If so, this might help to account for the stronger own-race bias among Euro than among Afro children. This and related matters will be considered in chapter 8 when we look at the inter-relationships among racial concepts.

Finally, the racial self-classification responses show again the presence of a pro-Euro bias among a significant number of preschool Afro children. In fact, the racial self-classification data provide one of the most dramatic examples of this bias. Even when preschool Afro-American children have demonstrated that they know how to use racial categories correctly, an appreciable number of them then say they are "white" rather than "black." Such responses indicate that racial self-classification involves affective as well as cognitive elements.

8.
Interrelationships Among Racial and Color Concepts

Our previous discussions of race and color concepts have ignored, for the most part, the question of interrelationships among the measures employed. In the present chapter we shall consider the relationships among the various concepts which we have studied and attempt to answer such questions as: Do children who display a strong pro-Euro/anti-Afro attitude tend to have a stronger tendency toward viewing the color white positively, and the color black negatively? Is a strong tendency to evaluate Euro figures positively associated with a high frequency of Euro choice on a racial preference task? What is the relationship between children's knowledge of racial classification and their racial attitudes and preferences?

It is unfortunate that we do not have more sound evidence concerning the interrelationships of the various race and color concepts we have reviewed. This paucity is due to several factors. First, some of the pairs of concepts have not yet been included in the same investigations and, thus, no data concerning their possible inter-relationships have been gathered. Second, in some studies where data have been gathered on more than one concept, no attempt has been made to study interrelationships. Third, in some studies where interrelationships were studied, the measurement of each concept was so crude (i.e., one or two test items) that little precision can be claimed for the relationships observed. Finally, most of the studies reviewed have not given adequate attention to possible order and sequence effects. For example, in several of the multiconcept studies noted in chapter 4, children were given a single racial similarity item at the end of the procedure after the child had already responded to a number of questions dealing with racial attitude, racial preference, etc. Under these conditions, one cannot but wonder whether the child's racial similarity responses might have been influenced by his earlier racial attitude and racial preference responses.

With the foregoing cautions in mind, we will now consider the available data concerning the interrelationships of color and racial concepts in young children. As an aid in explication, we have organized the various race and color concepts into two major classes. In the first group, we have placed those measures which appear to involve affective responses; in the second group, we have included those measures which seem to call for cognition and judgment. We will consider first the interrelationships among the various measures within each class and will then summarize the relationships between the two classes of variables. As we proceed, we will see that this manner of organizing our discussion is not arbitrary but anticipates one of our major conclusions; namely, that the correlations among the measures within each class are higher than the correlations between the classes.

MEASURES OF AFFECT

One group of measures consists of those research operations which seem to ask the child for an expression of his feelings about race and color. Included are the relatively direct measures of attitude and preference in which the child is asked which of the stimulus figures is the "good one," or which he prefers to play with. Also included are more indirect measures of affect in which the child is asked which figure he would "rather be," or is asked to pretend that he is one of the figures depicted and to indicate his choice. All of these measures seem to require the child to respond on the basis of his personal feelings about the stimulus figures rather than requiring him to make "objective" judgments concerning them.

Racial Attitude and Racial Preference

The first data involve the relationship of racial attitude to racial preference, i.e., between the child's evaluative tendencies toward light- and dark-skinned persons and his expressed preferences for them when asked, for example, with which child he would like to play. As we noted earlier, one must not assume that evaluation and preference behavior are identical, since both adults and children may, on occasion, choose things which are negatively evaluated. Deborah Best (1972) compared the PRAM II racial attitude scores of 120 Euro-American preschoolers (mean age 5-1) with their scores on a racial preference procedure. Following the administration of PRAM II, certain of the PRAM II pictures were presented again with the subject being asked to indicate which of the two figures he preferred as his teacher for next year, his companion on a picnic or at the movies, etc. Each child was given six opportunities to express a preference between the light- and dark-skinned PRAM II figures, with a score of 6 indicating all Euro choices and a score of 0 indicating all Afro choices. When these racial preference scores were correlated with the PRAM II racial attitude scores, a coefficient of .57 was obtained. This result indicated a clear tendency for the children who obtained the higher (E+/A−) racial attitude scores to show a greater preference for the Euro figures than did the children who obtained the lower (largely neutral) racial attitude scores.

John McAdoo (1970) studied a group of Afro pre-schoolers, median age 4-6, and compared their PRAM I racial attitude scores with what he called a "racial preference" score obtained by a Clark and Clark-type doll selection procedure. In the latter, the child was asked to select the "nice doll," the one he would "like to play with," the one which "looks bad," and the one which is a "nice color." McAdoo found that a composite pro-Euro choice score from the doll procedure showed a substantial positive correlation with PRAM I scores ($+.49$ to $+.63$ in various subgroups). This finding is important, since it indicates a general correspondence between racial bias scores obtained by the PRAM and doll selection procedures. On the other hand, it does not speak clearly to the relationship of racial attitude and racial preference, as we have defined them, because the doll selection procedure included some "attitude" items as well as some "preference" items.

Two recent studies have explored the relationship of racial attitude and racial preference among children in the early school grades. Alex Mabe (1974) studied second grade children in a desegregated school setting in North Carolina. The children were told that their teacher was planning to make some new class groupings and they were asked to choose the classmates they would "like to sit near," "like to work with," and "like to play with." Using each child's first three choices to each of the three questions, Mabe counted the number of times Euro children were chosen and correlated this measure with racial attitude scores from the PRAM II procedure which had been administered two weeks earlier. The result of this analysis indicated a tendency for a high frequency of Euro choice to be associated with high (E+/A−) attitude scores for both Euro ($r = .55$) and Afro ($r = .31$) children. Among the 20 Afro children, for example, the 10 children with the highest PRAM II scores (15 and up) chose an average of 4.5 Euro associates, while the 10 children with the lower attitude scores (14 and down) chose an average of only 2.9.

The second study to be noted here is an unpublished investigation in which we compared racial attitude and racial preference among Euro and Afro third graders in an interracial school setting in North Carolina. Children were asked to select the five classmates whom they would like to have ride in the car with them on an imaginary field trip. The children's choices were analyzed for frequency of Euro-American choice which was then related to the children's racial attitude scores which had been obtained from the PRAM II procedure administered six months earlier. The analysis of these data revealed nonsignificant correlations between PRAM II scores and frequency of Euro-American choice among both Euro-American and Afro-American subjects. While the lack of relationship of racial attitude and racial preference in this study might be attributed, in part, to the relatively long time interval between the collection of the two sets of measures, an analysis of the race of *first* choice in the third grade group yielded even more puzzling findings. Among the 47 Afro-American subjects, the 20 children who made an Afro first choice obtained a mean racial attitude score of 14.80, while the 27 children with a Euro first choice had a mean racial attitude score of 11.67. There was, in effect, more evidence of E+/A− bias in the group choosing Afros than in the group choosing Euros! A parallel effect was seen in the first-choice data of the 105 Euro-American subjects; the 96 children with a Euro first choice had a mean racial attitude score of 16.19, while the 9 children with an Afro first choice had a mean score of 18.67. Again, there was more evidence of E+/A− bias in the group making Afro first choices. While we cannot reconcile to our satisfaction the differences in the findings of the two studies just described, it may be important that the children in the first study felt they were making choices with real consequences, while those in the second felt they were responding to a hypothetical situation.* Whether one accepts this interpretation or not, it appears that there was a complex relationship between racial attitude and racial preference among those third grade children.

The evidence that individual differences in racial attitude and racial preference are highly correlated among preschool children has led us to conclude that the two concepts are essentially equivalent at this age level. It would seem that preschoolers generally prefer what is positively evaluated, but that this relationship becomes more complex during the early school years. Additional evidence in support of this latter conclusion is seen in the fact that the racial preferences of most Afro children shift from pro-Euro to pro-Afro during the early school years, while their racial attitudes remain pro-Euro.

Racial Attitude and Perceived Racial Similarity

The question of the relationship of racial attitude to perceived racial similarity was explored by Linda Mattson who conducted a study of 29 Euro and 28 Afro preschoolers who were administered PRAM II, followed by a "self and family" similarity measure. The latter procedure consisted of presenting the (male) child with one of the PRAM II pictures and saying, "Make believe you are one of these two little boys; which little boy are you?" The child was then shown additional PRAM II pictures and asked to make believe one of the figures was his (brother, sister, father, mother, etc.). Twelve similarity responses were obtained from each child, with a score of 12 indicating all Euro choices, and a score of 0 indicating all Afro choices. An examination of the similarity and

*Gordon Cantor reports two studies (Ball and Cantor, 1974; Cantor, 1972) of fourth and fifth grade boys in which the Euro-American subjects rated pictures of Afro boys more favorably than pictures of Euro boys, in terms of how much they liked the idea of having the boy pictured to go home with them.

attitude scores suggested that they were related in a linear fashion, and product moment correlation coefficients were used to assess the magnitude of the relationship. For all 57 subjects, the correlation coefficient between PRAM II racial attitude scores and the "self and family" similarity scores was .53. When the relationship was examined separately in the Euro and Afro subject groups, it was found that while a positive correlation was found in both instances, the coefficient was appreciably higher among the Euro children (.65) than among the Afro children (.34). The findings of the Mattson study thus indicate a relationship between the strength of the child's tendency to evaluate Euro figures positively and the strength of his tendency to perceive similarity between himself and the Euro figures.

Racial Preference and Self-Preference

Another opportunity to examine the relationship between two affective measures is provided by the playmate preference and "rather be" items of the Morland Picture Interview (MPI) procedure. As we observed in chapter 6, there is a tendency for preschool children generally to select the Euro figure more often than the Afro figure in response to both of these questions, with the tendency being more pronounced among Euro children than among Afro children. To what degree do the choices on these two items tend to correspond? In Table 8-1 are displayed the percentages of Afro and Euro preschoolers falling in each cell of the 2 x 2 table representing the children's choices on the preference and "rather be" items. With regard to the Euro children, it can be seen that 74% chose the Euro figure both times and 8% chose the Afro figure both times, for a total of 82% consistent choice on both items. Among the Afro children, 45% chose the Euro figure twice and 21% chose the Afro figure twice, for a total of 66% consistent choice on both

Table 8-1. MPI Studies:* Percent of Preschool Subjects Choosing Euro-American and Afro-American Children as the Ones They Prefer as Playmates, and Would Rather Be

		Rather Be	
		Afro	Euro
Euro-American Preschoolers (N = 353)			
Prefer	Euro	10%	74%
	Afro	8%	8%
		(Sum of Consistent Choices: 82%)	
Afro-American Preschoolers (N = 283)			
Prefer	Euro	18%	45%
	Afro	21%	15%
		(Sum of Consistent Choices: 66%)	

*The data in Table 8-1, and the other MPI tables in this chapter, are from the subject groups described in chapters 6 and 7. The variations in number of subjects in the tables are due to the fact that not all of the MPI studies contained data on all of the concepts being compared, and the fact that subjects in the "?" or "cannot say" categories were excluded from these analyses.

items. From this we can see that there was in both groups a tendency for the preference and "rather be" choices to be correlated, although the relationship was not as strong among Afro children as among Euro children.

The findings suggest there is considerable consistency in attitude, preference, and identification responses when preschool children are asked to choose between light- and dark-skinned human figures. The child who has a strong pro-Euro attitude is more likely to express a preference for Euro figures and to see himself as similar to them; the child who does not have a strong pro-Euro attitude is less likely to make Euro preference and similarity responses. We will now consider the question of the relationship of the child's attitudes toward racial figures and his attitudes toward the colors white and black.

Racial Attitude and Color Attitude

The data from studies of the relationship of racial attitudes and black-white color attitudes are reasonably

Table 8-2. Studies of the Relationship of Color Attitude and Racial Attitude Scores

Investigator(s)	Location	Date	Subject Characteristics	Instruments Employed	Correlation of Color Attitude and Racial Attitude Scores
Williams and Roberson (1967)	N.C.	1966	Euro-American Preschoolers (N = 111)	CMT I, PRAM I	r = .41
Vocke (1971)	S.C.	1970	Afro-American Preschoolers (N = 90)	CMT I, PRAM I	r = .41
Shanahan (1972)	Wash.	1972	Euro and Afro Preschoolers (N = 28)	CMT II, PRAM II	r = .21
Boswell, D. A.*	N.C.	1972	Euro and Afro Preschoolers (N = 45)	CMT II, PRAM II	r = .37
Boswell (1974)	N.C.	1973	Euro-American Preschoolers (N = 50)	CMT II, PRAM II	r = .76
Young, B.*	Ontario, Can.	1974	Canadian (Caucasian) Preschoolers (N = 23)	CMT II, PRAM II	r = .33
Best, Naylor, and Williams (1975)	Dijon, France	1973	French (Caucasian) Preschoolers (N = 65)	CMT II, PRAM II (translated)	r = .28
Best, Naylor, and Williams (1975)	Venice, Italy	1974	Italian (Caucasian) Preschoolers (N = 24)	CMT II, PRAM II (translated)	r = .30

*Unpublished studies.

good because sensitive, multiple-item procedures have been employed and order effects have been shown not to be of any consequence. The findings of these studies are summarized in Table 8-2. Note that in all studies reported a positive correlation was found between color attitude and racial attitude scores. This means that children who obtained high (W+/B−) color attitude scores tended to obtain high (E+/A−) racial attitude scores, and that children displaying low color attitude scores tended to obtain low racial attitude scores. On the other hand, it can be noted that, with one exception,* the correlation coefficients are not indicative of a strong relationship between color meaning scores and racial attitude scores.

*Boswell (1974) has speculated that the atypically high coefficient in her study may be related to the fact that the subjects were not "naive" but had taken one or both of the test procedures in earlier studies. This was not true in the other studies cited.

In view of the reliability of the measuring instruments, noted in chapters 3 and 4, it was possible for the color attitude and racial attitude scores to have correlated more highly than in fact they did. Thus, it seems clear that while the CMT and PRAM scores are to a degree measuring "the same thing," each measure also assesses "something" which the other measure does not. In other words, there is a discernible tendency for children with a strong positive attitude toward the color white to have a more positive attitude toward light-skinned persons. On the other hand, the two attitudes are sufficiently independent to indicate that the degree of racial bias shown by a child cannot fully be explained by reference to the strength of his tendency to view the color white as good and the color black as bad, and vice versa. These findings concerning the relationship of race and color attitudes are considered to be of critical significance and are pivotal to the theoretical discussion offered in chapter 10.

Color Attitude and Fantasied Color Identification

Williams and Rousseau (1971) explored the relation of attitude toward the colors white and black and fantasied identification with these colors among Afro-American preschoolers. In this study, color attitudes were measured by the standard CMT I procedure. Fantasied identification was assessed by using the CMT I pictures of white and black animals and asking the child to play a make-believe game: "Let's make believe you are one of these two (doggies). Which (doggie) are you?" The child had six opportunities to select a white or black animal in response to such questions. An examination of the fantasied identification and color attitude scores indicated a systematic relationship: those children who viewed white most positively relative to black showed a stronger tendency to identify with the white animals (r = .39, with age partialled out). Once again, we see evidence of a relationship between attitude and fantasied identification measures at the preschool level.

It seems safe to conclude that the observed correlations among these measures of affective responses of pre-schoolers to light- and dark-skinned human figures, and to the colors white and black, point to the presence of a common factor among them. The strength of the tendency to positively evaluate light-skinned persons relative to dark-skinned persons is related to the tendency to prefer and perceive personal similarity to light-skinned persons. Further, evaluative tendencies toward light- and dark-skinned persons are related to evaluative tendencies toward the colors white and black—which in turn are related to fantasied identification with these colors. In the next chapter we will speculate that the common factor underlying these relationships is a general tendency to respond more positively to light stimuli than to dark stimuli—a tendency which may originate in the early learning experiences of the child and become further strengthened and elaborated by cultural influences. This hypothesis is consistent with the finding that the affective measures we have discussed show, at most, only slight correlations with age across the preschool years, suggesting that the individual differences in these measures cannot be accounted for by cultural learning alone.

MEASURES OF COGNITION AND JUDGMENT

This group of measures consists of those research operations which test the child's knowledge of racial classification, or his ability to make judgments concerning racial figures. Included here is the child's ability to classify Euro- and Afro-American persons in response to common racial labels, and to classify himself appropriately. Also included is the racial similarity measure from the MPI in which the child is asked to select the figure which "looks like you."

We have seen in chapter 7 that the ability of preschool children to classify persons by race increases systematically with age during the preschool years: it is an uncommon three-year-old who can make accurate racial classifications and it is an uncommon six-year-old who cannot. To what degree does the child's ability to classify himself with regard to race correspond to his ability to so classify other persons? This can be studied by examining the degree of consistency in the children's responses to the racial classification and racial self-classification items from the MPI studies. In Table 8-3 are presented the percentages of Euro and Afro preschoolers falling in each cell of the 2 x 2 table representing the children's classification as high or low in racial classification ability and correct or incorrect in racial self-classification. It can be seen that a great majority of the children who were high in racial classification ability were correct in their own racial classification—98% of the Euro children and 77% of the Afro children. On the other hand, those children who were low in racial classification ability appeared to divide their self-classification responses in an essentially random fashion between the two alternatives. These data support the idea that the ability to use racial labels to classify other persons and the ability to engage in correct racial self-classification develop concurrently during the preschool years. In this respect, the learning of racial classification is probably no different from the learning of other classifications of social significance. For example, we saw earlier that knowledge of sex-role classifications increases regularly through the preschool years. Our society attaches importance to the classification of persons by race and the children gradually learn their lesson. It is interesting to note, however, that the racial self-classification findings are not identical among Euro- and Afro-American children. Among those preschoolers who know their racial labels, virtually all Euro-American children correctly identify themselves, while only about three-quarters of Afro-American children do so. This latter

Table 8-3. MPI Studies: Percent of Preschool Subjects High or Low in Racial Classification Ability Who Made Correct or Incorrect Racial Self-Classifications

		Self-Classification		
		Incorrect	Correct	
Euro-American Preschoolers (N = 430)				
Racial Classification Ability	High (N = 285)	2%	98%	(100%)
	Low (N = 145)	55%	45%	(100%)
Afro-American Preschoolers (N = 332)				
Racial Classification Ability	High (N = 163)	23%	77%	(100%)
	Low (N = 169)	57%	43%	(100%)

result suggests that some Afro children may have difficulty in identifying themselves with a racial label which has already developed some negative connotations for them.

Let us now consider the findings regarding the "look like" measure of racial similarity from the MPI. This measure has been included in this section because on its face it seems to ask the child to make an objective judgment about the degree of perceived similarity between himself and the Euro- and Afro-American persons in the stimulus photographs employed in the MPI. On the other hand, we should remind ourselves that there are many bases on which similarity can be judged other than the "racial" differences among the persons in the pictures.

A summary of the "look like" responses of preschoolers high and low in racial classification ability is given in Table 8-4. Consider first the findings for the Euro-American children who were low in racial classification ability. A strong majority (78%) of these children, who were generally oblivious to formal racial classification, said that they look like the Euro figure in the pictures.

Table 8-4. MPI Studies: Percent of Preschool Subjects, High and Low in Racial Classification Ability, Saying They "Look Like" Euro and Afro Figures

		"Look Like"		
		Afro	Euro	
Euro-American Preschoolers (N = 406)				
Racial Classification Ability	High (N = 279)	9%	91%	(100%)
	Low (N = 127)	22%	78%	(100%)
Afro-American Preschoolers (N = 314)				
Racial Classification Ability	High (N = 160)	56%	44%	(100%)
	Low (N = 154)	44%	56%	(100%)

Moving to the data for the Euro children who were high in classification ability, we note a further increase in the tendency to "look like" the Euro figure with 91% of the children so responding. Thus, it appears that the Euro children perceive a similarity to Euro figures which is not necessarily dependent on knowledge of formal racial classification. This could be based on similarity in physical features (including skin color), or the children could simply be saying that they "look like" the light-skinned, hence, "good" figure. It also appears that when the Euro child becomes aware of racial classification there is a further sharpening of this tendency to say that he "looks like" the Euro figure.

The Table 8-4 data for the Afro preschoolers are quite different from those just described. Viewed conservatively, all the observed percents could be said to be merely random departures from the 50% chance level; and, hence, that knowledge of racial classification has no relationship to racial similarity responses in Afro children. On the other hand, there is a small but interesting shift in the data: children low in classification ability were 56% Euro in their similarity choices, while children of high ability were 56% Afro, suggesting that a slight shift toward Afro similarity may accompany the development of racial awareness. Nevertheless, it is clear that the two variables are largely independent of one another—a conclusion which can encompass the racial classification/racial similarity findings for both Afro and Euro children.

The foregoing discussion calls into question the designation of the racial similarity measure as being cognitive-judgmental in nature. Some further light is cast on this by a consideration of the relationship of the children's "look like" responses to the affective variables of racial preference and racial self-preference. A comparison of preschoolers' responses to the racial similarity ("look like") and racial self-preference ("rather be") items of the MPI is given in Table 8-5. Among the Euro-American children, it can be seen that the great majority of those children who said they would rather be Euro also said that they looked like the Euro persons in the test pictures, while those children who chose the Afro figure as the one they would rather be, divided their "look like" responses rather evenly between the two types of figures. In all, 75% of the Euro children made a consistent choice of figures on the two items. The findings for the Afro-American children seem even clearer with about two-thirds of the children who would rather be Euro saying they looked like the Euro persons in the pictures and about two-thirds of the children who would rather be Afro saying they looked like the Afro persons. In other words, the children's racial similarity choices correlated substantially with their racial self-preference responses. In fact, this relationship seems stronger than the correlation between racial similarity and racial classification ability, which we noted above.

The data in Table 8-6 provide comparison of responses to the "look like" and playmate preference items of the MPI. Among Euro-American children, there was a high degree of consistency of response to the two items with

Table 8-5. MPI Studies: Percent of Preschool Subjects Choosing Euro-American and Afro-American Children on the Similarity ("Look Like") and Self-Preference ("Rather Be") Measures

		"Rather Be"	
		Afro	Euro
Euro-American Preschoolers (N = 430)			
"Look Like"	Euro	15%	62%
	Afro	13%	10%
		(Sum of Consistent Choices = 75%)	
Afro-American Preschoolers (N = 332)			
"Look Like"	Euro	12%	42%
	Afro	26%	20%
		(Sum of Consistent Choices = 68%)	

Table 8-6. MPI Studies: Percent of Preschool Subjects Choosing Euro-American and Afro-American Children on the Similarity ("Look Like") and Playmate Preference Items

		"Prefer"	
		Afro	Euro
Euro-American Preschoolers (N = 430)			
"Look Like"	Euro	15%	62%
	Afro	10%	13%
		(Sum of Consistent Choices = 72%)	
Afro-American Preschoolers (N = 332)			
"Look Like"	Euro	13%	42%
	Afro	20%	25%
		(Sum of Consistent Choices = 62%)	

almost three-fourths of the children saying that they looked like the pictures which they preferred. A similar relationship can be seen for the Afro-American children: a majority of those who preferred Afro said they looked like Afro; a majority of those who preferred Euro said they looked like Euro.

The relationships between racial similarity responses

and preference and self-preference responses suggest that there is a heavy affective component in the children's "look like" responses. In fact, the "look like" responses seem to have a stronger relationship to the two affective measures than to the children's ability to engage in formal racial classification. From this, we conclude that for many of the children the "look like" item was not primarily cognitive/judgmental but was heavily affective in nature. It is as though these children said, "I don't really look like any of the children in the picture so I will pick the one I prefer or would rather be." Let us offer one final bit of data in support of this conclusion. In the MPI studies, there were 125 Afro children who were high in general racial classification ability *and* who also classified themselves correctly. If the "look like" response is primarily a cognitive measure of racial awareness, we would expect that a very high percent of these children would say that they "look like" the Afro-American figures. In fact, almost half of this group said that they looked like the Euro-American figures—which they tend to prefer and with which they tend to identify. We must conclude that the so-called racial similarity measure based on the children's "look like" responses is more affective than cognitive in nature.

RELATIONSHIP OF MEASURES OF AFFECT TO RACIAL CLASSIFICATION ABILITY

The evidence reviewed in the preceding sections of this chapter has led us to conclude that the various measures involving children's responses to racial figures can be classified into two major categories: measures predominantly affective in nature and measures predominantly cognitive in nature. The affective class includes measures of attitude, preference, self-preference, fantasied identification, and—to a lesser degree—perceived similarity. The cognitive class is limited to measures of the child's knowledge of racial classification, as applied to other persons and to himself. We will now consider the relationship between these two classes of variables, a matter of considerable theoretical interest. Consider, for example, the question of the relationship of racial attitude to racial classification ability. If children's attitudes are highly correlated with their ability to classify persons by race, it is reasonable to speculate that the two are being learned concurrently; as the child learns the classification of persons by race, he also learns the attitudes toward the races provided by existing cultural norms. On the other hand, if racial attitudes and racial classification are found not to be closely related, it suggests that attitudes may be determined, at least in part, by factors which have nothing to do with race, per se. In this latter case, what we call racial attitudes in young children would not be "racial" in their origins, although they may be racial in their implications.

The first data consist of the performance of preschool children, high and low in racial classification ability, on the preference and self-preference ("rather be") items of the MPI. These data are summarized in Table 8-7 where it can be seen that the children's awareness of racial classification has little systematic relationship to their responses to the preference and self-preference items. Among the Euro-American subjects, the children with high racial awareness display a strong tendency toward Euro playmate preference and self-preference responses. It can also be seen, however, that this tendency is reduced only slightly among children with low racial awareness. In other words, it is evident that the tendency of Euro children to choose the Euro figure is influenced only slightly by the child's awareness of formal racial classification.

A similar conclusion can be offered for the Afro-American data in Table 8-7. The children's awareness of racial classification seems to have little relationship to

Table 8-7. MPI Studies: Percent of Preschool Children, High and Low Racial Classification Ability, Choosing Euro-American and Afro-American Persons on the Playmate Preference and Self-Preference ("Rather Be") Items

	Playmate Preference			Self-Preference		
		Afro	Euro		Afro	Euro
Euro-American Children						
Racial Classification Ability	High (N = 278)	11%	89%	High (N = 251)	15%	85%
	Low (N = 129)	25%	75%	Low (N = 130)	25%	75%
Afro-American Children						
Racial Classification Ability	High (N = 162)	33%	67%	High (N = 124)	44%	56%
	Low (N = 149)	41%	59%	Low (N = 182)	38%	62%

their playmate preference and self-preference responses which are moderately pro-Euro in all instances. This conclusion is further supported by a consideration of the responses of the 125 Afro children who were high in racial classification ability *and* were also correct in their racial self-classification responses. The preference and the self-preference responses in this group were 67% and 54% Euro, respectively.

The findings from a study by James Floyd (1969) provide a picture similar to that just described. Floyd studied 35 Afro-American preschoolers in Pennsylvania employing the MPI. Among the measures obtained were a racial preference score, indicating the frequency with which the subjects chose Euro children over Afro children as potential playmates, and a racial classification score based on the child's accuracy of response in picking out "white" and "black" persons from the stimulus pictures. Floyd's results indicated that the children's racial classification scores, which increased with age, did not correlate with the children's racial preference scores, which did not increase with age.

Having observed the relative independence of the affective and racial identification measures on the MPI, we will now consider the findings from other studies in which different assessment procedures have been employed to study the same question. An early study dealing with racial attitude and racial classification was conducted by Williams and Roberson (1967) who studied 111 Euro-American children, with a median age of 5-4. In this study, the PRAM I procedure was employed to assess racial attitude, while racial classification ability was measured by a 12-item procedure in which the child was presented with the PRAM stimulus pictures and was asked to indicate the "white" person, or the "Negro person," or the "colored person." The correlation between the racial classification and racial attitude scores was found to be only .24, and when age was partialled out this correlation dropped to .05. From these findings it appears that there was little systematic relationship between the child's ability to use racial labels to categorize persons and the degree of pro-Euro bias he expressed.

In a more recent investigation, Robert Baugher (1973) conducted a study of 83 Euro- and Afro-American preschoolers with a mean age of 4-6. One measure obtained was a PRAM-type racial attitude score, which indicated the child's tendency to associate "good" words with lighter-skinned figures and "bad" words with darker-skinned figures. A second measure was a composite racial classification score based on the frequency with which the child chose dark-brown figures when asked to indicate the "black," "Negro," or "colored" figures, and the frequency with which the pinkish-tan figure was chosen as the "white" figure.* When the racial attitude and racial classification measures were compared, it was found that the scores correlated .22, which indicated only a slight tendency for the degree of the child's evaluative bias toward the light and dark

*Baugher also included a "self-recognition" subscore which has been eliminated from the present "racial classification" score.

figures to be associated with his knowledge of racial classification. This evidence that racial attitude is largely independent of racial classification ability is further supported by Baugher's finding that while racial classification ability scores increased significantly with age ($r = .61$), racial attitude scores were found not to be associated with age ($r = .05$). These findings suggest that preschool children's increasing awareness of formal racial classification is not a major determinant of the degree of pro-light-skinned bias which they exhibit.

Another study comparing racial attitude and racial classification ability was conducted by Harriette McAdoo (1970) who studied 78 Afro children with a mean age of 5-6. McAdoo assessed racial attitude by the PRAM I procedure, and then used six of the PRAM stimulus cards to measure racial classification ability by asking the child to "Show me the white (black) girl." McAdoo noted that there was no appreciable correlation ($r = .09$) between racial classification scores and racial attitude scores, and went on to point out that this was probably due to the high level of racial awareness in these children—they obtained a mean of 5.65 on a 0–6 scale. McAdoo found, in effect, that there were wide individual differences in racial attitude among children who were generally quite aware of racial classifications, a result also obtained by Boswell (1974). This provides further support for the notion that individual differences in racial attitude are not closely related to individual differences in racial classification ability.

Studies by Vocke (1971), and by C. Firestone and C. Feinstein (unpublished), provide some additional data regarding the relation of racial attitude and racial classification ability. In these studies, the children were classified as "aware" or "not aware" of the use of conventional racial labels. This classification was made by presenting the child with the PRAM I stimulus materials and giving him four opportunities to select the "white" person, four to select the "Negro" person, and four to select the "colored" person. The subject was said to be "aware" if he selected "correctly" on all of the four white person trials and on all of the four Negro person or all of the four colored person trials. When Vocke's 90 Afro preschoolers were so classified, the 55 "aware" children were found to have a mean racial attitude score of 9.2 (on a 0–12 scale, with 6 as an unbiased midpoint), while the 35 "not aware" children had a mean attitude score of 8.3. Thus, while the racial attitude score was slightly higher in the "aware" group, there was clear evidence of the same pro-Euro bias in the "not aware" children. When Firestone and Feinstein's 16 Euro-American preschoolers were classified, the 10 "aware" children had a mean racial attitude score of 9.7, while the 6 "nonaware" children had a mean of 10.5.

In a generally similar investigation, Katz and Zalk (1974) studied 192 preschool children in New York City and obtained a low but significant correlation of +.27 between a racial attitude/preference measure and a racial classification/self-classification measure. From these studies we again see evidence that the attitude/preference responses of preschoolers are largely independent of their ability to classify persons according to common racial levels. It is clearly not necessary for preschool children to be aware of racial labels in order to have preferences and attitudes regarding racial figures.

Having reviewed the existing evidence concerning the interrelationships among the various measures involving children's responses to race and color, the conclusion is reached that measures of attitude, preference, self-preference, and perceived similarity all appear to share a common affective component which consists of a general tendency to feel more positively about light-skinned persons than about dark-skinned persons, a tendency which is also related to the children's tendency to view the color white more positively than the color black. Having examined the cognitive measures involving racial classification and found that the children's abilities to classify other persons and themselves are closely related, we conclude that there is little relationship between degree of racial awareness and the children's affective responses to Euro- and Afro-American persons. The general tendency of preshool children to respond more positively to light-skinned persons than to dark-skinned persons is quite evident among children who display no knowledge of formal racial classification. These conclusions provide a general framework for conceptualizing the inter-relationships among race and color measures. There are undoubtedly many additional, more subtle, effects, the demonstration of which awaits the application of more systematic and sophisticated research efforts than have yet been employed in this area.

9.
Synthesis and Interpretation of Research Findings

In the foregoing chapters, we have reviewed in detail the research evidence concerning the responses of young children to race and color, and have shared with the reader the complexities of the various research methodologies and empirical findings. Our intent was to let the children "speak for themselves" with a minimum of comment and theoretical speculation. We hoped this would minimize the "coloring" of the data by the authors' own views and would allow the reader to make his own interpretations of the research findings.

We turn now to our efforts at synthesis and interpretation. In this chapter we review the major phenomena revealed in our survey of the research literature and offer interpretative comments regarding them. This is an exercise in abstraction in which we emphasize the substantive findings, minimize methodological detail, and, at times, ignore some empirical inconsistencies. On the basis of this interpretive review, we offer in chapter 10 a general theoretical model encompassing what we believe to be the major determinants of the responses of young children to color and race.

The research evidence indicates that preschool children, as young as three years of age, respond differently to the colors white and black. White tends to be positively evaluated and black negatively evaluated (W+/B−); good things are associated with white, and bad things with black. Not all children display this tendency to the same degree; some children show a high degree of W+/B− bias, some show a lesser degree, and some show no consistent bias. On the other hand, it is very uncommon to encounter a child with a reverse (B+/W−) bias, even among Afro-American children.

The findings regarding the evaluative meanings of white and black among preschool children are generally similar to the findings from studies of young adults, which demonstrate a remarkably consistent, cross-cultural tendency to evaluate white more positively than black. In other words, most preschool children are already responding to these colors in the way most adults do. Does this mean that the preschooler has already learned these color meanings from the adult culture? Perhaps, but not necessarily. This could be a case of "the child being father to the man" in which symbols of the adult culture are extensions and elaborations of shared feelings which each adult has carried forward from his own early childhood where the feelings were acquired through individual experiences which had little or nothing to do with cultural symbols. This line of reasoning is supported by the findings that individual differences in W+/B− bias are correlated with individual differences in aversion to darkness, as this is represented in fear of the dark of night and thunderstorms.

This is not to say that the preschool child is oblivious to the color symbols of the general culture in which he is reared. The child is exposed to these symbols through contact with the mass media, children's literature, organized religion, and idiomatic speech—and we all know the propensity of young children for learning from their everyday experiences. It is not a question of whether cultural learning may be involved in the development of W+/B− bias in young children, but whether this explanation alone is sufficient to account for the color bias. The research findings suggest it is not. First, we note that W+/B− bias is evident in many three-year-old children whose contact with cultural symbols has certainly not been extensive. Second, we note that concepts and attitudes which preschoolers acquire by cultural learning tend to show a regular age progression, with the older children showing more evidence of learning than the younger children—and we have seen that there is only a slight tendency toward such an age progression with regard to W+/B− bias. Third, we note that the degree of learning of culturally determined concepts and attitudes will usually show a substantial correlation with IQ, with bright children showing more evidence of learning than dull children—but such is not the situation with regard to W+/B− bias, which is quite evident in children of all intellectual levels. These considerations have led us to conclude that cultural learning does not provide a complete explanation for the W+/B− bias displayed by young children.

It is plausible to speculate that the noncultural component of the W+/B− bias is attributable to a biologically based tendency to prefer light over darkness. The young Homo sapiens, after all, requires reasonably high levels of illumination to interact comfortably with his environment and may find darkness intrinsically aversive. Once the child has developed a preference for light over darkness (L+/D−), this bias may generalize to the colors white and black, and provide the initial foundation of the W+/B− bias which we observe. Subsequently, exposure to cultural usages in which white is employed to symbolize goodness, and black badness, would serve to consolidate the child's own personal inclinations. In this sense, we believe the child is "father to the man" and that the general, pan-cultural tendency to symbolize goodness with white and badness with black may originate in experiences of peoples throughout the world with the light of day and darkness of night.

We are all aware that the human is an organism highly dependent on his visual sense for orientation to the environment and interpretation of events occurring in it. In addition, the human is, biologically speaking, a diurnal or "daytime" organism with a visual apparatus which requires relatively high levels of illumination in order to function effectively. Because of this highly visual nature and the diurnal retina, the human becomes disoriented under conditions of darkness when he can no longer monitor the environment. This loss of stimulus control in the face of potentially harmful situations is fear-provoking, and the human learns to be fearful of darkness and to avoid it.

The orientation and control associated with light and the lack of control associated with darkness also can be related to psychoanalytic concepts. In theorizing about the negative affective meaning of black, Faye Goldberg has written:

. . . the color black may evoke feelings of fear and discomfort because its association with darkness elicits the unconscious struggle against the yielding to the impulses of aggression, sex, soiling, and passivity (death) which is heightened in darkness. These impulses, strongly socialized and controlled during the day, find their expression in dreams and fantasies in childhood, and adult activities of impulse expression are given legitimate expression at night. . . . I am suggesting, then, that whiteness is associated with "super-ego" values around cognitive control and "good," i.e., socially acceptable, behavior and thus is associated with purity, innocence, and supra-human or theistic concepts. Black, on the other hand, is the shadow self (in Jungian terms) and represents emotions associated with the expression of our anti-social impulses—fear, guilt, hate—and, hence, is associated with evil and sub-human, devil-type of images (1973, p. 135).

While W+/B— bias has been observed in all groups of children studied, the presence of this bias in young Afro-Americans deserves special comment. The major findings indicate that W+/B— bias is generally evident among Afro preschoolers, but not to the same degree as among Euro preschoolers. In view of our previous theorizing, the presence of W+/B— bias in Afro children is not at all surprising since they would have the usual childhood experiences with light and darkness and would develop an L+/D—bias, which would generalize as a W+/B— bias. In addition, they are exposed to the general cultural symbolism which employs white positively and black negatively. In other words, we would expect W+/B— bias to develop in Afro children for the same reasons that it does in Euro children. On the other hand, the evidence of less W+/B— bias in Afro children than in Euro children suggests the operation of subcultural experiences which serve to mitigate the effects of the general determinants which we have noted. This could be due, in part, to the Afro child's positive experiences with dark-skinned parents and playmates which act to weaken the initial development of L+/D— bias. It is possible that another offsetting influence could be the Afro child's exposure to the "Black is beautiful" rhetoric of the Black Identity movement. On the other hand, it is clear that this rhetoric has had, as yet, no major impact on the evaluative responses of Afro preschoolers to the colors black and white; we saw earlier that less than 1% of the 180 Afro preschoolers tested in the 1972–73 CMT II standardization study showed clear evidence of a B+/W— bias. We also saw that most Afro preschoolers tend to identify themselves with the color white rather than the color black, probably as a result of wanting to be identified with the "good" color rather than the "bad" color.

Let us comment briefly upon an alternative interpretation which is sometimes offered for the presence of W+/B− bias in Afro children. It is proposed that the Afro child should have a "natural" inclination toward B+/W− bias but that his contact with the "white is good, black is bad" symbolism of the general culture overrides this inclination and teaches him a W+/B− bias. In refutation of this idea, first, we note that, if such an effect occurs, it is remarkably efficient since virtually no Afro child shows any residual of the "natural" B+/W− bias. Second, we can inquire as to why the Afro child who, it is argued, is so powerfully influenced by the general culture, is so unresponsive to the "Black is beautiful" messages from his racial subculture. For these reasons, we tend to reject this alternate interpretation. It seems more parsimonious to conclude that there are some general conditions which act to produce W+/B− bias in both Afro and Euro preschoolers, with the further amplification or suppression of this effect by subcultural influences.

On the development of black-white color bias beyond the preschool level, we note that prior to the Black Identity movement, Afro-American college students displayed essentially the same W+/B− bias as did their Euro-American counterparts. With the development of this movement, the evaluative meanings of the color names began to shift, and our most recent data indicate that black is now evaluated more positively than white by Afro-American young adults. Since the Afro preschooler displays pro-white bias, and the young adult shows pro-black bias, where does the "crossover" take place? The limited data available suggest that this occurs during the junior high school years. By this time the Afro teenager may have had sufficient exposure to the rhetoric of the Black Identity movement to lead him to accept black as a personal identity term with the result that he now evaluates black more positively than white. That the affective meanings of the colors can change is not at all surprising, since we have demonstrated that W+/B− bias can be modified—even among preschoolers—whenever the necessary reinforcement contingencies are present. On the other hand, the persistence of W+/B−bias through the childhood years seems to point up the strength of its determinants.

The course of development of white-black color bias among Euro-Americans seems quite clear: the W+/B− bias of the Euro preschooler persists through childhood and into young adulthood. It can also be noted that there is no evidence that the Black Identity movement has had any effect on the evaluative responses of Euro-American adults to the colors white and black; the colors continue to be evaluated as "very good" and "somewhat bad," respectively.

With respect to the findings regarding black-white color bias, let us be reminded again that we have been talking about children's responses to the colors white and black. Strictly speaking, these responses tell us little about the children's responses to persons of different races. We think, however, that there are some causal links between white-black color bias and racial bias. We observe the parallel between the lightness of white vs. the darkness of black and the lighter, pinkish-tan skin of the Euro-American vs. the darker, brown skin of the Afro-American. The opportunity which this provides for primary stimulus generalization seems quite evident.* We also note the current practice of designating racial groups by color names, with Euro-Americans labeled "white" and Afro-Americans labeled "black"—a clear invitation to generalize color bias to racial groups. Under these conditions, it seems most unlikely that the preschool child who views white as good and black as bad could avoid generalizing some of his color bias to persons who differ both in skin color and in the color labels by which they are designated. This conclusion is supported by the research

*Primary stimulus generalization is used by psychologists to refer to a situation where a response which has been conditioned to a given stimulus can also be elected by other physically similar stimuli.

findings indicating that there is a positive correlation between the degree of children's white-black color bias and the degree of their racial bias (see chapter 8), and that the modification of color bias is accompanied by a change in racial bias (see chapter 5). On the other hand, the reader should not conclude that we propose to explain racial bias on the basis of color bias alone. The racial concepts and attitudes of children are much more complex than this, and we merely assert that the child's preference for light over darkness and white over black creates a general evaluative context within which more specific learnings about race may occur.

RACIAL CLASSIFICATION ABILITY

While it might seem more logical to proceed directly from a discussion of color bias to a consideration of racial bias (i.e., attitude and preference), we wish first to consider the research findings regarding racial classification ability. Our reason for doing this is to develop a guideline to employ when we consider whether children's evaluative and preference responses to Euro and Afro figures are due to the racial classification of the figure, or to their color. In other words, we are interested in whether the child needs to be aware of conventional racial classifications in order to make evaluative responses to the light- and dark-skinned persons which adults would classify as representing members of different racial groups.

We have defined racial classification ability in terms of the child's choice of appropriate figures when asked to select according to popular racial labels. The child who regularly selects light-skinned, Euro-American persons as "white persons," and darker-skinned Afro-American persons as "black persons" demonstrates that he has learned to classify persons according to "race." We must be cautious, however, in the interpretation of the significance of this behavior. The ability to use racial labels correctly does not mean that the child is aware of all of the meanings adults attach to racial classification any more than a child's ability to classify persons by sex means that he is fully aware of sex-stereotypes. Nevertheless, a child's ability to employ racial labels does indicate that he has at least a beginning awareness of the manner in which persons are assigned to racial groups in our culture.

The research findings regarding racial classification ability are relatively straightforward and indicate a gradual increase in this ability through the preschool years. At age three, it is a rare child who can reliably designate persons according to conventional racial labels. There are marked increases in classification ability at ages four and five, and by age six it is a rare child who does not show a high degree of accuracy in racial classification. This high correlation of age and racial classification ability seems obviously to reflect cultural learning. Preschool children in our society are in contact with a culture in which racial labeling is frequently encountered, and the children gradually learn to make racial classifications in the same way in which they learn to make other classifications of high social significance.

The regular increase in racial classification ability across the preschool years provides a valuable yardstick against which to compare attitudinal and preference responses toward "racial" figures. To the degree that children's attitudinal and preference responses are related to racial classification ability, it is plausible to attribute these responses to the cultural messages which they have received about race, per se. To the degree that attitude and preference behavior is not related to classification ability, we must look beyond direct, verbalized cultural messages about race in our search for an explanation.

Racial attitude is defined in terms of the figure chosen in response to descriptions which include positive and negative adjectives, while racial preference is defined in terms of the figure chosen as the one with which the child would like to play, or would himself rather be. Because the research procedures employed to assess these concepts are operationally distinct, we chose to discuss them separately earlier in the book. For purposes of the current summary, however, we choose to discuss them together, because we have concluded that, at the preschool level, the attitude and preference procedures assess essentially the same tendency, i.e., preschoolers prefer persons whom they positively evaluate—and vice versa. This view is supported by the research findings which indicate that the racial attitude scores and racial preference scores of preschool children correlate about as highly as possible, given the reliabilities of the assessment procedures. On the other hand, we have seen that the racial attitudes and racial preferences of Afro children diverge during the early school years and, thus, must be considered separately at this age level.

The research findings on racial attitude and racial preference indicate that from age three onwards preschool children show a positive attitude toward—and preference for—light-skinned as opposed to dark-skinned persons. This phenomenon is equally evident whether one uses stimulus figures which differ only in skin color, or figures which differ in skin color and other racial characteristics. The implication here is that skin color is the most salient cue determining the children's responses to the figures. This interpretation is supported by the finding that older preschool children show no hesitancy in applying racial labels to human figures which differ only in skin color.

The positive attitude/preference for light-skinned persons is evident among both Euro- and Afro-American children, but is less pronounced among the latter. On the PRAM II racial attitude measure, for example, 73% of Euro children were pro-Euro in bias and 7% were pro-Afro, while the Afro children were 52% pro-Euro and 12% pro-Afro. The playmate preference data from the MPI procedure yield a generally similar picture: the preferences of Euro preschoolers were 74% Euro and 13% Afro, while the preferences of Afro preschoolers were 57% Euro and 30% Afro. On the self-preference, or "rather be," item of the MPI, the preferences of Euro preschoolers were 70% Euro preference and 18% Afro preference, while the preferences of Afro preschoolers were 57% Euro and 37% Afro. As we attempt to explain these findings, we must account both for the general tendency toward pro-Euro bias and also for the lesser degree of this bias among Afro children.

In seeking an explanation for the pro-Euro bias observed in both Euro and Afro children, we turn first to a consideration of American social structure in which Euro-Americans occupy the dominant position. Cross-cultural data from England, South Africa, New Zealand, and Hong Kong, as well as America, support the generalization that young children of both dominant and subordinate racial groupings tend to prefer and perceive themselves similar to those in the dominant racial grouping. This theorizing proposes that, since Euro-Americans occupy a dominant position in American society, preschool children would become aware of this fact and would develop a pro-Euro bias. Further, it would appear that the child's learning from the social structure is more indirect than direct, resulting more from informal observation than direct instruction concerning the favored position of Euro-Americans—Allport's (1954) "caught not taught" hypothesis. Support for this idea is found in the relationship of attitude and preference scores to racial classification ability. Pro-Euro bias is almost as strong in children who cannot classify persons by race as it is in children who can. On the MPI playmate preference measure, for example, Euro children with low classification ability were 65% pro-Euro and 22% pro-Afro, while those with high classification ability were 80% pro-Euro and 10% pro-Afro. By comparison, Afro children with low classification ability were 51% pro-Euro and 35% pro-Afro, while those with high classification ability were 62% pro-Euro and 31% pro-Afro. These findings suggest that while a knowledge of racial classification terms may act to *enhance* pro-Euro bias, it is not necessary in order for the bias to exist. Children who seem oblivious to racial classification can and do express strong pro-Euro biases. It can be argued, therefore, that the social structure has an impact on attitude and preference before the child becomes aware of racial classification terms.

While social structure theory seems adequate to explain the general phenomenon of pro-Euro bias, other findings seem difficult to reconcile with an exclusive emphasis on cultural learning. We note that the findings concerning racial attitude and preference show little evidence of systematic change with increasing age across the preschool years. While the early studies with the PRAM racial attitude procedure showed a slight tendency toward higher (more pro-Euro) scores among older preschoolers, racial attitude and chronological age were found to correlate only .08 in the PRAM II standardization study. Likewise, studies of racial preference using the MPI show, at most, only slight increases in pro-Euro bias with increasing age. Generally, then, racial attitude and preference measures do not show the sizable, systematic age progression expected when one is studying the development of concepts which preschoolers are learning solely as a result of cultural influences. A related finding is that individual differences in racial attitude scores show little relationship to individual differences in intelligence—and when something is being learned from the culture, bright children usually learn it better. Another relevant finding is that the racial attitudes and preferences of preschoolers have not been found to vary significantly with the geographical areas of the United States in which studies have been conducted and, thus, seem to have little relation to regional variations in patterns of racial composition and interaction. In addition, we note that in France and Italy where there is little or no involvement of race in social structure the preschool children display a pro-light-skinned bias similar to that found in American children.

Our findings are not easily embraced by a theory which places exclusive reliance on the American child's experience with the pro-Euro social structure in explaining pro-Euro bias. This leads us to propose that there is another factor operating to produce the tendency to view light-skinned persons more positively than dark-skinned persons, namely, a generalization of the child's preference for light over darkness to the lighter skin of the Euro-American relative to that of the Afro-American. As Baugher (1973) has shown, preschoolers tend to prefer lighter-skinned people to darker-skinned people; a light brown figure is the "bad" one when it is paired with a pink-tan figure, but it becomes the "good" one when it is paired with a dark brown figure. Support for the implication of the child's light-dark preferences in the expression of racial bias is found in the relationship between individual differences in black-white color bias and in racial attitudes. Children who view white positively relative to black have stronger pro-Euro attitudes; children with less pro-white bias show less pro-Euro bias. Additional support is found in the findings that the alteration of color bias via behavior modification techniques usually results in at least some modification of race bias. If, as we have argued earlier, the degree of the child's pro-white bias reflects a general preference for light over darkness, then the correlation between color bias and racial bias suggests that the relative lightness of the Euro-American figure may contribute to the pro-Euro bias observed in preschool children.*

We do not wish to overstate the case for the implication of color bias in the determination of racial bias. Several research findings indicate that color attitudes and racial attitudes are related but not identical phenomena. While color attitude scores and racial attitude scores are positively correlated, the magnitude of the correlation is not as high as it could be, considering the reliabilities of the respective measurement procedures. Thus, the color attitude scores and racial attitude scores seem in part to be measuring the same thing, and in part something different. A second finding supporting this view is that when children's color bias is reversed from W+/B− to B+/W− via behavior modification procedures, the racial attitude scores do not necessarily reverse from E+/A− to A+/E−, but often merely move toward a neutral or unbiased position. A third finding concerns a small but perhaps important difference in the distributions of color and racial attitude scores at the preschool level where it is found that low (A+/E−) racial attitude scores occur more frequently than low (B+/W−) color attitude scores in both Afro and Euro children. (A small number of children of both races show evidence of a definite A+/E− bias, but B+/W− bias is almost never found.) A fourth finding is that the pattern of correlations with other variables is not the same: Boswell (1974) demonstrated that color attitude correlates with aversion to darkness, but racial attitude does not, while racial attitude correlates with mother's racial attitude, but color attitude does not. These research findings are consistent with the view that color attitudes

*The question is sometimes asked, "Why do light-skinned persons seek suntans?" This seems to be a culturally determined preference which is attributable to the suntan being associated with youth, health, and leisure. Historically, light-skinned persons have often gone to great lengths (e.g., women's hats, parasols, and gloves) to avoid a sun-darkened skin because of its association with the outdoor labor of the lower classes (note the pejorative term "red-neck").

constitute one—but only one—determinant of the pro-Euro bias of the preschool child.

The two factors cited thus far, namely, the favorable position of Euro-Americans in the social structure and the generalization of W+/B− bias to lighter-skinned persons, are considered adequate to account for the general tendency toward pro-Euro bias of Euro- and Afro-American children. We have noted, however, that the pro-Euro bias is not so strong among Afro as among Euro preschoolers. We believe that a third factor can help to account for this difference. This factor is the norm in American culture that every person should identify with the racial category to which society has assigned that person and be proud of such identification, especially if the race is a minority one; in no sense should a person reject or be ashamed of his racial membership. In chapter 1 we cited the renewed emphasis in American society on preserving and promoting one's racial and cultural heritage. It is probable that some of this emphasis gets through to preschool children, although it is doubtful how effective this cultural message is unless the children are aware of racial classification and know clearly to which race they "belong." At the same time, Afro preschoolers might well be receiving subcultural messages that "black people are beautiful" and that "whitey is bad." Also, it was noted earlier that Afro children display a lesser degree of W+/B− color bias than Euro children, which suggests that their preference for light over darkness is somewhat weaker and hence would not generalize as strongly to the light-skinned models. We suggest that some combination of these factors is responsible for the lower degree of pro-Euro bias in Afro preschoolers.

We can summarize our interpretation regarding racial attitude and preference at the preschool level as follows. The young preschool child's general bias in favor of light over darkness generalizes to the relatively lighter skin of the Euro-American and establishes a diffuse pro-Euro bias. This pro-Euro bias is further strengthened by cultural messages regarding the favored position of Euro-Americans in the society and is supplemented by the current practice of designating dark-skinned persons as "black" and light-skinned persons as "white." In view of these factors, the pro-Euro bias of American preschool children is not surprising: Euro-Americans are viewed more positively than Afro-Americans because they are light-skinned, because they are called "white," and because they are "on top." Little wonder that pro-Euro bias is so pervasive among preschool children in America. But there is also a cultural message that Americans should identify with and be proud of their own racial category. For Euro preschoolers this message further promotes their pro-Euro bias; for Afro children it, along with the Black Identity movement, weakens the pro-Euro bias.

We have seen that the research findings indicate that racial attitude and racial preference are virtually synonymous at the preschool level. This is also true for school-age Euro children who continue to be pro-Euro in both attitudes and preferences. On the other hand, there is a clear separation in these concepts for Afro children following entry into the multiracial public school. This divergence takes the following form. At the preschool level, Afro children express pro-Euro attitudes and pro-Euro preferences. After entry into school, the preference pattern shifts dramatically to pro-Afro, while the attitude pattern remains pro-Euro. At the third grade level, for example, Afro children, as a group, express a definite pro-Afro preference, while still showing a tendency toward a pro-Euro attitude. Some years later, the attitude appears to "catch up" with the preference, and we once again find a congruence between the two which are now both pro-Afro. Apparently, the Afro child in the early school years develops a preference for Afro persons which is based on something other than his having a positive attitude toward them. Such a development might well be an expression of the norm that Americans should identify with their own racial grouping. In public schools, especially those that employ racial balance, racial affiliation of each student is made crystal clear, since such affiliation is a basis for assignment to a particular school and to classrooms within the school. Another line of speculation is that the pro-Afro preferences of Afro school-age children may have "defensive" determinants; it may be safer to choose Afro playmates because they lessen the possibility of rejection or unsuccessful competition. Our inclination is to favor the former (racial identification) hypothesis, which seems supported by the racial similarity findings to be reviewed later. The latter (defensiveness) hypothesis does not seem consistent with the racial acceptance data.

RACIAL ACCEPTANCE

The measure of racial acceptance differs from that of attitude and preference in that it is a nonchoice procedure in which the subject is presented with a photograph of a single child or group of children and is asked whether he would like to play with the person(s) depicted.

Preschool children express a high degree of general acceptance of other children as potential playmates, and accept Euro children more frequently than Afro children. This difference is not large, however, in the case of Afro-American preschoolers who accept Euro-American playmates only slightly more frequently than they do children of their own race. The difference in racial acceptance is greater in the case of the Euro preschoolers, who display considerably less acceptance of Afro-Americans than Euro-Americans. It must be stressed, however, that this is only a relative difference and that a large majority (about 80%) of Euro-American preschoolers express acceptance of Afro-American children as playmates.

In moving from the preschool to the early school years, we observe a moderate decline in cross-race acceptance: Euro children are now less accepting of Afro children, and Afro children are less accepting of Euro children. The general picture, however, remains one of acceptance rather than rejection, with a large majority of both races expressing acceptance for persons of the other race. On the other hand, the picture is not a symmetrical one: Afro children in the early school grades continue to be much more accepting of Euro children than the Euro children are of Afro children.

The juxtaposition of these conclusions regarding acceptance with our earlier conclusions regarding attitude and preference indicates that a negative attitude or preference does not necessarily imply active rejection. At the preschool level where both Afro and Euro children tend to be pro-Euro in their attitudes and preferences, they still express a high degree of acceptance of Afro playmates. At the early school level, where the preference of Afro children shifts to pro-Afro, the great majority of Afro children are still accepting of Euro playmates. While the absolute levels of measured acceptance may be somewhat inflated by the "yea saying" bias noted in chapter 6, it seems safe to conclude that active rejection must not be inferred from the presence of negative racial attitudes or preferences in young children.

The shift of Afro children to a pro-Afro preference when they enter public schools is not accompanied by a rejection of Euro playmates. In effect, the Afro children are saying they prefer Afro playmates but Euro playmates are O.K., too. This returns us to the idea that the pro-Afro preference of Afro children which appears in the early school years is most likely related to the child's clear recognition of his own racial classification and the realization that persons should identify with the racial category to which they belong. This hypothesis receives support from the findings on racial similarity or "self-identification."

RACIAL SIMILARITY

As noted earlier, we prefer the term racial similarity to the term racial self-identification. The latter term, taken literally, seems to imply that children are aware of race and that they are telling us the race with which they identify themselves. In practice, the procedures employed simply ask the child which of the figures he (or his father, mother, etc.) looks like, without any determination of the child's awareness of racial classification, per se. In effect, this provides a measure of perceived similarity between the child and the light- and dark-skinned figures. Thus, the Afro child who says that he looks like the light-skinned Euro figure is not necessarily "identifying with the other race"; he may be merely saying that he is like the "good" one. For these reasons, we have used the more descriptive term racial similarity in referring to the research findings and reserve the term racial self-identification for use as a theoretical construct.

Euro-American and Afro-American preschoolers behave differently on racial similarity tasks. The great majority of Euro-American preschoolers say that they (and their fathers and mothers) look like the Euro figures. This is quite consistent with their behavior on attitude and preference tasks where they express a positive evaluation of, and preference for, the light-skinned figures. Is the choice of the Euro figure on the racial similarity task due to a matching by race, or are the children merely saying that they look like the light-skinned, "good" figure? The answer seems to be "both." We have seen that about two-thirds of Euro children who are low in racial recognition ability say that they are more similar to the Euro figure, while about four-fifths of children high in racial recognition ability make Euro choices. From this, it is evident that Euro children have a tendency to say they look like Euro figures which is independent of their knowledge of racial classification. On the other hand, an awareness of racial classification seems to enhance the tendency of the children to select the Euro figures as similar to themselves.

Afro-American preschoolers tend to divide their racial similarity choices rather evenly between Afro and Euro figures. For example, the "look like me" responses of the Afro children taking the MPI were 47% Euro, 41% Afro, and 12% choice unclear. These racial similarity results, thus, contrast with the behavior of these children on the playmate preference task (57% Euro choice, 30% Afro choice); on the self-preference ("rather be") task (52% Euro choice, 34% Afro choice); and on the PRAM II racial attitude task (52% pro-Euro, 12% pro-Afro).

Two general interpretations can be offered regarding the tendency of these Afro preschoolers to choose Euro and Afro figures with about equal frequency on the racial similarity task. The first interpretation is that the racial similarity data may reflect nothing more than the random choices of children who see no similarity between themselves and the figures presented, with some children choosing one figure and some the other, on a chance basis. A second interpretation is that the data may represent the pooled responses of two subgroups of Afro children: one, which is not aware of race or skin-color similarity, and which is choosing the "good" (Euro) figure; the other, which is aware of race and/or color similarity and which is choosing the Afro figure. The available evidence provides some slight support for this second interpretation: the MPI racial similarity choices of Afro children who were low in racial classification ability were 40% Afro and 50% Euro, while the choices of Afro children high in racial classification ability were 50% Afro and 40% Euro. An awareness of racial classification, thus, seems to produce a slight shift toward perceived similarity to the Afro figures. On the other hand, it is clear that many Afro preschoolers—even if they are aware of racial classification—do not perceive themselves as being similar to the dark-skinned Afro-American figures. Related to this is the fact that only 76% of Afro preschoolers who were high in racial classification ability applied a correct racial label to themselves, compared to 98% of Euro preschoolers. We can interpret these findings as indicating that a large number of Afro preschoolers have not yet identified themselves as belonging to a dark-skinned racial group. Thus, when the Afro child expresses pro-Euro attitudes and preferences he is not necessarily "putting down his racial group"—he may be quite oblivious to the whole matter of "his race" and be choosing only in terms of a general pro-light-skinned bias and/or the pro-Euro messages which he has picked up from the culture. Scholars who see evidence of "self-hatred" or "self-rejection" in the pro-light-skinned bias of the Afro child are guilty of a serious over-interpretation of the research data.

The racial similarity picture for the Afro child changes during the early years in a multiracial public school. Early school-age Afro children revealed the following choices in response to the "look most like" item of the MPI: 77% Afro; 10% Euro; and 13% uncertain. The comparable figures for Euro school-age children were: 79% Euro; 7% Afro; and 15% uncertain. From this, we see that the children in both groups are now generally "identifying" with their own racial groups, and to about the same degree.

Among Afro school-age children, it is interesting to note the parallel between the increased frequency of Afro choice on the racial similarity measure, and their previously noted shift in racial preference from pro-Euro to pro-Afro. This is consistent with our speculation that the preference shift is related to a change in racial identification. In other words, we could say that the early school-age Afro child now recognizes his racial identity. He also seems to accept his racial identity (66% would "rather be" Afro; only 30% Euro) and prefers playmates of his own race (58% prefer Afro; only 21% Euro). On the other hand, we have seen that a pro-Euro attitude appears to persist long after the observed changes in racial identification and preference, and does not become pro-Afro until the teenage years. This seems to portend a problem in self-esteem for the school-age Afro child who identifies with, and chooses to associate with, a racial group which he still evaluates somewhat negatively, relative to the majority racial group. These conclusions suggest that the critical period for the development of self-esteem in the young Afro-American is not—as is often proposed—in the preschool years, but in the early school years when his Afro identity has been established but his pro-Euro attitudes continue to linger. Is it possible to change these pro-Euro attitudes at an earlier age? An affirmative answer is suggested by the findings of studies of the modification of race and color concepts.

MODIFICATION OF RACE AND COLOR ATTITUDES

The research evidence indicates that the tendency of preschool children to evaluate light-skinned Euro persons more positively than dark-skinned Afro persons can be changed by individually administered behavior modification procedures in which the proper learning contingencies are employed. Further, the evidence indicates that such procedures produce a general attitude change, rather than the mere mechanical alteration of the trained responses, and that measurable effects can be observed one year following the attitude modification procedure. In addition, it has been shown that E+/A− bias can be weakened, and perhaps eliminated, through the modification of the child's tendency to view the color white more positively than the color black. Thus, while we may be forced to conclude that the development of E+/A− bias is "natural" in young American children, we must not conclude that it is immutable.

In contrast to the effectiveness of the individually administered behavior modification procedures, group-administered curriculum procedures have generally been found not to be effective in the modification of E+/A− bias in preschool children. Classroom procedures involving stories of Afro-American heroes, play activities aimed at developing positive associations to dark colors, etc., have generally been found to leave E+/A− bias unchanged in both Afro and Euro children. It is our opinion that the classroom procedures used to date have been ineffective because they have not required the children to make active responses to race and color stimuli, and because they have failed to provide clear and consistent training in the direction of the desired attitude change. In other words, we believe that it is possible to develop effective group procedures if sufficient care is given to basic learning principles. On the other hand, we must question, realistically, the extent to which attitude change accomplished in the classroom can be expected to have socially significant effects unless it is accompanied by changes in existing patterns of social structure and interracial interaction outside the school setting.

The variety of research findings summarized in this chapter seem to fall into a reasonably coherent pattern. While the picture is an incomplete one, the known phenomena seem adequate to form a general outline of a theory of the development of color and race bias in young children.

10.
A Developmental Theory of Color and Race Bias

We will now integrate the research findings and our previous interpretations into a general theory of the development of children's responses to color and race. In constructing this theory we have employed three general classes of determinants: the biologically based early learning experiences of the child with light and darkness; the messages regarding color and race which the child receives from the general culture; and the amplification or suppression of the general cultural messages as a result of subcultural and family member- ship. Most previous theorizing in this area has placed exclusive emphasis upon the latter categories, i.e., upon cultural, subcultural, and familial influences. While such factors are of importance in shaping the child's concepts of color and race, a strict cultural influence theory is inadequate in explaining all of the observed phenomena, e.g., the absence of a clear age progression in pro-Euro bias in the preschool years, the lack of correlation between race or color bias and IQ, the general cross-cultural tendency toward the positive evaluation of white relative to black, etc. On the other hand, facts such as these can be explained by consideration of the child's early learning experiences with light and darkness.

Our theory involves a consideration of both cultural and

biological factors. The emphasis on cultural factors reflects our belief that human behavior is shaped in large part by social interactions with other human beings and that an adequate explanation of human behavior cannot be achieved without a heavy emphasis upon social and cultural considerations. To believe this, however, in no way precludes the necessity for a consideration of the biological make-up of human beings and the manner in which this interacts with culture to determine human behavior. For example, our entire discussion of the possible influence of cultural variables upon the young child is predicated upon a basic biological fact—the incredible learning ability of the young Homo sapiens. Were it not for this genetically determined characteristic of the human nervous system, the whole notion of cultural influences would be void. It is important to recognize that human behavior is always a joint function of biological make-up and culture, or heredity and environment, or nature and nurture. We may ask whether biological make-up or culture is *more* important in the determination of a given type of behavior, but to ask whether a given behavior is the product of heredity *or* environment is to pose a useless question, since the answer must always be "both." The relationship between biological make-up and culture is often direct, as in the case where one factor facilitates or sets limits upon the development of the other. Anthropologists agree that the evolution of the opposable thumb, upright posture, and large brain which enabled our ancestors to learn to manipulate tools was a necessary condition for the development of human culture as we know it. On the other side, it is clear that social norms relating to such matters as family size in various segments of a population can alter the nature of the general gene pool, with possible consequences for such matters as the health and intellectual level of future generations. The recognition of the joint influence of biological make-up and culture in determining human behavior makes us comfortable in proposing a model which emphasizes the role of both factors in the development of race and color concepts in young children.

The Effects of Early Experience

We propose that virtually every child has experiences early in life which lead to the development of a preference for light over darkness. This is based, primarily, on the child's visual orientation to his environment and the disorientation which he experiences in the dark, and may be further strengthened by the fact that his major need satisfactions occur during the daylight hours. In addition to a learned preference, one can speculate that the young human may have an innate aversion to darkness, perhaps based on an evolutionary history in which avoidance of the dark was an adaptive characteristic. Although the demonstration of other innate fears in children (Jersild and Holmes, 1935) makes such speculation plausible, we know of no empirical findings with children which require such a theory. On the other hand, there are findings from studies of nonhuman primates which suggest the operation of innate factors in the responses of these species to darkness and the color black.

In a series of studies conducted with the squirrel monkey, a diurnal primate with a visual apparatus highly similar to our own, Parker (1966) first demonstrated that the onset and duration of light were highly reinforcing events, i.e., the monkey would learn to press a bar in order to illuminate the otherwise dark chamber in which he was placed. Parker then conducted a study in which the animal could obtain light or obtain food, but not both simultaneously. This was done by placing the monkey in a box-like apparatus, at one end of which there was a food dish and at the other end a perch with a switch connected to the light which illuminated the box. When the monkey was on the perch, the light remained on; when he left the perch, the light went off and the box was totally dark. The food cup could be reached only by leaving the perch. Under these conditions, Parker demonstrated that the squirrel monkey remained on the perch and endured long periods of extreme hunger rather than experience the darkness which occurred when he left the perch. It is clear that for this diurnal primate, total darkness elicits an aversive reaction which is sufficiently strong to compete successfully with the primary drive of hunger.

Zimmermann's (1973) findings with neonate rhesus monkeys are also relevant here. Each monkey received his food by learning to go into one of two boxes, one white and one black, attached to his home cage. Half of the monkeys received their food in the white box, while the others were fed in the black box. After twenty days of training, the situation was reversed so that each monkey now had to learn to go into the other box for his food. Under these conditions, the monkeys trained in the white box and shifted to the black took over twice as long to learn to go to the new box as the monkeys who were shifted from black to white. By inference, these infant monkeys had an attraction to the white box relative to the black box which facilitated the shift to the white box and/or retarded the shift to the black. Such a clear "preference" for white over black in these infant primates is provocative and worthy of additional investigation.*

These findings with nonhuman primates suggest that we should not be too quick to assume that there is no innate fear of darkness in the human. Nevertheless, we prefer to begin our theorizing, more conservatively, with a consideration of ways in which an aversion to darkness and attraction to light may become established through learning experiences.

*The work of George Ungar and his associates at the Baylor University Medical School suggests that there may be a biochemical basis for dark avoidance. These investigators have isolated and synthesized a brain protein, called *scotophobin*, which when injected produces dark avoidance in the rat, a nocturnal animal, which normally prefers darkness to light (see summary in McConnell, 1974, pp. 472–74).

Fear of the dark is so commonplace in young children that most parents show no concern when it appears and pay little attention to it, other than to buy a night-light and grumble about the inconvenience involved. Interestingly, evidence of aversion to darkness is not usually observed during infancy, but seems to appear first, in most children, between the ages of two and four. By this time the child has acquired a primarily visual orientation toward his environment, has learned through experience that there are frightening things which may be encountered, and has developed an active imagination. Alone in the dark, the child imagines or dreams of a frightening situation—is there a lion under the bed? Being unable to make a satisfactory visual check, the child calls for assistance. The parents respond, turn on the light, comfort the child, and make a check which proves negative for lions. Note the learning situation. The darkness was associated with fear, and the light was associated with fear reduction. The effect on the young child is much the same as if there *had* been a lion in the dark, and turning on the light had made it disappear. After such an experience, we are not surprised to find the child requesting that a light be left on and remaining at least mildly phobic about darkness. This experience, with minor modifications, probably happens to children the world over since the necessary conditions—visual orientation, frightening things, and darkness—are certainly pan-cultural in nature. Further, since not all children have identical learning experiences involving darkness, we are not surprised to find that children differ in degree of aversion to darkness, which may vary from little or none to the extreme cases of nyctophobia seen in the child guidance clinic.

The association of darkness with loss of visual orientation and control is not the only reason why a child might develop a preference for daylight over darkness. The frightening sounds associated with the darkness of thunderstorms could be another source of reinforcement.

Or consider the child's needs for activity and stimulus change, for human interaction and contact comfort. The satisfaction of all of these needs occurs primarily during daylight hours. Nighttime—even when it's not frightening—is frustrating, while daytime is "where the action is." (The popular song, "Thank the Lord for the Nighttime," was not written by a three-year-old.) The gist of our argument is that the early experiences of the typical young child with the light of day and dark of night cause the development of a strong preference for light over darkness $(L+/D-)$.

There are two major consequences of these virtually universal human experiences with light and darkness. First, there is the cumulative, historical-cultural consequence which results in the pan-cultural tendency to use darkness and dark colors as negative symbols, and light and light colors as positive symbols. Viewed in this way, these color symbols are seen not as arbitrary conventions, but as cultural elaborations of shared human feelings. Further, there is little danger of the symbols losing their meanings because positive feelings for light and negative feelings for dark are continually being reestablished in successive generations of young children.

The second, and individual, consequence of the child's early experiences with light and darkness is that he develops a personal predisposition to evaluate light things more positively than dark things. Thus, if we present the three-year-old with a picture of a white animal and a black animal, he is likely to select the white one as the "good" one and the black as the "bad" one on the basis of the relative lightness and darkness of the stimulus figures. Likewise, if we present the child with pictures of light-skinned and dark-skinned persons and ask him to make a choice between them, we are likely to see evidence of a pro-light-skinned bias on whatever measure we are employing (attitude, preference, similarity, etc.). We propose that the child who has had little exposure to cultural messages regarding color and race may still display a pro-white color bias and appear to display a pro-Euro racial bias simply on the basis of his inclination to view light things as more positive than dark things. In sum, what appears to be racial bias in the young preschooler is not racial in its origins—although it later becomes racial in its implications.

Two other observations are to be made concerning the early-experience subtheory. First, it is assumed that all young humans have generally similar experiences with light and darkness and hence that the preference for light over darkness will develop in children of all racial groups. Second, the strength of the aversive response to darkness may differ in children according to the details of their learning experiences and such individual differences may be related to the individual differences observed later in the race and color concepts they develop. Such an effect would, in fact, help to explain the otherwise puzzling individual differences in the racial attitude scores of preschool children which do not correlate with age or IQ. If the individual differences were being produced to some degree by determinants operating prior to the preschool years, they would, to that degree, tend not to correlate with age during the preschool years. And we doubt that individual differences in such variables as fear of the dark are sufficiently cognitive to be expected to correlate with IQ.

We do not want to overstate our case and imply that the light-dark preference of the young child is the sole—or even the principal—determinant of his race and color biases. All we wish to do is point out that the child is not a tabula rasa at the time he starts receiving race and color messages from the culture. Rather, he is already predisposed by his early learning experiences toward a pro-white, pro-light-skinned bias, and it is against this background that the cultural messages are received and interpreted.

General Cultural Influences

The preschool child in contemporary America is surrounded by a welter of cultural "messages" regarding color and race. We suspect that the child is receptive to messages concerning color before those concerning race, and we shall discuss these two types of general cultural influences in that order.

We noted in chapter 2 the wide variety of situations where the young child is exposed to the cultural practice of employing the color white (or light) to symbolize goodness and the color black (or darkness) to symbolize badness. Such symbolism abounds in the mass media, in children's literature, in Judeo-Christian religion, and, through idiomatic speech, in the very fabric of human communication. What is the impact of this symbolism upon the preschool child?

The research evidence suggests that contact with the black-white symbolism does not initiate the child's tendency to evaluate white more positively than black, since this tendency is already evident at the age of three when the cultural impact of color terminology cannot as yet be very great. Also, the cultural influence does not appreciably affect the *degree* of W+/B− bias, since there is little increase in such bias across the preschool years, a period in which the child is in increasing contact with the culture and is learning a great variety of cultural concepts, including, for example, sex roles and racial classification. We believe that the main impact of the cultural symbolism is to confirm the child's own feelings regarding light and darkness and to consolidate this learning in conceptual form. Prior to the cultural messages, the child *feels* that white is good; following the cultural message, the child *knows* that white is good. The preschooler who is told, for example, that angels are white and evil witches are black responds, in effect, "I understand; it makes sense to me."

The earliest cultural messages regarding race received by young American children probably derive from the advantaged position that Euro-Americans traditionally have enjoyed in American society. We shall not take the time to attempt to detail the many ways in which young children may become aware that Euro-Americans have occupied a more favorable position than Afro-Americans. This fact is so thoroughly woven into the fabric of American life that it is doubtful whether any American social scientist can be fully aware of all of its manifestations. There are the subtle lessons to be learned from the fact that Euro-Americans have tended to monopolize positions of power and prestige and to have better houses, clothes, and education than Afro-Americans. In the past, the type of racial contact young American children have had with adults across racial lines probably has helped to communicate the advantaged position of Euro-Americans. Prior to attending public school, Euro-American children often encountered Afro-American adults in menial positions in their homes and nursery schools and rarely as guests in their homes. Afro-American children tended to have contact with Euro-Americans as professional people of high status and rarely in a setting of social equality. In the past, we believe these pro-Euro messages from the culture have combined with the child's earlier bias toward light-skinned persons and consolidated further the pro-Euro bias of the preschool child. Hopefully, the experiences of preschool children today are different from those of yesteryear in that contemporary children have the opportunity to experience dark-skinned persons in a variety of high-status roles, ranging from professional and business people to the superstars of athletics and entertainment. We believe that today's children are receiving, at least, mixed messages with regard to the relationship of race to social status and are no longer subject to the subtle but powerful message that dark-skinned people must somehow be inferior since they are almost always found in low-status roles.

There may be, however, other influences acting to promote increased racial bias in today's young children. One such factor may be the current heavy emphasis upon the importance of race as a social classification. Such an emphasis may serve to alert young children to the "importance" of race and sensitize them to racial messages, including those which contain racial bias. The unwitting reinforcement of the notion of the importance of race is illustrated in the anecdote reported in chapter 1 where a teacher who was required to determine the number of Euro- and Afro-American children in her class accomplished this by first asking all the "white" children to stand and be counted, and then asking all the "black" children to do the same. The children could hardly escape the message that there were two different kinds of children in the classroom, and that it was important to classify each child into his appropriate group before proceeding with other matters. What lessons were these children now ready to learn because of this emphasis on race?

It seems likely also that the semantics of present-day racial classification act to reinforce racial bias in young children. The practice of designating Euro-Americans as "white" and Afro-Americans as "black" invites the child to generalize the color meanings to the racial groups: "If these people are called 'white,' they must be the good ones, and if these people are called 'black,' they must be the bad ones." Thus, the lesson of racial classification is learned in an intrinsically evaluative context which combines with the child's existing bias toward lighter-skinned figures to confirm, and to some degree heighten, his tendency toward pro-Euro bias. The use of white and black as racial designation terms also tends to produce an "over-discrimination" for the child. The opposite nature of these words seems likely to lead the child to think that the groups of persons so designated must be radically different from one another. On the other hand, terms such as Euro- and Afro-American recognize the existence of subgroup differences among persons who participate in the same general American culture.

We are aware that our comments may be disturbing to some Afro-Americans for whom the term black has become important because of its use as a racial identity term in recent years. We have, of course, no quarrel with efforts to promote a sense of subcultural identity in any group of Americans. We believe, however, that a positive sense of self-identity in young Afro children can be accomplished more easily by using a term such as Afro-American than by using the negatively loaded word black. To tell an Afro preschooler that he is black and that black is beautiful may be understood by the child as "I am bad and it is good to be bad," or some other similarly garbled message.* And, on the other hand, telling the Euro child that he is white puts him "on the side of the angels" in a quite unrealistic fashion.

What about the cultural norm which says that one should identify with and evaluate positively one's own racial category? This poses no problem for the Euro-American child. As he becomes aware of racial classification and of his own racial affiliation, the Euro child discovers that he is a member of the group which is light-skinned, is called "white," and is socially favored. He thus finds support for evaluating Euro-Americans positively and for identifying with this racial group. He learns that he belongs to the "good club," and he has no difficulty in accepting his membership.

The situation is much more complex for the Afro-American child. We have seen that, as a preschooler, he also has a noticeable pro-light-skinned bias. As he becomes aware of racial classification and of his own racial membership, he faces the difficult problem of feeling positively about, and identifying with, a group which is

*Could this be related to the recent development of the slang usage of bad (pronounced ba-a-ad) to communicate approval, among some young Afro-Americans?

dark-skinned, is called "black," and which is often in a socially disadvantaged position. He is therefore faced with conflicting cultural messages. On the one hand it is "preferable to be white," but on the other hand a person is expected to identify with his own race. This conflict takes some time to resolve, if indeed, it is resolved. By the early school years, the Afro child has become well aware of racial classification, has recognized his similarity to Afro-Americans, and has developed a preference for Afro playmates. At the same time, he still retains his tendency to view Euro persons more positively than Afro persons. The scanty research evidence suggests that it is not until the teenage years that his attitude shifts to pro-Afro and he finally fulfills the cultural norm of both identifying with and making a positive evaluation of his own racial category.

Other Influences

In the foregoing discussion of general cultural influences, we have attempted to explain the general pattern of race and color concepts found in young American children. Black-white symbolism, the importance of race, the favored status of Euro-Americans, and the norm of racial self-acceptance impinge upon American children generally. While these broadly based determinants are useful in accounting for the development of similarities in race and color concepts, and for some of the differences between Euro- and Afro-American children, they are not adequate to explain all of the observed variation in these concepts. To account for such variation we need to look at other influences such as racial membership, socioeconomic status, and family membership. There has been little empirical research relating these factors to color and race concepts in young children. Our discussion of them is in recognition of our belief that a full explanation of how race and color concepts develop will require a consideration of such influences.

Racial Membership / While the color and racial biases of preschool Euro and Afro children are in the same direction, i.e., pro-white and pro-Euro, they are less marked in Afro than in Euro children. This suggests that there may be factors involved in racial membership which weaken or reinforce the effects of the general cultural influences. This should not surprise us considering the continuing importance of racial membership in American society, which we documented in chapter 1.

With such strong emphasis on the importance of race and with Euro-Americans generally occupying a position of greater prestige than Afro-Americans, we can assume that Afro and Euro children experience American life differently because of their racial membership. We have already pointed out the probable effect of the Black Identity movement on young Afro-Americans. Yet this movement does not touch all preschool Afro-American children equally. Some Afro children attend all-Afro "freedom" schools in which racial identity and racial pride are stressed, while others attend interracial Headstart programs in which racial identity is not so strongly emphasized. Lipscomb (1972) showed that Afro children in these different types of schools in the same town developed somewhat different racial concepts. Some Afro-American communities feel the impact of the pro-Afro and, at times, anti-Euro, teaching differently. For example, it is probable that children of Black Muslims encounter such teaching more than other Afro children.

Euro-American racial membership, as we have noted, gives additional positive reinforcement to the general cultural influences. At the same time, there are attempts by some groups within that racial category to strengthen the pro-Euro and anti-Afro biases, and there are attempts by other groups to weaken them. Thus, there are organizations like citizens' councils and all-Euro private schools that seek to protect and maintain the privileged position of Euro-Americans. On the other hand, there are human relations councils and educational and religious groups which promote equality of treatment. Euro-American children vary in the exposure they have to such groups, and, as a result, they are likely to vary in the degree of pro-Euro bias which they develop.

We conclude that the young child's racial membership is likely to lead to certain special experiences which modify the effects of general cultural influences. Further, it appears that, within each racial group, there is variable exposure to such racially specific influences which may contribute to the individual differences which we observe in the race and color concepts of young children.

Socioeconomic Status / We have spoken of the privileged position of Euro-Americans and the disadvantaged position of Afro-Americans in American society. This generalization is, of course, an oversimplification. It means that, proportionately, there are more Euro- than Afro-Americans of high status and more Afro- than Euro-Americans of low status, although these proportions are probably changing under the impact of civil rights legislation and affirmative action programs that actively recruit minority Americans for upper-status positions. Our point here is that within each racial category there are socioeconomic status differences which may be related to racial concepts and attitudes in young children.

A considerable amount of research, especially by sociologists, shows variation by socioeconomic status in many behavioral domains; for example, in occupational and educational aspirations, political affiliation and attitude, and religious belief and activity. Therefore, we might well expect some variation in race and color concepts according to socioeconomic status. Logically, it might be expected that lower socioeconomic Euro-Americans would have a stronger pro-Euro and anti-Afro bias than upper-status Euros. Lower-status Euro-Americans probably are thrown into more direct competition for jobs with Afro-Americans than are upper-status Euro-Americans. Also, some lower-status Euros may feel the need to look down on Afro-Americans as a means of compensating for their own low status in the Euro group. On the other hand, upper-status Afro-Americans might feel the effects of racial discrimination more keenly, since they are in a position to see it more clearly, and might therefore experience more resentment than lower-status Afro-Americans.

While numerous studies relating racial attitudes of adults to socioeconomic status have been reported, there is little consistent empirical support for the foregoing speculations. Simpson and Yinger (1972, pp. 131–38) have reviewed and summarized much of this research and have noted the problems in comparing results from studies which use different ways of determining status, and the lack of control of other factors that might influence attitudes. Their review does not reveal any generally consistent relationships between status and attitudes, perhaps due to the linear model which most researchers have assumed. This is suggested by the research of Vanneman and Pettigrew (1972) who found a curvilinear rather than a linear relationship between socioeconomic status and racial prejudice. They reported that skilled or "affluent" workers were more prejudiced than those of either higher or lower status. Perhaps this explains the findings in MPI studies where children's racial bias scores usually have not been found to be related to "high" and "low" socioeconomic status, while, on the other hand, Porter (1971) found evidence of relationships when she employed a middle-class, working-class, and lower-class status analysis. This suggests that the use of more sophisticated status classifications may reveal that there are systematic relationships between socioeconomic class and racial bias in young children.

Family Membership / We suspect that most of the preschool child's earliest learning about race occurs through contact with other members of his family. In this sense, the family serves as a principal communicator of what we have called general cultural influences, as well as the subcultural influences related to race and social class. If this were the only communication function served by the family, we would expect to find that children of the same race and social class would display highly similar racial concepts and attitudes, but they do not. Boswell (1974), for example, found wide individual differences in racial attitude scores among her middle-class, Euro-American preschool subjects. Thus, when we speak of family membership variables we are concerned with the possibility of other more idiosyncratic family influences which may act to amplify or suppress the effects of the general cultural and subcultural influences. This line of thinking is consistent with the intuitive reaction of the layperson who encounters evidence of strong racial bias in a young child and infers that his parents must be highly prejudiced persons.

Our discussion of possible family influences is quite speculative, since there is little empirical evidence bearing directly on this point. However, we would like to propose three general ways in which the family may influence the development of racial concepts and attitudes in young children. Although, for convenience, we will speak of the parents and the young child as constituting the family, it is obvious that other persons regularly present in the home (siblings, other relations, etc.) may also have a significant influence on the young child.

It would appear that parents may influence the manner in which the child thinks about racial groups, as well as the way he feels about them. An example of the former is the frequency with which the parents talk about race and the amount of importance which they attach to racial classification. We know people, both Euro- and Afro-American, who seem to find it virtually impossible to speak about persons or their deeds without alluding to their race. To such persons, race has the character of a basic human classification which seems as fundamental to them as the classification of persons according to sex. It should be added that these people are not necessarily overtly prejudiced—perhaps not even covertly so. We suspect that in a home in which one or both of the parents have such a preoccupation with race, the child develops an awareness of racial categories at an early age and comes to view race as something of great importance. This, in turn, may alert the child to cultural messages concerning race, and lead to the acquisition of a greater degree of conventional racial bias. Perhaps such a factor was at work in the study by Floyd (1969) who concluded that the greater the commitment of Afro-American parents to black activism, "the more the child wants to be white." The same mechanism may have been at work when John McAdoo (1970) found that a "Black consciousness" curriculum did not reduce pro-Euro bias in Afro preschoolers but, if anything, appeared to move the bias a bit further in the pro-Euro direction.

The precocious learning of racial categorization may have other effects. We know the conceptual behavior of young preschool children is rather simple in nature and often reveals what Piaget has called "transductive reasoning," i.e., the generalization from the particular to the particular. This type of thinking is shown by the three- or four-year-old child who assumes that because a group of objects are alike in one respect, they must be alike in other respects. Phyllis Katz (1973) has noted the close parallel between such transductive reasoning in preschool children and what Gordon Allport (1954) has called "overcategorization" in prejudiced adults who assume that all persons placed within a given class behave in the same way and exhibit the same traits. This leads to the hypothesis that premature learning of racial categorization may establish transductive reasoning patterns regarding race which may persist through later childhood and into adulthood. In sum, a parental preoccupation with race may have the effect of sensitizing the child to the reception of cultural messages regarding race during a developmental period in which he is likely to process such information in an overly simplified manner. With reference to this, Mary Ellen Goodman has written:

> While Johnny is very young his grown-ups probably do well to stay clear of race-group labels, of whatever variety. No matter what the nature of the labels, they imply sharply separated categories or kinds of people. . . . What we actually have here is a brownness continuum which proceeds without a break from dark brown to the extreme bleach of the extreme blond. If Johnny gets this picture firmly fixed in his mind *before* he gets used to race-group labels, he will be able to use them later without being misled by them. He will know that they represent shorthand designations for socially defined race groups made up of people whose color actually varies over a wide range. We hope he will also know that their other characteristics vary widely too (Goodman, 1964, pp. 224–25).

A second way in which parents may influence their children in the development of racial bias is in terms of the feelings which they communicate concerning persons of different races. While the research evidence is sparse, Boswell (1974) has shown that the racial attitudes of middle-class Euro-American preschoolers correlate with their mother's attitudes; mothers who are relatively negative toward Afro-Americans have children with a similar bias. We suspect that racial bias is transmitted in both direct and indirect ways. Any kindergarten teacher can attest to the frequency with which her children deliver parental quotations on the subject of race (and all other "important" matters). We know from research findings that preschool children respond to their world in a highly evaluative manner and are, thus, attuned to the reception of evaluative messages concerning other persons. The preschool child is already busily engaged in the basic human enterprise of sorting out the "good guys" from the "bad guys," and mother's evaluative comments concerning members of racial groups fall on receptive ears.

We believe, also, that feelings about racial groups can be transmitted in various indirect ways. Mother and father may never speak harshly of persons of the other race, but the look on mother's face or the way that father laughs, may carry the affective message. One can even argue that nonverbal cues such as voice, facial expression, and body tension and posture may be more important than verbal cues in the communication of feelings to young children. The mother who fears large dogs can hardly fail to communicate this fear to her preschool child—regardless of her verbal protestations to the contrary. In somewhat less dramatic ways, we suspect that parents often communicate negative feelings regarding race while never overtly verbalizing their feelings. Exposure to such a parental model may not only facilitate the development of negative affect in the child but also suggest to him that one is supposed to keep such feelings secret and pretend that they do not exist. This, it would seem, saddles the child with a double burden to carry forward into his life in an interracial world.

In addition to the communication of racial attitude, per se, there is the possibility that certain parental personality traits and related child-rearing practices may contribute to the development of racial bias in young children. Let us use the concept of the "authoritarian personality" as an illustration (Adorno, Frenkel-Brunswik, Levinson, and Sanford, 1950).* The authoritarian personality charac- terizes a person who views human beings as basically weak and untrustworthy and who places great reliance on the use of external authority in the direction and control of human behavior. Ethnocentrism is a focal trait in the authoritarian personality in which general apprehensions concerning human nature tend to become focused on

*While the original work of Adorno et al. has been criticized on both theoretical and methodological grounds, we feel that the general concept of authoritarianism is sufficiently sound to serve as an illustration in this context.

persons who are "different" from him, including persons of other races. From this, it is deduced that acceptance of an authoritarian approach to life and racial prejudice will be found to be related, and this prediction has been confirmed in studies at the adult level.

How does experience with authoritarian parents lead to the development of racial bias? First, there is the obvious point that since authoritarian parents are themselves biased, they may communicate this bias to their children in the direct and indirect ways noted above. But there is more. Phyllis Katz (1976) has summarized the dynamics, as follows: "The theory assumes that prejudice in children is generated by harsh and rigid parents. The child is viewed as having to continually submit to arbitrary and often severe parental authority. Because of the parents' uncompromising natures, the resultant hostility of the child is never permitted direct expression. Accordingly, as a defense mechanism, the child identifies with the frustrating authority figures, tends to idealize them, and displaces his aggression towards out-group persons" (pp. 133–34). It follows that children of authoritarian parents should have a high degree of racial prejudice, and Katz cites several studies of school-age children in which evidence of such a relationship has been found.* For example, Harris, Gough, and Martin (1950) studied children in grades four through six and found that the mothers of high-prejudiced subjects preferred quiet children to noisy ones, stressed the importance of obedience, and discouraged sex-play in their children, often by means of physical punishment. The mothers of low-prejudiced children were much more permissive in their child-rearing practices. The findings from a 1974 study by Barbara Young suggest that similar relationships may be demonstrable at the preschool level. Young studied 23 Canadian preschoolers and their parents, and

*Katz notes that authoritarian attitudes are related to other variables such as intelligence, educational level, and social class which makes it difficult to interpret these findings in a simple manner.

found that the children's PRAM II scores correlated with the parents' scores on measures of authoritarianism and ethnocentrism. Children whose parents were judged high in authoritarianism and ethnocentrism showed a higher degree of pro-Euro bias than did children whose parents were judged low in these characteristics.

The foregoing discussion of the authoritarian parent is intended to be illustrative rather than conclusive, and there are other parental personality traits and behavior patterns which may influence children's orientation toward persons of other races. It seems that we often speak too simplistically and mechanically about the "transmission" of race bias from parents to child. While the parents' racial concepts and attitudes constitute important models, other parental dynamics and child-rearing practices may influence the evolving racial concepts and attitudes of the young child.

As we noted earlier, there is little empirical research evidence bearing on many of the points we have discussed. There is a great need for additional investigation in this area in order to determine the degree to which differences in racial concepts among children may be attributed to familial influences. Such research may go far toward explaining the individual differences in race and color concepts found among children of the same race and age groups.

A THEORETICAL MODEL

We have outlined what we believe to be the major factors which contribute to the development of color and race bias in young children. We have noted that such bias may originate in the child's natural tendency to develop a general preference for light over darkness based on his biological status as a diurnal animal. We have described the various cultural, subcultural, and familial influences which may shape the subsequent development of the child's concepts and attitudes relating to color and race. The major features of the theory which we have proposed are represented in Figure 10-1, the consideration of which provides a convenient way to summarize what we have said. Young children display a preference for light over darkness (L+/D−) which develops initially as a result of aversive early experiences involving darkness and positive experiences with light (A). General cultural norms (B) equating light with goodness and dark with badness also may contribute to the L+/D− bias which, once established, may generalize directly (C) to light-skinned (Euro) and dark-skinned (Afro) persons, initiating a pro-Euro/anti-Afro (E+/A−) bias. The L+/D− bias also generalizes (D) to the colors white and black and contributes to the development of a pro-white/anti-black (W+/B−) bias, which is further strengthened by the child's exposure to the general cultural symbols (E) which employ white to signify goodness, and black, badness. The W+/B− bias may be further influenced by subcultural norms and family experiences (F) which may act either to enhance or suppress the bias. Generalization of the W+/B− bias to light- and dark-skinned persons (G) is greatly facilitated by the general cultural practice (H) of designating light-skinned persons as "white" and dark-skinned persons as "black," with subcultural and family influences (I) again acting to strengthen or weaken this effect. Finally, development of E+/A− racial bias occurs not only via the two generalization effects (C and G) but also as a result of messages regarding race, per se, which the child receives from the general culture (J) and the subcultures and family (K) with which he is in contact.

It is our view that this theoretical model is adequate to explain the fact that most preschool children exhibit a pro-Euro bias, while also accounting for the different degree of this bias in Euro and Afro children, and allowing for individual differences in bias among children. The

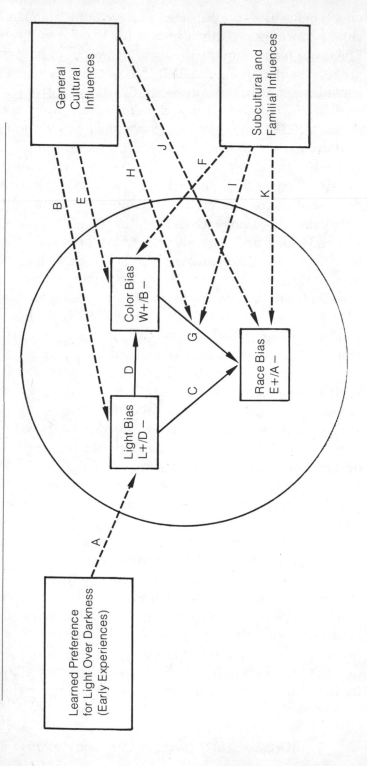

Figure 10-1. Theoretical Model of the Development of Race Bias in Young Children

model suggests that what appears to be racial bias in preschool children may initially be only a pro-light/pro-white bias which may have nothing to do with race and, hence, should not be interpreted as evidence of "racial prejudice" among Euro children or "negative self-concept" among Afro children. Later, however, this initial bias may contribute to the development of true racial bias as the child learns of the importance of race in our society and encounters the various cultural, subcultural, and familial messages which are associated with racial classification. We propose that the "racial bias" exhibited by young children is not primarily racial in its origin, but becomes racial in its effect as children learn about race and their own racial identity.

In concluding this chapter and the book proper, we wish to call the reader's attention to Appendix A in which we outline our thoughts concerning future research. We discuss there the need for improved methodology and research design and point out a variety of substantive questions which require investigation. Beyond our present efforts to summarize and interpret existing knowledge stands our hope that this work will be of value to future researchers as they attempt to answer the many remaining questions concerning the development and modification of color and race bias in young children.

APPENDIXES

APPENDIX A:
FUTURE DIRECTIONS FOR RESEARCH

Research conducted to date has resulted in the development of a sizable body of knowledge concerning the development and modification of race and color concepts in young children. On the other hand, the overall picture is incomplete, and many important questions remain unanswered. In the authors' view, there is a need both for more research and better research in this area. By more research, we mean an attack on the many facets of these topics which are not yet well understood. By better research, we mean the development and use of improved assessment procedures and research designs. One would expect that in approaching a topic of obvious social significance researchers would be doubly careful in the construction of their instruments and the design of their studies. Unfortunately, this has not always been the case and there are instances where the importance of the subject matter seems to have bedazzled the researcher, with the result that basic research principles have been ignored and violated. In this appendix we will offer our suggestions for future research, dealing first with the matter of methodological improvements, and second with the substantive questions which need further exploration.

METHODOLOGICAL IMPROVEMENTS

We will deal with needed improvements in the assessment procedures ("tests") used in this research area, with problems in general research design, and with the use of more sophisticated data analysis procedures. In setting the level of this discussion, we have been guided by two considerations: first, the observation that much previous research in this area has been characterized by a relatively low degree of methodological sophistication; and, second, the fact that persons interested in research in this area come from a wide variety of academic backgrounds and disciplines including anthropology, child development, education, psychology, and sociology. In view of this, we have chosen to emphasize certain basic methodological matters and have given little attention to many of the more sophisticated methods available to the behavioral scientist.

Assessment Procedures

The starting point for the development of more adequate procedures for assessing racial concepts is the recognition that one is involved in the general area of psychological testing and that all the familiar questions regarding validity and reliability need to be asked. Testing psychologists have long recognized that meaningful inferences about behavioral traits can only be made from adequate samples of behavior. The idea that one can usefully determine a child's racial preference by obtaining his response to one or two questions is as far-fetched as attempting to assess his vocabulary level by asking him the meaning of one or two words. All indications suggest that the racial and color concepts of young children should be conceptualized as *variables*, that is, behavioral tendencies which vary not only in direction but in degree or consistency. Thus, the question of racial preference should not be thought of as a categorical matter in which the child prefers one race or the other, but as a variable in which the child displays a degree of preference for one race or the other. The necessity for this view is seen whenever multiple-item measures are employed. For example, when Best (1972) gave Euro preschoolers her 12-item racial preference procedure, the children did not always choose the Euro figures but displayed varying degrees of tendency to prefer them. Racial preference clearly cannot be conceptualized as categorical, but must be thought of as a matter of degree. The same basic argument can be advanced for the other racial and color concepts with which we have been concerned.

If race and color concepts are to be conceptualized as variables along which children differ as to degree, it follows that one must provide the child with sufficient response opportunities to allow a reasonably sensitive assessment of his position along what-ever continuum is being studied. Just as one could not make a sensitive assessment of intelligence using a 3-item intelligence test, one cannot make a sensitive assessment of racial attitude using a 3-item racial attitude test. Bearing in mind the dictum that, other things being equal, the longer a test, the greater its reliability, what guidelines can be offered about the length of procedure necessary for the assessment of race and color concepts in young children?

Since a majority of the race and color concept assessment procedures have been of the two-choice (Euro or Afro figure) variety, the binomial distribution can be of assistance in establishing guidelines for test length. Let us consider the case of a 6-item test of, say, racial attitude which is scored in terms of number of pro-Euro responses and, thus, generates scores of 0 through 6, with a score of 3 as a neutral, or nonbiased midpoint. Within this score range, when can we be confident that the child is displaying a significant behavioral consistency as opposed to merely responding at random? A consideration of the binomial distribution informs us that if we were testing a group of completely unbiased children, who were responding randomly to the test, we would expect to obtain the following chance distribution of scores:

Number of Euro Choices	Percent of Children
0	2
1	10
2	23
3	31
4	23
5	10
6	2

This indicates that if we employ a conventional level of statistical significance (say .05), it is only when a child obtains a score of 0 or of 6 that we can conclude with any confidence that his behavior cannot reasonably be attributed to chance. This illustration indicates the degree to which scores on a 6-item procedure may be influenced by random choice behavior. Let us consider another example: the case of a racial attitude test of 24 items, scored in terms of pro-Euro responses with a score range of 0–24 and a neutral midpoint of 12. Reference to the binomial distribution informs us that, in a group of children responding by chance, less than 5% would obtain scores of 17, less than 5% would obtain scores of 7, and even fewer would obtain scores of 18 and up, or 6 and down. Thus, we can establish two ranges of significant scores—17 and up, 7 and down— with reasonable confidence that obtained scores falling in these ranges are not attributable to chance but are very likely indicative of a consistent bias in favor of Euro (17 and up) or Afro (7 down) persons. In this way, the 24-item procedure yields two ranges of scores within which all scores are indicative of significant bias, but with some scores indicative of less bias than others.

Another way to note the advantage of the 24-item as opposed to 6-item procedure is in terms of reliability of test scores. While this relationship can be described mathematically, the following illustration may be generally more instructive. Suppose we are testing two children both of whom have a very strong pro-Euro/anti-Afro bias, so that we would expect them to make a maximum E+/A− score on whatever procedure we employ. One child is given a 24-item test and, as expected, obtains a score of 24. The second child is given a 6-item test and obtains a score of 6. Subsequently, each of the children is retested and in both cases there is a minor disturbance in the room next to the testing room, which distracts the child and results in a change in three of his choices on the test. For the child taking the 24-item test, this would result in a score drop from 24 to 21, which is still indicative of his high E+/A− bias. On the 6-item procedure, the same disturbance would result in the child's score dropping from a top score of 6 to a midpoint score of 3, which is no longer indicative of his strong bias but suggests that he is unbiased. It can thus be seen that the investigator using relatively short procedures to assess racial concepts in young children runs a strong risk that the true individual differences in the trait which he wishes to assess may be masked by errors of measurement.

In view of the foregoing observations, we offer the following guidelines regarding the number of two-choice items used for the assessment of racial concepts in young children. The guidelines are expressed in multiples of 6 since tests of 6, 12, and 24 items have been used in a number of previous studies. It is our recommendation that 6 items be considered the minimum acceptable test length. Although still subject to considerable distortion by chance responding, scores from a 6-item test seem to be adequate for studies in which one wishes to identify molar phenomena by an examination of differences in the mean performance of groups, i.e., does one group of children tend to have higher racial attitude scores than another group?

A 6-item test is considered inadequate when one is interested in relating individual differences in racial concepts to individual differences in other subject characteristics, and a 12-item test is recommended as minimally adequate for this purpose (e.g., correlating individual differences in racial attitude and individual differences in age or intelligence). For situations where an even greater degree of sensitivity to individual differences is needed, a 24-item test is recommended. For example, a 24-item procedure would be needed to study the relationship of individual differences in children's racial attitude scores to individual difference in parental characteristics. A testing procedure of more than 24 items for assessing a single racial concept is not recommended since it is our experience that beyond this number the attention of the young child tends to flag, and additional items may act to reduce the validity of the resulting test scores. It is possible, however, to use research procedures of 36 or even 48 items if the overall procedure is being used to assess more than one concept, and if there is sufficient variety of format among the items representing the different concepts. For example, preschool children have no difficulty maintaining attention and interest on the Preschool Racial Attitude Measure II which contains 24 racial attitude items and 12 interspersed sex-role items.

A different instrument-related problem concerns the nature of the stimulus materials employed in research on racial concepts in preschool children. The nonliterate status of the young child precludes the use of written stimulus materials and, as a result, researchers have employed a variety of visual materials (dolls, puppets, artist's drawings, photographs, etc.) to represent the Euro and Afro persons about whom questions are asked. There are several problems surrounding the choice of stimulus materials for the type of research we are discussing. It might be thought that photographs of actual persons would be the obvious solution, but then the question arises as to which Euro person is to be paired with which Afro person. An attempt to answer this question by saying that we will use persons who are as similar as possible except for race merely compounds the problem, for now we must decide what personal features are to be considered racial—skin color? hair texture? hair style? facial structure? etc. If one wants to assess the child's evaluative response to persons of different races, then the persons photographed should be equally attractive to the child apart from "racial cues"—but what are racial cues and how are we to determine the attractiveness of the persons apart from racial cues?

Inability to achieve a satisfactory answer to these questions has led many investigators away from the use of "real-life" photographs, and toward the use of dolls, puppets, or artist's drawings by which one attempts to represent certain racial characteristics while keeping the figures highly similar in other respects. In these procedures, skin and hair color have been the characteristics most often employed to represent race, with light skin and hair intended to represent Euro-Americans, and dark skin and hair used to represent Afro-Americans. This approach has the merit of being able to specify the stimulus difference which leads to any differential behavior observed. On the other hand, one can ask whether two figures which differ only in skin color are perceived by the child as being of different "races," whatever that means to the young child. A partial answer to this question is provided by the findings of a number of studies which indicate that preschool children will choose a dark-skinned figure when asked to select the "black doll" or the "Negro doll," and will select a light-skinned figure when asked to select the "white doll." In other words, the fact that skin color remains the primary and most compelling basis for racial classification may mitigate the artificiality of the specially prepared stimulus materials.

The problem we are discussing is a reflection of one of the basic issues in social science research: verisimilitude to real life situations with less knowledge of the variables operating vs. greater control and knowledge of relevant variables with some tolerance for artificiality. In the present instance, empirical data could be of assistance in weighing this issue. No study with which we are familiar has employed both photographs of real persons and drawings or dolls in order to judge their comparability as stimulus figures in studies of racial concepts in young children.

Before leaving the question of visual materials, let us offer a criticism—and a plea. Researchers studying racial concepts in young children have been unusually lax in their descriptions of the physical characteristics of the stimuli employed to represent persons of different races. Thus, in one study the two dolls are described, respectively, as "brown and white," in another study as "black and white," in another study as "medium brown and light," and in another study as "black and flesh-colored." Were the dolls in the first study literally white, or were they pinkish-tan colored? Were the dolls in the second study actually black, or were they brown in color? What does "light" mean, and whose flesh is being referred to? This type of descriptive imprecision is unpardonable in good research of any sort, and doubly so in an area of social significance. (Hopefully, the researchers were not as careless elsewhere as they were in the description of their stimulus materials!) We are not arguing for some elaborate calibration of skin color or other stimulus characteristics; such is not yet warranted in this research area. Rather, our plea is for reasonably accurate verbal descriptions of the physical characteristics of the stimuli employed.

Finally, there is the general question of the two-choice-item format of most race and color concept assessment procedures. In most such procedures the child is asked to choose between Euro and Afro figures ("Which is the good man?"), rather than responding directly to a single figure ("Is this a good man?"). The usual two-choice procedures are, in effect, "forced-choice" procedures with several associated advantages and disadvantages. The general advantage in forced-choice procedures lies in the recognition that the significance of human behavior is often most clearly revealed "at the choice point"—that is, when a decision must be made between alternatives. We would not expect to learn a great deal about a child's interests if we ask him, "Would you like to have a new bicycle?" for the answer almost certainly would be "yes!" Neither would we expect to learn much by asking him whether he would like to have a new stereo. But if we ask the child, "Which would you prefer—a new bicycle or a new stereo?" his choice behavior may tell us something about the types of activities in which he is most interested. In the same way, if we ask a child whether he would like this (light-skinned) child as a playmate, and then ask whether he would like this (dark-skinned) child as a playmate, we may get a "yes" to both questions. Only by asking the child to choose between the two figures can we determine whether the child finds both playmates equally attractive, or whether one is substantially more attractive than the other.

The principal disadvantage of forced-choice procedures is that they generate scores which may be misinterpreted by the uncritical observer. Consider as an example a child who has a tendency to evaluate Euro persons relatively more positively than Afro persons. If we administer a 24-item forced-choice racial attitude test—such as PRAM II—the child will tend to choose the Euro figure when a positive adjective is used and the Afro figure when a negative adjective is used. This will result in the child obtaining a PRAM II score which is said to be indicative of a pro-Euro/anti-Afro (E+/A−) bias. This interpretation is correct as long as we recognize that we are speaking of *relative* bias. It does not necessarily indicate that the child has a negative attitude toward Afro persons, in any absolute sense. The child could, for example, feel that Euro persons were "very good" and Afro persons only a "little bit good," and the forced-choice test procedures might yield the same high score as if he felt that Euros were "somewhat good" and Afros were "somewhat bad." Thus, for example, when we find an Afro child who displays an E+/A− bias we must not interpret this as a definite indication that he has a negative attitude toward his own racial group, but rather as an indication that he views Afros less positively than Euros.

Another related problem is involved in the use of forced-choice procedures. Does a child who obtains a very high PRAM II score have a more "intense" E+/A− bias or merely a more "consistent" bias than the child who obtains a moderately high score? That the forced-choice procedure requires the child to make *some* response to each item makes this question difficult to answer. On the other hand, the distinction between consistency and intensity of attitudes may not be as important as one might think. Attitude research with young adults indicates that racial attitude measures which allow the subject to express the intensity of his agreement or disagreement with the statements presented yield essentially the same results as simpler procedures which allow the subject only two response alternatives—agree or disagree. This suggests that the logical distinction between attitude consistency and attitude intensity may not be important psychologically. Perhaps all we mean when we say that a child has a "strong" E+/A− bias is that he has a consistent and broadly generalized bias which is revealed whenever he is required to make an evaluative distinction between Euro and Afro persons.

Some of the problems associated with nonforced-choice, or free-choice, procedures can be illustrated by the findings from a study by Kathryn Williams (Williams, Williams, and Beck, 1973) in which a modified "signal detection" version of the PRAM II procedure was employed. In the standard PRAM II procedure, the child is asked to choose between Euro and Afro figures as the one described in the accompanying story, e.g., "Which is the good man?" or "Which is the mean man?" In Williams's study, she presented each of the PRAM II figures singly and asked, e.g., "Is this a good man?" or "Is this a mean man?" with the child responding "yes" or "no." The reader will note that with this procedure the child is not required to make a racial choice and is free to respond positively, or negatively, to any or all of the figures.

The data for the Euro-American preschoolers in Williams's study are summarized in Table 10-1 which shows the mean number of "yes" responses out of twelve opportunities for each of the following adjective-racial figure combinations: positive words with Euro figures; negative words with Euro figures; positive words with Afro figures; negative words with Afro figures. The most striking result is that all mean scores were on the high side of the chance midpoint of six, indicating a tendency for these preschoolers to answer "yes" rather than "no" regardless of the question asked. A second interesting finding is that the preschoolers were much more likely to answer "yes" when the question involved a positive word than when it involved a negative word, regardless of the race of the depicted figure. Thus, we see that the "free" responses of these preschool children were, in fact, not so free, but were heavily influenced both by a general "yea-saying" set, and by a more specific "positive-adjective yea-saying" set. This tendency has been further documented in an investigation by Marlena

Table 10-1. Mean Number of "Yes" Responses Given by Euro-American Children to Four Combinations of Adjective Type and Race of Figure   (Williams, Williams, and Beck, 1973)

| | Adjective Type | |
Race of Figure	Positive	Negative
Euro-American	11.2	8.1
Afro-American	10.7	8.5

Cannon and Vickie Cheek. In this study, 54 preschool children, aged 4-5 to 6-4, were asked twelve yes-or-no-type questions about pictures taken from magazines and picture books. For four of the items, the answer was obviously "yes," and for four it was obviously "no." The remaining four items were ambiguous, in that there was no objective basis on which the child could answer "yes" or "no." On these latter items, where the children should have responded on a chance or 50–50 basis, they in fact gave 75% "yes" answers and only 25% "no" answers. This tendency of preschoolers, when in doubt, to say "yes" may have contributed to the high levels of racial acceptance seen in the studies, reviewed in chapter 6, in which children were asked, "Would you like to play with this child?" On the other hand, the evidence of differential acceptance of Euro and Afro playmates obviously cannot be attributed to a general "yea-saying" response set.

The findings of the Kathryn Williams and Cannon and Cheek studies demonstrate a major problem in using nonchoice test procedures with young children, particularly when the research design does not permit an assessment of the magnitude of the response sets. The "yea-saying" response set is, in effect, a pitfall for the unwary investigator who asks a yes-or-no question of young children, and proceeds to draw conclusions based on the fact that most of them say yes.

Before leaving Kathryn Williams's study let us ask whether the "yea-saying" response sets completely dominated the behavior of the children in the free-choice situation. The answer is "no"; a careful examination of Table 10-1 reveals that the pattern of means was what would be expected from studies employing the standard PRAM II procedure: the children's responses indicate that positive adjectives were more often associated with Euro figures than with Afro figures; and negative adjectives were more often associated with Afro figures than Euro figures. On the other hand, it can be observed that these effects, while statistically significant, were not large in absolute terms and do not appear as dramatic as the usual findings from the forced-choice PRAM II procedure where, for example, positive adjectives are associated with Euro figures about 75% of the time and with Afro figures only about 25% of the time. This illustrates the dilemma very nicely—shall we use a free-choice procedure in which response sets may mask the phenomena in which we are interested? Or shall we use a forced-choice procedure which may appear to exaggerate the magnitude of the phenomena? On balance, we come out favoring the latter. While forced-choice procedures provide only relative measures and may, on occasion, appear to amplify the magnitude of the phenomena being studied, they are generally recommended because of the psychological significance of choice behavior and because of the strong possibility that data obtained by free-choice procedures will be distorted by the response sets noted above.

In chapter 5, we noted a different type of forced-choice racial attitude measure, developed by Thomas Parish (Parish, 1972; Parish and Fleetwood, 1975), which may prove useful in some research applications. In this procedure, the child is presented with a drawing of a single Afro person and is asked to choose between a positive and a negative evaluative adjective, e.g., "Is this a good boy or a bad boy?" This procedure does not require the child to make a racial choice, and thus permits an assessment of attitude toward Afro persons which is operationally independent of attitude toward Euro persons. To date, this method has been employed only in the assessment of the attitudes of Euro children toward Afro persons and needs to be extended to the assessment of the attitudes of Euro and Afro children toward persons of both races.

Research Design

A basic problem in past research studies of children's racial concepts has been inadequate attention to subject selection procedures. Too many studies have been conducted on a "target of opportunity" basis, in which the children studied are those which happen to be most accessible to the investigator. While the authors are all too familiar with the problems associated with obtaining access to young research subjects, we feel that investigators could and should exert more effort toward obtaining the most appropriate subjects for whatever research study is being planned. We must be careful not to create a research analog of the story about the drunk who had lost his cuff link in a bar, but explained that he was searching for it under a street light "because the light is better out here." *Who* serves as our research subjects is probably as important as *how* we go about measuring what we are interested in.

Researchers need to give more systematic attention to relevant subject characteristics such as age, sex, intelligence, family composition, social class, and so forth. These variables are known to be associated with a wide variety of children's behaviors and it is certainly unwise to attempt to develop an understanding of racial concepts in young children without proper reference to such variables. For example, Porter's (1971) research suggests that children's racial attitudes are significantly related to their social class backgrounds. Even when it appears that the racial concept under study is not related to one of these basic subject variables, it is best to continue to take it into account in the design of research. For example, the data to date suggest that the racial attitudes of young children have little correlation with their IQs. Does this mean we would be safe in ignoring IQ in the future studies of racial attitudes? No, because we may someday discover that bright children and dull children develop similar racial attitudes for quite different reasons.

We offer two related recommendations concerning this matter. First, when composing comparative research groups, we should make every reasonable effort to match the groups on basic subject characteristics. Admittedly, it is easier to do this in some research situations than in others. In experimental investigations (e.g., attitude modification studies), it is relatively easy to compose highly similar "experimental" and "control" groups by assigning the available subjects to the two groups on either a random or a representative sample basis. The principal problems arise when we are conducting correlational research, e.g., when we are making a comparative study of some racial concept in Euro and Afro children. In this case such variables as age and sex-ratio are rather easily equated. On the other hand, variables such as IQ and socioeconomic status are much more difficult to equate across racial groups. This leads to our second recommendation which concerns the practical situation where the researcher has found it impossible to equate his groups on some basic subject variable, such as IQ. Even though he cannot match his groups on IQ the researcher can still correlate IQ with his racial concept measures *within* each of his research groups. One is usually but not always safe in inferring that when racial concept scores do not correlate with IQ scores within each of two research groups, the racial concept differences *between* the two research groups are probably not attributable to the IQ difference between the groups. In other words, whenever the groups in a correlational study cannot be equated on a given basic subject variable, the variable should still be measured so that within-group comparisons can be made between it and the racial concept scores being studied.

A different problem in research design has to do with order (and sequence) effects in studies in which more than one racial concept is being assessed in the same subjects. We are aware of the general effects of set upon behavior—that the orientation with which we approach a task often influences the way we perform. Unfortunately, this principle has often been ignored in studies assessing more than one racial concept. Thus, we find studies in which a child's racial similarity ("look like") responses have been assessed after he has responded to items dealing with racial preference or racial attitude. Before a researcher can make any confident conclusions regarding his racial similarity findings, he must demonstrate that these results are independent of the order in which the concepts were assessed.

Fortunately, there are basic research designs that enable one to study order effects and to determine the degree to which they are operating to influence the child's behavior in a multiconcept testing situation. The basic idea in such procedures is that of "counterbalancing." In the simplest case where only two racial concepts are being assessed, counterbalancing involves testing a random half of the children on concept A followed by concept B, and the other half on concept B followed by concept A. Statistical procedures can then be employed to determine whether the order of administration affects the scores which the children make on the two concepts. A proper treatment of order effects is essential if we are to accomplish the careful study of the interrelationship of the various racial concepts with which we have been concerned. If one wishes to study the relationship between racial attitude and racial self-classification, for example, one must measure both concepts in the same child; when this is done, order effects must be properly assessed if the research is to be of maximum value.

We have the impression that sometimes researchers do not study order effects because they are afraid they will find them—and that this will complicate the interpretation of their findings. Our response is that research designs should be selected to accurately reveal the phenomena under study, and not to make life easy for the investigators. If order effects are present, we should find this out and deal with them. Second, order effects are not always found. This was demonstrated in a study by Donna Boswell who administered both PRAM II and CMT II to a group of 45 Euro-American preschoolers. Boswell's study employed a counterbalanced design in which half the children took PRAM first and CMT second, while the other half took them in reverse order. The findings of the study were quite clear in indicating no evidence of order effects. For example, the children obtained highly similar mean scores on the racial attitude measure whether or not it was preceded by the color meaning assessment procedure. With replication, Boswell's findings will indicate that we need not be concerned about order effects in future studies in which PRAM II and CMT II are administered to the same children.

Another general recommendation for improved research is to make greater use of multivariable research designs in conceptualizing the studies. Imagine that we are planning to conduct a study to determine the effectiveness of a special "race-related" curriculum in reducing E+/A− bias in a group of 100 Euro kindergarten children. We recognize the need for a control group of children, who also receive a special curriculum which is nonrace-related. We also think that the race of the teacher might be important, and we will study this also. Conceptually, we are considering a two-dimensional design where one dimension is the type of curriculum, and the second is the race of the teachers. We can represent this design pictorially as follows:

		Euro	Afro
Curriculum	Race-related	N = 25	N = 25
	Nonrace-related	N = 25	N = 25

Race of Teacher

The figure helps us see that we must think in terms of four basic research groups of 25 each, to which we would ideally assign our subjects at random. If random assignment is prevented by practical considerations, we may be able to employ four intact kindergarten classes which are reasonably equivalent on relevant subject variables.

Should we decide that we would like to extend our study to include 100 Afro kindergarten children as well, our design will have still another dimension. We can represent this three-dimensional design as follows:

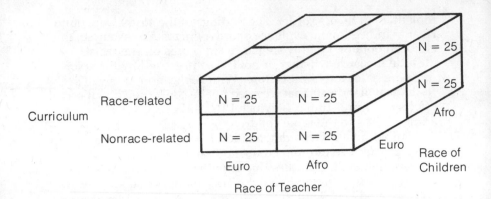

Curriculum

Race-related — N = 25 | N = 25 | N = 25 | N = 25 (Afro)

Nonrace-related — N = 25 | N = 25 | (Euro)

Euro   Afro

Race of Teacher

Race of Children

The figure indicates that our study now requires four groups of Afro children, in addition to four groups of Euro children. For purposes of conceptualization, we may want to describe the design to ourselves in other terms. We can say, for example, that we are studying our special curriculum as a joint function of race of teacher and race of child. Or, we can say that we are studying the effect of race of teacher as a joint function of special curriculum and race of child. The value of casting our research plans in terms of such multiple-variable designs is not limited solely to advantages in conceptualization. There are also important statistical advantages.

In the foregoing examples, we have been describing what is called a "post-only" design. By this, we mean that the children's racial attitudes were assessed only once, at the end of the study. This design can be compared with a "pre-post" design in which the children's attitudes would be assessed before and after their exposure to the special curriculum. What are the relative advantages of these two types of designs?

The principal advantage of the pre-post design is that it creates what is known as a "within-subjects" design where, in effect, each subject serves as his own control. The subjects are assessed before the curriculum and again afterwards, and we compare their scores to see what change has occurred. The within-subjects feature of this design greatly increases its statistical precision and makes it possible to demonstrate significant effects with relatively small numbers of subjects. On the other hand, the principal disadvantage of the pre-post design is the possibility that the administration of the "pre" measure may itself have some effect on the child, either by establishing a set which might influence his response to the curriculum procedure, or by influencing his response to the second ("post") administration of the assessment procedure. In the latter case, if the child receives the identical procedure at pre and post points, he may feel that he is expected to make the same responses the second time as the first, and this could serve to obscure the changes in which the researcher is interested. This problem is offset in large part whenever different but equivalent forms of the procedure are given at the two assessment points. For example, the 24-item PRAM II procedure can be divided into two equivalent 12-item short forms and used in this way.

The principal advantage of the post-only design is that it avoids any possible effects of repeated testing. The principal disadvantage is its extreme dependence on proper sampling procedures. When one can assign subjects to groups on a genuinely random basis, there are few problems. On the other hand, when true random sampling is not possible, the researcher becomes highly vulnerable to sampling errors. Consider the situation where practical considerations dictate that one intact kindergarten class is to receive a race-related curriculum and a second intact class is to receive a control curriculum. In this case, any difference in the groups on a post-only evaluation can be as easily attributed to preexisting differences in the two samples as to the differential effects of the two curricula.

What general guidelines can be offered for choosing between pre-post and post-only designs? The post-only design is recommended whenever the researcher has access to a large number of subjects who can be assigned to treatment groups on a truly random basis. For practical purposes, we can define a "large" number of subjects as the number sufficient to produce 25 subjects or more in each subgroup (or "cell") of the research design. The pre-post design is recommended whenever the number of subjects is small and/or the subjects cannot be assigned to the treatment groups at random.

There are other, more complex, research designs which are applicable to investigations of the development and modification of race and color concepts in young children. The interested reader is referred to Campbell and Stanley's (1966) excellent review which describes strategies such as "cross-lagged panel correlation," a technique which, contrary to the old dictum, permits the inference of causal relations from correlational data.

Data Analyses

The primitive assessment techniques which have often been used in research on racial concepts in young children have had their counterpart in the use of unsophisticated data analysis procedures. The parallel is not accidental. If a researcher's assessment procedures are crude and categorical, then about all he can do is to count the number of children falling into his categories and use relatively insensitive statistical procedures such as chi-square and proportion tests. If, on the other hand, he uses procedures that assess variables and makes use of multivariable designs whenever appropriate, then much more powerful data analysis procedures can be employed.

The family of analysis procedures known collectively as correlational methods has had, as yet, little impact in this area, even though most of these methods have been available for many years. The technique of partial correlation, for example, could be employed to study the relationship of two variables (say racial attitudes and black-white color attitudes) with a third variable (say racial self-classification) held constant. Such studies could do much toward clarifying the complex relationships among the several racial concepts we have studied. Another powerful correlational tool is the technique— or group of techniques—known as factor analysis. This procedure is particularly useful when one has assessed a variety of behavioral variables in the same subjects and wishes to establish the smallest number of basic "factors" that underlie the measures obtained. Assume, for example, that we have measured the performance of 100 children on a group of ten operationally distinctive tasks, all of which seem to have something to do with intellectual functioning. Does this mean we are assessing ten distinctive types of intellectual per-formance? Probably not; some of the tasks may be assessing essentially the same thing. Factor analysis will help us decide the smallest number of "factors" or types of intelligence we need to postulate in order to account for the data in hand. Similarly, factor analysis could be used to help answer some of the questions with which we wrestled in earlier chapters. For example, if one developed an adequate measure of each of the racial and color concepts we have discussed, and then administered these measures to a group of children, one could intercorrelate all of the scores and perform a factor analysis to determine if there is a primary factor which underlies all of them, whether there are secondary factors shared by certain subgroups of measures, and so forth. The use of such correlational methods could contribute greatly to the develop-ment of conceptual clarity in this area of study.

The formulation of research in terms of the multidimensional designs described earlier permits one to employ the powerful data analysis tool known as analysis of variance. This technique permits the concurrent assessment of the effects of each of several variables on the behavior of interest and, even more importantly, permits an assessment of any "interaction" effects among the variables. We can explain this by returning to the illustration of the two-dimensional research design (p. 297). In the example, we talked about a hypothetical study of the effects on racial attitude scores of two factors: type of curriculum (race-related vs. nonrace-related); and race of teacher (Euro-American vs. Afro-American). An analysis of variance of the racial attitude scores from such a design would permit the separate assessment of the "main effects" of each variable considered separately, e.g., the mean racial attitude scores for all subjects who had the race-related curriculum might be found to be significantly lower than the mean score of subjects who had the nonrace-related curriculum. Similarly, we might find a main effect of race of teacher with the mean score of children with Afro teachers being significantly lower than the mean score of children taught by Euro teachers. Thus far, our analysis of variance has served as nothing more than a somewhat more precise version of the familiar t test for assessing the significance of differences in means. The great value of analysis of variance becomes apparent whenever the data suggest an interaction between the variables under study. The hypothetical data in the following diagram illustrate an interaction effect, as well as the two main effects we have described. The evidence of an interaction here is seen in the fact that the two lines are not parallel; that, while both groups of children who had the race-related curriculum scored below the two groups who had the nonrace-related curriculum (the main effect), this effect seems more pronounced when the teacher was Afro than when the teacher was Euro. Analysis of variance enables us to determine whether this observed interaction is statistically significant, that is, unlikely to be due to chance factors.

The value of analysis of variance is even greater when we are dealing with three-dimensional designs as in the figure on page 298. For example, we might find that the interaction between race of teacher and curriculum, illustrated above, seems to occur among Euro children but not among Afro children. In this case, we will want to assess the significance of this "triple" interaction among the three variables of race of subject, race of teacher, and curriculum. If the triple interaction is significant, it means that we cannot talk about the effect of the race-related curriculum upon racial attitude scores without taking into account both the race of the person who teaches it and the race of the child who participates in it. If all this seems complicated, one should not blame the analysis of variance procedure. To the contrary, this procedure assists us in clarifying the natural complexity of the relationships among the variables which affect our subject matter.

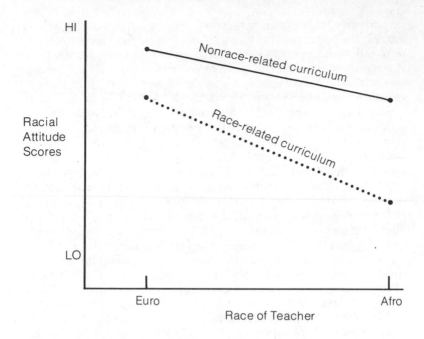

HI

Racial
Attitude
Scores

LO

Nonrace-related curriculum

Race-related curriculum

Euro   Afro

Race of Teacher

SUBSTANTIVE QUESTIONS FOR FUTURE RESEARCH

Our review of the research findings on race and color concepts in young children and our consideration of theoretical alternatives to explain these findings have pointed up a large number of unanswered questions to which future researchers can address themselves. It is our hope that our efforts will result in a more systematic approach to research in this area. We feel that the time is now past for "purely empirical" studies of race and color concepts; it is no longer productive for a researcher to set up some makeshift assessment procedure, administer it to some available children, and then speculate widely (wildly?) about the implications of his "findings." What is needed now is theory-guided, programmatic research which will systematically explore the major areas in which questions remain unanswered. We will first discuss questions dealing with the origin and development of race and color concepts under natural conditions, then questions relating to the modification of race and color concepts by means of specially designed programs.

A major question is, how many different concepts must we study if we are to gain a reasonably complete understanding of the way young children respond to race and color? The answer is closely tied to certain methodological considerations we have already considered. We must first develop reasonably reliable measures of the various operationally distinct concepts such as racial attitude, color attitude, racial preference, racial acceptance, racial similarity, etc. Once these measures are available, we need to conduct studies of young children in which all of the measures are given to each child, with proper attention being paid to order and sequence effects. With such data in hand, one can proceed to examine the interrelationships among the various measures to determine the degree to which they are reflecting the same or different concepts in various subpopulations. For example, let us assume we are employing six operationally distinct measures and have administered all six to a large number of preschool children. We would then intercorrelate the scores for each measure with the scores for every other measure and examine the patterns of intercorrelations. On the one hand, we might find that all of the measures intercorrelate as high as their respective reliabilities permit; in this case, all of our scores would seem to be reflecting a single concept, or measuring the same thing. At the other extreme, we might find no correlation among any of the measures which would indicate that we are assessing six distinctly different concepts. A third and more likely possibility is that we would find high correlations for certain pairs of measures, and low correlations for other pairs of measures, pointing to the existence of less than six—but more than one—distinctive concepts. If the pattern of intercorrelations is complex, we might wish to employ factor analysis to determine how many basic "factors" are being assessed by our six operationally distinct measures. If this were done and factors were found which do not coincide with one or more of our original measures, we might need to develop revised, "factorially pure" measures aimed directly at the assessment of the major factors which have been identified.

While the final answer about the number and nature of race/color concepts among young children must await research of the type just described, we can offer two preliminary observations based on our review of the existing data on concept interrelationships from chapter 8. First, we note that racial attitudes and white-black color attitudes, while related, appear to be sufficiently independent to warrant their consideration as separate behavioral tendencies. Second, we note that, within the general domain of racial concept/attitudes, the measures appeared to fall into two general classes: a group of measures which seemed to be primarily affective in nature and which involved a tendency to feel more positively about light-skinned persons than dark-skinned persons; and a second group which appeared to be primarily cognitive in nature and involved the child's knowledge of racial classification. In any event, we will not approach a complete understanding of the development of race and color concepts in young children until we have determined how many concepts there are and how they can best be assessed.

Studies at the Preschool Level

Measurement Studies / A continuing line of research at the kindergarten level involves the periodic monitoring of race and color concepts for evidence of systematic changes related to general cultural or subcultural influences. Of particular interest here is the question of the impact of the Black Identity movement upon the Afro-American child. For example, we saw in chapter 4 that there was some slight evidence of a decline in pro-Euro/anti-Afro bias among Afro preschoolers tested in 1971–72 compared with those tested a few years earlier. Has this apparent trend continued? Or will the Black Identity movement continue to have its main impact on children in the later school years? These questions are worthy of careful study.

Another line for future research involves the study of the affective meanings of white and black among preschool children in other cultures. We saw in chapter 3 that French and Italian children display a pro-white, anti-black bias similar to that found among Euro- and Afro-American children. This line of research needs to be extended to non-Western preschoolers, for example, from Africa or India. Given the opportunity, there is no great difficulty in conducting such studies since it is relatively easy to adapt the basic assessment procedure (CMT II) to other languages and cultures. Closer to home, it would also be interesting to assess the affective meanings of black and white among other American groups such as Indian-Americans, Mexican-Americans, and Oriental-Americans.

Generality of Light-Dark Bias / We speculated earlier that many preschool children may have a pro-light/anti-dark bias which is related to their tendency to evaluate white animals more positively than black animals and light-skinned persons more positively than dark-skinned persons. The further exploration of this hypothesis constitutes an important line of future research, with several different approaches being evident. One approach would explore the generality of the tendency to view light-colored things more positively than dark-colored things. Illustrative here is an unpublished study of Euro-American preschoolers conducted by Frank Kuhn in 1975. Using a PRAM-like picture-story procedure, Kuhn demonstrated a pro-light/anti-dark bias not only for pictures of persons and animals, but also for inanimate objects, geometric figures, and nonsense figures. In addition, Kuhn demonstrated that the light-dark bias was not confined to stimulus figures differing in "race-related" colors (pink *vs*. brown, white *vs*. black, etc.) but was also evident in the children's responses to light and dark green, blue, red, orange, etc. A related question concerns the relative nature of the light-as-good, dark-as-bad judgment. We have Baugher's findings (see chapter 4) indicating that a light-brown human figure is judged positively when paired with a dark-brown figure and negatively when paired with a pinkish-tan figure. Would this evidence of a light-dark evaluation gradient find further support in a study involving a large number of skin tones representing many different positions along such a gradient?

A serendipitous finding by Phyllis Katz (1973) suggests a different approach to this same question. In a discrimination learning study presented as a "trip to the moon" game, Euro and Afro preschool children were required to learn which of two schematic faces ("moon people") was the correct one ("the one we should take back"). The two faces were light and dark pink for some subjects, light and dark brown for others, and light and dark green for others. For each child, the experimenter decided, arbitrarily, whether the lighter face or darker face was to be reinforced as the correct one. In analyzing the learning data, Katz found that children for whom the lighter figure was correct learned the discrimination more easily, i.e., it was more difficult for the children to learn that the darker face was the correct one. Similar findings were obtained in an unpublished study by Susan Selvey and Charles Richman who studied the effect of white and black stimuli on discrimination learning in two groups of four-year-old children. Using white and black geometric forms, it was found that the 16 children for whom the white form was correct took an average of 16.1 trials to learn the discrimination, while the 16 children for whom black was correct took an average of 39.2 trials. When the situation was reversed so that each group was now rewarded for responding to the other cue, it was found that the group trained on black and switched to white shifted more rapidly (mean trials = 17.7) than the group trained on white and shifted to black (mean trials = 21.2). Thus, in both the original learning and the shift, it appeared that the white cue facilitated learning and/or the black cue inhibited learning. The findings by Selvey and Richman, and those of Katz, suggest that the discrimination learning paradigm may provide another useful approach to the study of light-dark bias in young children.

Additional studies with nonhuman primates may be instructive in developing an understanding of light-dark bias in young children. Research patterned after that of Parker (1966) with squirrel monkeys and Zimmermann (1973) with rhesus monkeys would be of value, particularly in attempting to assess the role of biological factors in the development of light-dark bias.

Race of Examiner Effects / The puzzling question of race of examiner effects in the assessment of racial and color concepts deserves further systematic attention. The reader who has followed our earlier reviews of the research literature is well aware of the inconsistent evidence regarding such effects. When these effects occur, they seem to make sense, but they are exceedingly elusive. We saw in chapter 4 that the preschool children in the PRAM II standardization study expressed significantly less E+/A− bias in the presence of an Afro-American examiner, but that Deborah Best was unable to replicate this finding with other preschoolers, and that school-age children showed some evidence of the effect but it was significant only among third graders. To compound the confusion, there has been no evidence of race of examiner effects for CMT II, the companion procedure of PRAM II, or for the MPI. How can results such as these be explained?

We have no firm hypotheses to offer but two general observations may be of assistance in solving the race of examiner puzzle. First, while some measures of race and color concepts may be sensitive, at times, to race of examiner effects, others may not be. For example, measures of racial attitude may be more susceptible to such influence than are measures of racial preference or color attitude. Second, we can note that there has been no really careful research on the effects of the examiner's race, per se. No study with which we are familiar has carefully matched examiners on all nonracial variables in order to isolate the effect of race. Instead, researchers have allowed the race variable to be confounded with a variety of other examiner characteristics (e.g., ease in relating to young children) which may affect the child's response on the test procedures. That a personally attractive and skillful Afro examiner obtains different results from an unattractive and unskillful Euro examiner does not tell us much about race of examiner effects.

In addition to the possibility of isolating the race of examiner variable by matching, another approach may prove useful. Our pilot studies indicate that the PRAM II racial attitude test can be administered by a semi-automated "teaching machine" procedure with no examiner being personally present. This, in turn, should make it possible to conduct experimental studies of the influence of various examiner characteristics, including racial ones, by gradually reintroducing the examiner into the testing situation.

Finally, let us note that misery loves company and that ours is not the only area in which confusing race of examiner effects are found. As Sattler's (1970) review demonstrates, race of examiner effects are generally unreliable phenomena, even in the area of intelligence testing where many people believe that reliable effects have been demonstrated. While careful systematic research will be required to answer the race of examiner question, we can conclude our comments by noting that this is not a question of major consequence. The research evidence indicates that race of examiner effects—when they occur—do not have a major influence on the racial responses of young children.

Correlational Studies / Studies to date have demonstrated reliable individual differences among kindergarten-age children in racial/color concepts; for example, some Euro children consistently display a high degree of pro-Euro/anti-Afro bias, others show a moderate degree, and others appear to be unbiased. Additional research is needed to clarify the meaning of these individual differences. One important line of investigation would involve the study of other behaviors of the child in relationship to the racial/color concepts which he displays. Another line of study would involve the assessment of various parental and peer characteristics which might be related to the racial/color concepts displayed by the child. While the findings from such correlational studies would not be conclusive regarding cause and effect relationships, they could be helpful in the refinement of theoretical alternatives and in the generation of further experimental research. We have already seen how this can happen in our theoretical discussion where the absence of an appreciable correlation between racial attitude scores and IQ served to cast doubt upon the adequacy of a general normative theory of racial attitude development.

The list of child characteristics or behaviors which might be examined in relationship to racial/color concepts is extensive and we will here note only two general classes, with illustrations of each. The first class consists of nontest behaviors that appear to have some relevance to race or color. For example, one could ask whether interracial behaviors in kindergarten or primary-grade classes are related to degree of racial bias as assessed by test procedure. Do Euro-American children with a high degree of pro-Euro/anti-Afro bias interact less, or differently, with Afro children than do other less biased Euro children? With racial attitudes being measured by the PRAM II procedure, one could assess the interracial behaviors by a variety of techniques ranging from direct observation during free-play periods to sociometric procedure to teacher's ratings. The limited research of this type conducted to date (e.g., Mabe, 1974) suggests that there are some interesting relationships to be explored. Another line of investigation involving the relation of racial/color test scores to nontest behaviors is the further study of the relationship of individual differences in white-black color attitudes to individual differences in aversion to darkness. The findings from Donna Boswell's (1974) study, described in chapter 3, suggest that there is a significant link here which bears further exploration.

Another class of child behaviors which might be examined are those which have no obvious relationship to race or color but are of the type which may reflect personality and/or cognitive characteristics of the children. In the personality area, for example, one could attempt to determine whether individual differences in aggressiveness are related to racial attitude test scores, or whether individual differences in anxiety are related to black-white color meaning scores. In a different area, one could study whether individual differences in cognitive style (e.g., categorical thinking) are related to the tendency of children to make extreme scores on the racial/color concept measures.

The second major area in which correlational studies are needed involves the relationship between the racial/color concepts of children and parental characteristics such as those mentioned in our discussion of theory in chapter 10. There are certain obvious relationships to be studied such as the further investigation of Donna Boswell's (1974) finding of a significant relationship between the racial attitudes of preschool children and their mothers. Beyond this, there are a large number of personality and/or cognitive variables which might be assessed in the parents and related to the racial/color concepts displayed by the child, for example, the degree of importance which parents attach to racial classification, or the effect of authoritarian child-rearing practices. Certain parental characteristics may be related to socioeconomic status which should be given more careful attention in future research studies. This general line of research might best be pursued by first conducting broad "dragnet" studies to identify the general type of related parental variables, followed by a more detailed exploration of the relationships discovered.

Studies of Very Young Children

Little is known concerning the responses of children below age three to racial figures or to the colors black and white. The reason is obvious; the techniques that have been developed for assessing racial/color concepts in older preschool children require an attention span and verbal comprehension not usually found in these younger children. Thus, the first order of business here is the development of research techniques which can be employed with children in the first three years of life.

The limited amount of work we have done with children of about 24 months of age suggests that careful observation in a free-play situation may provide some useful data. We described in chapter 3 some of our findings regarding the responses of these two-year-olds in a situation where they were permitted to play freely with toys, some of which were white in color and some of which were black. Additional studies of this sort need to be conducted with two-year-olds using, for example, human-like dolls which differ in skin color. We have found, however, that it is difficult to work with two-year-olds in a "laboratory" setting with no familiar adults present. It would be interesting to conduct the toy play studies in the familiar surroundings of the child's own home with the parents nearby but interacting only minimally.

If the search for the earliest evidence of differential responses to white and black, or to light- and dark-skinned persons, requires one to go back beyond the limits of the free-play method and into the early months of life, additional techniques will be required. One approach would involve the use of classical conditioning procedures to determine, for example, whether aversive conditioning develops more rapidly to a black conditioned stimulus than to a white conditioned stimulus. Such a finding might be considered consistent with the idea that the color black already has aversive qualities to the infant. Another promising approach is the application of discrimination learning procedures which have been successfully employed with children as young as 6 months of age (see review by Reese and Lipsitt, 1970, 172 f.). Do infants, as was true of Selvey and Richman's four-year-olds (see p. 305) learn a discrimination more rapidly when the reinforced cue is white rather than black? Do human infants, like Zimmermann's (1973) infant monkeys, find it easier to shift from a black to a white stimulus than to shift from white to black?

One might also attempt to employ some of the sophisticated visual attention techniques which have been developed for use with infants in other research areas (see Bond, 1972; Thomas, 1973). For example, Hershenson (1964) has shown that newborn infants give less attention to a dim light than to lights of medium or bright intensity, while Spears (1964) has demonstrated that four-month-old infants pay greater attention to the colors red and blue than to the color gray. Would infants show a differential distribution of attention to black and white stimuli when they are presented simultaneously? Such a finding would be interesting, but not easily interpreted, since attention cannot necessarily be equated with preference. If, for example, the infant attends more to the color black, is this because he finds black pleasing, or are we observing a vigilance response toward an aversive stimulus? These are but a few general suggestions for research at the infant level. Should it become necessary to conduct studies at this level, investigators who are experienced in infant research can undoubtedly devise adequate techniques for the study of such questions.

Studies of School-Age Children

As we have seen, studies of race and color concepts in young children have tended to focus on children in the three- to six-year-old age range. In addition to the need for studies of children below this age range, there is a similar need for additional studies of older children, that is, children in the early grades of school. Research methods are less troublesome here since many of the techniques which have been developed for use with preschool children (e.g., PRAM II and the MPI) are also useful with school children through the third or fourth grades. There are available, in addition, other research methods which have been designed expressly for children of this age level, e.g., Koslin's (1969) "Pick a Class" technique.

The increase in the number of interracial public elementary schools creates a pressing need for increased understanding of the racial concepts and attitudes among children in the early school years. The limited previous research on this topic has raised a number of questions for further study. Is it generally true that the pro-Euro/anti-Afro bias of Euro-American children increases from preschool to second grade level and then declines? Is it true that many Afro-American children maintain a pro-Euro racial attitude even after their racial preference has shifted to pro-Afro? If so, what is the implication of this for self-concept development in Afro children during the early school years? In what way is racial bias affected by the racial composition of the classroom or the race of the teacher? To what degree are the tested individual differences in racial bias related to various indices of interracial behavior in the school setting? Can effective classroom procedures be developed for the modification of racial bias among early school-age children? These and many other fascinating questions can now be studied wherever investigators are able to gain access to the necessary subjects. Unfortunately, the children in many school systems are not available to interested researchers since such research is still considered "controversial" and some school administrators are reluctant to give permission for such studies. The researcher who finds himself thus frustrated might remind himself that school-age children are not the exclusive property of the school system and that access to school-age children may be obtained by direct contact with their parents. Although this approach is much more difficult in a practical sense, we have found it necessary to employ it in some of our studies of school-age children.

There is also a need for a regular monitoring of attitudes among teenagers and young adults to ascertain whether systematic changes in race and color concepts continue to take place. We reviewed earlier the evidence which suggested that it is during the early teen years when the young Afro-American first demonstrates a positive evaluation of his own racial group relative to Euro-Americans. Will this finding be replicated in future studies, and will the continuing influence of the Black Identity movement cause this effect to appear among younger children? Similar questions can be posed concerning the affective meanings of white and black. For example, the evidence to date indicates that there has been no change in Euro-Americans' responses to white and black during the evolution of the Black Identity movement. Will the influence of this movement continue to be subcultural in nature, or will it eventually have an impact on color meanings among Euro-Americans?

We need additional evidence regarding the cross-cultural meanings of white and black among young adults. Having seen that young adults in the Far East tend to evaluate white more positively than black (see chapter 2), it would be interesting to extend this work to Africa. Anthropological descriptions are replete with illustrations of the use of white to symbolize goodness among many African groups. Can this be documented in a more systematic fashion via empirical techniques similar to those we have described?

As a final point regarding the natural development of race and color concepts, we would like to emphasize the need for longitudinal investigations in which the same children are studied beginning in the preschool years and continuing through the early school years on to young adulthood. Longitudinal research can be contrasted with the more familiar cross-sectional research in which developmental questions are investigated by the study of groups of children of different ages tested at the same time. While cross-sectional methods are useful because of their efficiency in giving quick estimates regarding developmental questions, they have severe limitations whenever there is reason to believe that significant and relatively rapid changes are occurring in the phenomena under investigation. This may well be the case in the area which we are discussing. Such factors as the recent increase in racial desegregation and the development of the Black Identity movement make us hesitant to assume that six years from now today's four-year-old children will act and feel like today's ten-year-old children, which is, of course, the basic assumption of the cross-sectional method.

Modification Studies

The phrase "modification of racial bias" can be understood in two different ways. It can refer to efforts to prevent the natural development of racial bias by interfering with its determinants, and there are many testable hypotheses of this sort which can be derived from the theory outlined in chapter 10. The other meaning of the phrase refers to efforts to use special retraining procedures to change racial bias which has already developed. It is this second type of modification which we wish to discuss here.

There are many unanswered questions about the conditions necessary for the modification of racial/color concepts in young children, and about the persistence and consequences of such changes. The behavior modification studies we have reviewed (see chapter 5) have been valuable in demonstrating that racial/color concepts are rather easily changed in one-to-one laboratory situations where the experimenter has full control of the necessary reinforcement contingencies. To put it succinctly, children who have a pro-Euro/anti-Afro bias or pro-white/anti-black bias will rather quickly give up these biases (or even reverse them) whenever adult approval is contingent on such change. While this general fact is well established, there remains a need for additional parametric studies concerning the relative efficacy of various types of reinforcers and reinforcement schedules. For example, would the use of partial reinforcement in this situation lead to more persistent behavioral change, as it often does in other learning situations?

Another important line of behavior modification research concerns the need for the presence of an adult to personally conduct the procedure and deliver the reinforcements. Can race and color concepts be effectively modified by an audiovisual "teaching machine" procedure in which the child's responses are followed by machine-delivered reinforcements such as: the giving or withholding of token rewards; the playing of tape recorded comments ("right" or "wrong"); or, simply, the advance (or lack of advance) of the machine to the next audiovisual presentation. Our pilot studies dealing with the automated presentation of the PRAM II picture-story procedure, and the successful modification study conducted by

Suellen Smith (see chapter 5), have made us optimistic regarding the development of an effective semiautomated behavior modification system. Such a procedure would have a great practical advantage over the one-to-one interpersonal procedure in that the former would require very little "teaching time," a commodity which is always in short supply.

The second major approach to the modification of race and color concepts is by means of special classroom procedures which are incorporated into kindergarten or school curricula. As we saw in our earlier research review in chapter 5, there remain many unanswered questions regarding effective techniques to employ for this purpose, since a number of apparently promising procedures have not had the desired effects. On the other hand, we do know that at least one curriculum procedure has worked. We now face the difficult task of isolating the crucial variables from the successful curriculum packages and finding even more effective ways to manipulate these variables. In the modification of racial attitudes, for example, the exposure of preschoolers to stories in which dark-skinned persons are described in positive terms—the "black heroes" approach—has been found to have little measurable effect on the children's tendency to evaluate dark-skinned persons less positively than light-skinned persons. An hypothesis for further study is that the black heroes curricula have not succeeded because they do nothing to reduce the children's unrealistically high positive attitude toward light-skinned persons. In other words, the curricula may indeed promote a somewhat more positive view of Afro persons, but this is still not sufficient to compete with the much stronger tendency toward the positive evaluation of Euro persons that already exists. This line of reasoning suggests that the successful elimination of racial bias may require the partial extinction of pro-Euro attitudes as well as the reinforcement of pro-Afro attitudes. In effect, the children may need to be exposed to stories involving "white scoundrels" as well as "black heroes." An extension of this would be a curriculum in which an attempt would be made to teach the children that race is irrelevant to the evaluation of persons—sometimes Afro persons are good, and sometimes they are bad; sometimes Euro persons are good, and sometimes they are bad. Through such an extinction procedure the children might come to feel that race provides no reliable indication of a person's worth—which might be the most valuable lesson that could be learned.

The reader who is particularly interested in future curriculum research will want to review some of the other observations which we made in chapter 5 as we reviewed the evidence from previous curriculum studies. For example, the degree of teacher commitment and pupil involvement are no doubt as important here as they are in any other classroom learning situation. Curriculum research is effortful, time-consuming, and loaded with practical difficulties. It must be conducted, however, if we are to find ways of modifying race and color concepts using our greatest available tool—the school classroom.

Let us turn now to the important and "wide-open" research area dealing with questions of the persistence and consequences of changes in race and color concepts. Suppose we have employed some racial attitude change procedure with preschool children and have succeeded in eliminating their original pro-Euro/anti-Afro bias as assessed by the PRAM II test procedure. How long does the modification persist? To what degree are the changes in the test behavior mirrored in changes in nontest behaviors; e.g., interracial interaction patterns? There is little information concerning the persistence of attitude change in young children, and research on this topic is badly needed. We note that techniques are available to assist in answering these questions; the PRAM II procedure has sufficient test-retest reliability, over a one-year interval, to make it a useful tool for this purpose. We also note that research on this topic should be guided by learning theory. In dealing with the elimination of racial bias, one is considering the extinction of certain response tendencies. Learning theory proposes that extinguished response tendencies will not become reestablished *unless* they are once again reinforced. In this connection, we can note the results of the Smith study described in chapter 5, in which it was demonstrated that a teaching machine procedure was successful in eliminating pro-Euro/anti-Afro bias among kindergarten children. However, when the children were retested one year later as first graders it was found that a pro-Euro bias had been partially restored. Herein may lie the difficulty. The child whose bias has been eliminated by some special procedure may continue to be in contact with other influences which act to again reinforce his original response tendencies and, hence, restore his racial bias. These comments are not offered to discourage the interested researcher but, rather, to remind him of the complexity of his task. To find that a child whose bias was removed by a special procedure has once again become biased does not necessarily indicate a fault in the modification procedure, but may only reflect the malleability of the child's behavior in response to the reinforcement patterns with which he comes into contact.

The general question of transfer effects constitutes another major area for future research. Consider the instance of a group of formerly biased children who have been through a special attitude change procedure and now show an unbiased performance on test procedures. What other behavioral changes do they show? Do they interact more frequently or in a different manner with children of the other race? Do sociometric patterns show an increase in cross-race choices? Is it now easier to obtain cooperative behavior in interracial groups? These and many other related questions await the attention of the investigator who is willing and able to conduct the elaborate studies necessary for the proper exploration of this research area. In such studies, the researcher should recognize that he is not coping with a novel problem but is dealing with one of the oldest questions in education and psychology—generalization of training—and should be guided by the extensive literature on this topic.

A BROADER VIEW

We believe that the theory proposed in chapter 10 embraces the major influences upon the development of race and color concepts in young children. On the other hand, the theory is quite general and far from complete. In particular, there is little research evidence relating the development of these concepts to the more basic processes involved in the general perceptual, cognitive, and emotional development of young children. Concepts and attitudes relating to race do not develop in isolation, nor are they acquired by osmosis. Young children learn these concepts along with a myriad of others as a result of their own perceptions, thoughts, and feelings and their need to develop an understanding of these experiences. While it may be useful, at times, to speak of children being "receptive to cultural messages" regarding race, we recognize that such highly abstract theorizing must eventually be related to the concrete transactions between the child and his environment— particularly his interpersonal environment.

A fully adequate understanding of the development of race and color concepts will require that our knowledge in this special area be integrated with that of general developmental psychology. As an example, our knowledge concerning racial bias in preschool children needs to be related to the general tendency for children, aged three to six, to group objects on the basis of color rather than form (Brian and Goodenough, 1929). In elaboration of this point, Phyllis Katz has written: ". . . we will probably not have an adequate understanding of how children acquire racial attitudes until we begin paying more than lip service to the multiplicity of concomitants and give much more attention to the developmental context in which acquisition takes place. . . . A child's perceptions and concepts about people should follow the same rules as their perceptions and concepts about other kinds of stimuli. The processes underlying the effects of reinforcement should not differ whether the child's social learning concerns table manners or who is welcome as a friend in the house. Interestingly, however, psychologists have preferred to study the processes of concept formation, perception, and learning in children by observing their reactions to neutral stimuli. Those interested in racial attitudes, on the other hand, have tended to investigate these as if they existed apart from other ongoing processes in the child. Attitudes about other people do not exist or develop in a vacuum" (Katz, 1976, p. 145). Dr. Katz practices what she preaches and her paper on the acquisition of racial attitudes constitutes the best effort to date to place racial concepts in a general developmental context.

TECHNICAL SUMMARIES OF RESEARCH PROCEDURES

GENERAL CHARACTERISTICS OF PRAM AND CMT PROCEDURES

The Preschool Racial Attitude Measure (PRAM) has been developed in order to assess the attitudes of preliterate children toward Euro-American and Afro-American persons. The Color Meaning Test (CMT) is a companion measure which has been developed to assess the attitudes of such children toward the colors white and black. Both procedures are picture-story techniques, and they share the same general rationale in which attitudes are assessed by means of the child's response to simple evaluative adjectives contained in the stories which he is told. A child who consistently selects one type of stimulus figure in response to positive evaluative adjectives and a different type of figure in response to negative adjectives is, in effect, displaying a positive attitude toward the former and a negative attitude toward the latter. This approach represents a simplified, downward extension of the evaluation factor of the semantic differential which has been shown to be an effective way of assessing attitudes among older children and young adults (e.g., Osgood, Suci, and Tannenbaum, 1957). The use of the evaluation factor rationale at the preschool level is supported by a series of studies which have demonstrated the existence of the evaluation factor in the semantic space of the five-year-old child (Edwards and Williams, 1970; McMurtry and Williams, 1972; Gordon and Williams, 1973).

The same sets of evaluative adjectives are used for the PRAM and CMT procedures. The stimulus figures differ with the PRAM pictures representing light- and dark-skinned human figures while the CMT pictures represent white and black animal figures. In the original version of both procedures, twelve evaluative adjectives were employed to produce score ranges of 0–12. Both procedures have been revised and doubled in length to produce score ranges of 0–24. We will describe the two revised procedures—known as PRAM II and CMT II. Additional details concerning PRAM I and CMT I may be found elsewhere (Williams and Roberson, 1967). Both PRAM and CMT have usually been administered by young women, but sex of examiner seems to have no effect on the scores obtained.

PRESCHOOL RACIAL ATTITUDE MEASURE II
(PRAM II)

PRAM II is an individually administered, picture-story procedure for the assessment of racial attitudes in young children (Williams, Best, Boswell, Mattson, and Graves, 1975). The procedure also yields a measure of the child's awareness of sex-typed behaviors which serves as a useful control measure of general conceptual development. PRAM II has been used successfully with children as young as three years of age and as old as nine. Administration time is approximately twenty minutes. The procedure is so designed that the first and second halves of the procedure constitute parallel short forms which may be administered separately, at different times.

Test Materials

The PRAM II test materials consist of 36 colored photographs and 36 associated stories. Twenty-four of the pictures and stories are used in the assessment of racial attitude while the remaining 12 are used to obtain the control sex-role score. The 24 racial attitude pictures each depict drawings of two dark-haired human figures which are identical in all respects, except that one has pinkish-tan skin color ("Euro-American") while the other has a medium-brown skin color ("Afro-American").

In the series of 24 racial attitude pictures, figures of both sexes are employed, and a variety of ages—from young children to "grandparents"—are represented. The figures in the series are drawn in a variety of sitting, standing, and walking positions, with the pictures being otherwise generally ambiguous as to any activities in which the persons represented might be engaged. The 12 pictures used for the sex-role items each display a male and a female figure of the same general age and of the same race, with half of the pictures representing Euro-Americans and half Afro-Americans.

The size of the pictures in the standard PRAM II set is 8 x 10 inches. The size of the photograph does not appear critical, however, since it has been demonstrated that virtually identical scores are obtained when 5 x 7 photographs are used.

The 24 evaluative adjectives used in the PRAM II procedure are shown in Table B-1. The full set of 36 stories is found in Table B-8.

Administration

The standard procedure for the administration of PRAM II is as follows. The child is taken to a private room where he or she and the examiner are seated at a low table.

Table B-1. Adjectives Used in PRAM and CMT Procedures

Positive Evaluative Adjectives (PEA's)	Negative Evaluative Adjectives (NEA's)
clean	bad
good	dirty
kind	mean
nice	naughty
pretty	stupid
smart	ugly
friendly	cruel
happy	sad
healthy	selfish
helpful	sick
right	unfriendly
wonderful	wrong

Note: All 24 adjectives are used in PRAM II and CMT II procedures. Adjectives above dotted line were also used in PRAM I and CMT I.

After some initial conversation to build rapport, the examiner places the PRAM II picture notebook, stories, and answer sheet on the table and says:

"What I have here are some pictures I'd like to show you, and stories to go with each one. I want you to help me by pointing to the person in each picture that the story is about. Here, I'll show you what I mean." The examiner then opens the notebook to the first (sex-role) picture of a little boy and a little girl seated, and reads the first story: "Here are two children. One of these children has four dolls with which they like to have tea parties. Which child likes to play with dolls?" After recording the child's response, the examiner displays the second picture of two little boys, one Euro- and one Afro-American, walking, and reads the second story: "Here are two little boys. One of them is a *kind* little boy. Once he saw a kitten fall into a lake and he picked the kitten up to save it from drowning. Which is the kind little boy?" After recording the child's response, the examiner proceeds to picture three and story three, etc., until all 36 items (12 sex-role; 24 racial attitude) have been presented.

It has been shown that PRAM II can also be administered by a "teaching machine" (Behavioral Controls, Inc., Model SR 400). In this application the smaller (5 x 7) PRAM II pictures are attached to the program paper so that only one picture is visible at a time. The stories are read to the child by a coordinated tape-recorder. After a given story is read, the child indicates his choice of figures by pressing a panel under the selected figure, the machine automatically records his response, proceeds to the next picture, reads the next story, etc. In a study of the comparability of this procedure to the standard interview procedure, 56 preschool children were administered PRAM II with half of the test given by machine and half by the standard method. The two half-score racial attitude means were 8.07 for machine administration and 8.41 for standard administration, a nonsignificant difference. It was concluded that the machine administration procedure yields PRAM II scores which are comparable to those obtained from the standard administration procedure.

Scoring

The PRAM II racial attitude responses and sex-role responses are scored in the following manner. The racial attitude score is determined by counting one point for the selection of the light-skinned figure in response to a positive adjective, and one point for the selection of a dark-skinned figure in response to a negative adjective. The racial attitude total (RA-T) score based on all 24 items thus has a range of 0–24, with high scores indicating a pro-Euro/anti-Afro bias (E+/A−), low scores indicating a pro-Afro/anti-Euro bias (A+/E−), and midrange scores (around 12) indicating no bias. The 12 sex-role items are scored by giving one point for each conventional sex-appropriate response, yielding a possible score range of 0–12.

Due to the two-choice nature of the PRAM procedure, the binomial distribution provides a convenient way to determine when an individual child is responding in a manner which would be unlikely on a chance basis. With 24 racial attitude response opportunities, the probability of an unbiased child obtaining a score of 17 or up is only .033; the same probability exists for scores of 7 or down. Thus, scores in the former category (17 up) are taken as evidence of a "definite" E+/A− bias, while scores in the latter category (7 down) reflect a "definite" A+/E− bias. Likewise, scores of 15 and 16, 8 and 9, are taken as evidence of "probable" bias, while the 10–14 midrange is characterized as "unbiased." It should be noted that this classification applies to the performance of the individual child and does not apply to group means. For example, a group mean of 14 may be significantly higher than 12 and, hence, indicative of a group tendency toward a E+/A− bias.

Normative Data

The basic standardization group for PRAM II consists of 272 preschool children from Winston-Salem, North Carolina, who were tested in 1970–72. The children ranged in age from 37 months to 85 months, with a mean age of 65 months (S.D. = 7.64). Half of the children were Euro-American and half were

Afro-American, with each race group composed of equal numbers of males and females. Half of each race-sex group were tested by female Euro examiners, and half by female Afro examiners.

The frequency distributions of racial attitude scores obtained by these children are shown in Table B-2. In Table B-3 are given the percent of children scoring in each of the five score ranges described above. Further analyses and discussion of these preschool data and a summary of PRAM II scores at the early school-age level will be found in chapter 4 of the text.

Table B-2. Frequency Distributions and Means of PRAM II Racial Attitude Scores for 272 Subjects Classified by Race of Subject, Race of Examiner, and Sex of Subject   (M = male; F = female)

	Euro-American Subjects (N = 136)						Afro-American Subjects (N = 136)					
RA Score	Euro Examiner			Afro Examiner			Euro Examiner			Afro Examiner		
	M	F	Tot.	M	F	Tot.	M	F	Tot.	M	F	Tot.
24	1	3	4	1	1	2	3		3	2		2
23	4	5	9	1		1	2	2	4		1	1
22	2	4	6	1	5	6	3	1	4		2	2
21	6	2	8	3	1	4	1	2	3	2	1	3
20	2	1	3	2	1	3	2		2	3		3
19	4	2	6	1	3	4	3	3	6	3		3
18	5	2	7	2	3	5	2		2	1	4	5
17	4	2	6	4	1	5	2	4	6	4	1	5
16	1	2	3	3	1	4		5	5	1	2	3
15	3	4	7	3	2	5	3		3	3	3	6
14		4	4	1	2	3	5	4	9	3	3	6
13	1	1	2	7	2	9		5	5	1	7	8
12	1	1	2		4	4	1	1	2	2		2
11				1	1	2	1	1	2	1	1	2
10				1	2	3	4	2	6	3	3	6
9				2	1	3				2	1	3
8				1		1						
7										1		1
6										1		1
5		1	1	1	1	1	1			1	1	2
4					1	1	1		1	1	1	2
3				1	1	2				1		
2								2	2			
1							1		1	1		1
0							1		1			
X̄ RA	19.0	18.3	18.7	15.7	15.0	15.4	16.2	14.3	15.3	14.8	13.5	14.2

Table B-3. Percent of PRAM II Scores of Euro- and Afro-American Children, Tested by Euro- and Afro-American Examiners Falling into Each of Five Categories

		Euro Children		Afro Children	
Score Range	Chance Expectancy	Euro Examiner (N = 68)	Afro Examiner (N = 68)	Euro Examiner (N = 68)	Afro Examiner (N = 68)
0–7	3.3	1.4	5.9	8.8	11.8
8–9	12.1	0.0	5.9	0.0	4.4
10–14	69.2	11.8	30.9	35.3	35.3
15–16	12.1	14.7	13.2	11.8	13.2
17–24	3.3	72.1	44.1	44.1	35.3

Internal Consistency

The internal consistency of the 24-item RA-T scale was examined using the data from the 272 children in the basic standardization study plus data from an additional 120 subjects who were subsequently examined. The total group of 392 children had a mean age of 64 months. The analysis was conducted by comparing the subjects' responses to two halves of the scale, with the data divided in several different ways: odd items vs. even items; "old" adjectives used in PRAM I vs. "new" adjectives added in the PRAM II revision; positive adjectives vs. negative adjectives; and first half (Series A) vs. second half (Series B). In each of these comparisons a product-moment correlation coefficient was computed between scores on the two 12-item halves, and the Spearman-Brown correction for doubled length was then employed to estimate the internal consistency of the total 24-item scale.

The results of these comparisons are summarized in Table B-4. These findings indicated that the racial attitude scale possesses a high degree of homogeneity. The Spearman-Brown estimates for the usual "split-half" comparisons (odd-even; first half–second half) indicate that the internal consistency "reliability" of RA-T scores is of the order of .80.

The findings for the old-item vs. new-item comparisons provide satisfactory evidence that the 12 items added in the PRAM II revision are measuring the same thing as the old items from PRAM I. The results for the positive adjective vs. negative adjective comparison indicate that scores on these two subscales are substantially related, indicating that children who choose light-skinned figures in response to positive adjectives also tend to choose dark-skinned figures in response to negative adjectives, and vice versa. Thus, the positive and negative items appear to be assessing different aspects of the same trait.

The results of the Series A vs. Series B comparison are of particular interest since the series had been designed to provide alternate short forms of the procedure. The high correlation between A and B scores (.71), the virtually identical means (A = 8.20; B = 8.24) and standard deviations (A = 2.74; B = 2.79), indicate that the two scales can be considered as equivalent 12-item short forms of PRAM II.

A comparable degree of internal consistency was found in the study of 483 primary school children described in chapter 4. For example, the correlation coefficients for Series A vs. Series B

Table B-4. Internal Consistency Measures for Racial Attitude Scale: Correlation Coefficients (r), and Spearman-Brown Estimates (r SB)

Odd-Numbered Items vs. Even-Numbered Items

	$\bar{X}$ Odd	$\bar{X}$ Even	r	r SB
Euro Ss (N = 252)	8.86	8.55	.61	.76
Afro Ss (N = 140)	7.38	7.31	.76	.86
Total Ss (N = 392)	8.33	8.11	.69	.81

Old Items vs. New Items

	$\bar{X}$ Old	$\bar{X}$ New	r	r SB
Euro Ss	9.23	8.18	.70	.78
Afro Ss	7.64	7.04	.68	.81
Total Ss	8.67	7.77	.70	.82

Positive Items vs. Negative Items

	$\bar{X}$ Positive	$\bar{X}$ Negative	r	r SB
Euro Ss	8.91	8.50	.53	.69
Afro Ss	7.56	7.11	.68	.81
Total Ss	8.45	8.00	.61	.76

First Half (Series A) Items vs. Second Half (Series B) Items

	$\bar{X}$ Series A	$\bar{X}$ Series B	r	r SB
Euro Ss	8.62	8.79	.65	.79
Afro Ss	7.45	7.24	.75	.86
Total Ss	8.20	8.24	.71	.83

scores for children in grades one through four were .78, .76, .67, and .64, respectively.

Stability

The stability of the RA-T scores across a one-year interval (12.8 months) was assessed using 57 subjects (29 Euro; 28 Afro). At the time of first testing, these subjects had a mean age of 56.8 months; at the second testing, these subjects had a mean age of 69.6 months. The mean RA-T score at the first testing was 15.30 while the mean at the second testing was 16.93, a statistically significant ($p < .05$) increase of 1.63 points. This finding suggests that there may have been a slight positive practice effect for the RA-T scores. It does not seem likely that the increase was attributable to the fact that the children were a year older, since RA-T scores have not been found to be correlated with age, during the preschool years.

Three scores (Series A, Series B, and Total) from the first administration were each correlated with the same three scores from the second administration, as shown in Table B-5. The correlation of .55 between total scores at the two administrations

Table B-5. Test-Retest Correlation Coefficients for Series A, Series B, and Total Racial Attitude (RA-T) Scores Across a One-Year Interval

	Retest		
Test	Series A Scores	Series B Scores	Total Scores
Series A Scores	.56†	.28*	.45†
Series B Scores	.50†	.41†	.42†
Total Scores	.60†	.40†	.55†

*$p < .05$
†$p < .01$

provided the best available estimate of test-retest reliability, although the relative youth of the subjects suggested that this may be a minimum estimate. As is usual, this value was lower than the estimated internal consistency of .80, noted above. The most demanding reliability test for any measure is the coefficient of "equivalence and stability," i.e., the correlation between different forms of the test at two different administrations. As indicated in Table B-5, the correlation between Series A scores from one administration and Series B scores at the other administration was statistically significant, indicating that the children's responses to one set of items were related to their responses to the second set of items given one year later.

The relationships of PRAM II racial attitude scores to other subject variables are discussed at some length in chapter 4 of the text. In general, the racial attitude scores have not been found to be related to the sex, age, or IQ of the children studied. On the other hand, the scores are related to the race of the children with Euro children demonstrating a higher degree of E+/A− bias than that found among Afro children. Racial attitude scores are also related to color attitude scores from the CMT procedures (see Table 8-2 in text).

Race of Examiner Effects

Race of examiner effects were found in the preschool standardization study and to a lesser degree in the primary school study discussed in chapter 4 of the text. In both cases, it was found that children, both Euro and Afro, obtained higher racial attitude scores when tested by Euro examiners. On the other hand, Deborah Best (1972) conducted a study designed specifically to explore the race of examiner effect and failed to find any evidence of it. In this study, each of 60 preschool Euro children was administered PRAM II by two examiners. The first examiner gave standard instructions and administered the first half of PRAM II. At this point, a second examiner entered the room, replaced the first examiner, and administered the second half of the procedure. One-quarter of the subjects were tested by each of the following race of examiner combinations: two Euros; two Afros; Euro then Afro; and Afro then Euro. The analyses of the data obtained under these conditions provided no evidence of race of examiner effects. For example, the mean racial attitude score obtained by the two Euro examiners was 17.6, compared with 17.9 for the two Afro examiners. In addition, there was no evidence of a tendency to shift scores up or down when the race of examiner was changed. In view of these findings, one must be cautious in assuming that the race of examiner effects will necessarily be found whenever PRAM II is administered. An additional discussion of these effects will be found in Appendix A.

Sex-Role Scores

As noted earlier, the PRAM II procedure includes 12 sex-role items which appear as items 1, 4, 7, 10, etc. in the series of PRAM II stories found in Table B-8 at the end of this appendix. With one point scored for each sex-appropriate response, the possible range of scores is 0–12 with high scores indicative of high sex-role awareness and midrange scores (around 6) indicative of no sex-role awareness. Virtually all preschool children score in the 6 to 12 range, with a majority obtaining scores of 9 and up. In spite of this restricted range, the sex-role score has been shown to be a useful measure of general conceptual development, correlating positively with both age and IQ among preschool children (see chapter 4).

COLOR MEANING TEST II (CMT II)

CMT II is an individually administered, picture-story procedure for the assessment of young children's attitudes toward the colors white and black. (Williams, Boswell, and Best, 1975). It requires approximately fifteen minutes to administer and has been used successfully with children as young as three years of age. The procedure is designed so that the first and second halves constitute parallel short forms which may be administered on two different occasions.

Test Materials

The CMT II test materials consist of 12 8" x 10" colored photographs and 24 associated stories. Each photograph depicts a drawing of two animals which are identical except that one is colored white while the other is colored black. The animals depicted are: horses, dogs, kittens, rabbits, cows, bears, ducks, pigs, chicks, mice, sheep, and squirrels. The 24 CMT II stories are given in Table B-9 at the end of this appendix. The 12 stimulus pictures are used in the order indicated for stories 1–12 and then are used again in the same order for stories 13–24. The twenty-four evaluative adjectives employed in the stories are the same as those used with PRAM II (see Table B-1 above). The full set of 24 stories is found in Table B-9.

Administration

The general administration conditions for CMT II are the same as those described above for PRAM II. The instructions to the subject are as follows: "What I have here are some pictures I'd like to show you, and stories to go with each one. I want you to help me by pointing to the animal in each picture that the story is about. Here, I'll show you what I mean." The examiner then places the notebook flat on the table in front of the child, opens to the first picture and reads the first story, ending with the key question. After the subject has responded, the examiner records the choice on the record sheet, then presents the second picture and story, following the same procedure until the first 12 stories have been told, and responses recorded. The examiner then starts again with the first picture and story number 13, and continues through story 24.

Scoring

CMT II is scored by counting one point for the selection of the white animal in response to a positive adjective, and one point for the selection of the black animal in response to a negative adjective. The score range is 0–24 with high scores indicative of a pro-white/anti-black attitude (W+/B−), low scores indicative of a pro-black/anti-white attitude (B+/W−) and midrange scores (around 12) indicative of no consistent color attitude. As with PRAM II, the binomial distribution has been used to establish the following categories for the CMT II scores: 0–7, definite B+/W− bias; 8–9, probable B+/W− bias; 10–14, no bias; 15–16, probable W+/B− bias; 17–24, definite W+/B− bias. These categories apply to the score obtained by an individual child, and should not be applied to the interpretation of group means. For example, a group mean of 13 or 14 might prove to be significantly different from the chance mean of 12.

Normative Data

The basic standardization group for CMT II consists of 320 preschool children from Winston-Salem, North Carolina, who were tested in 1972 and 1973. The children ranged in age from 40 months to 91 months, with a mean age of 61 months. Half of the children were Euro-American and half were Afro-American, with each race group composed of an equal number of males and females. Half of each race-sex group were examined by female Euro examiners, and half by female Afro examiners.

The frequency distributions of the color meaning scores obtained by these children are shown in Table B-6. Analyses of these data indicated nonsignificant effects for race of examiner and sex of subject. There was a significant effect of race of subject with Euro-American children scoring significantly higher than Afro-American children.

Table B-7 presents the percents of Euro-American and Afro-American children falling into the five score categories formed from the binomial distribution.

Internal Consistency

The internal consistency of the 24-item CMT II scale was examined using data from the 320 subjects in the standardization study. This was done by comparing the subjects' responses to two halves of the scale, with the data

Table B-6. Frequency Distributions and Means of CMT II Color Attitude Scores for 320 Subjects Classified by Race of Subject, Race of Examiner, and Sex of Subject   (M = male; F = female)

	Euro-American Subjects (N = 160)						Afro-American Subjects (N = 160)					
CM Score	Euro Examiner			Afro Examiner			Euro Examiner			Afro Examiner		
	M	F	Tot.	M	F	Tot.	M	F	Tot.	M	F	Tot.
24	1	1	2							1		1
23	2	1	3	3	2	5					1	1
22	4	3	7	4	2	6		2	2	1	1	2
21	2	2	4	4	1	5		1	1	3		3
20	3	3	6	5	5	10	4	1	5	1	4	5
19	6	5	11	1	2	3	1	1	2	1	2	3
18	4	2	6	5	3	8		2	2	4	2	6
17	4	5	9	3	4	7	5	6	11	5	3	8
16	3	5	8	4	2	6	2	2	4	4	6	10
15	3	5	8	3	2	5	6	7	13		1	1
14	1	3	4	2		2	4	7	11	1	3	4
13	3	1	4	4	8	12	7	1	8	5	7	12
12	1	2	3	2	6	8	8	5	13	3	3	6
11	1	1	2		2	2	2	1	3	4	3	7
10		1	1		1	1	1	2	3	1	3	4
9	2		2					2	2	4	1	5
8										1		1
7										1		1
6												
5												
4												
3				no children scored in 0–6 range								
2												
1												
0												
X̄ CM	17.5	17.2	17.3	17.9	16.0	16.9	14.5	15.0	14.8	14.7	15.1	14.9

divided in two different ways: odd items vs. even items; and first half (Series A) vs. second half (Series B). In each of these comparisons a product-moment correlation of .46 was obtained between scores on the two 12-item halves. From this, the Spearman-Brown formula for doubled length was employed to estimate the internal consistency of the total 24-item scale at .63.

Table B-7. Percent of CMT II Scores of 160 Euro-American and 160 Afro-American Preschool Children Falling into Each of Five Categories

Score Range	Category	Chance Expectancy	% Euro Children	% Afro Children
0–7	Definite B+/W− bias	3.3	0	0.6
8–9	Probable B+/W− bias	12.1	1.2	5.6
10–14	No bias	69.2	24.4	43.8
15–16	Probable W+/B− bias	12.1	16.9	17.5
17–24	Definite W+/B− bias	3.3	57.5	32.5

Relationship of Color Attitude Scores to Other Subject Characteristics

In the standardization group, the correlations between CM scores and chronological age were .20 ($p < .05$) for Euro children, .11 (n.s.) for Afro children, and .14 ($p < .05$) for all subjects combined. The correlations between CM scores and Peabody Picture Vocabulary Test-IQ were .29 ($p < .01$) for Euro children, .27 ($p < .01$) for Afro children, and .27 ($p < .01$) for all subjects combined. CM scores have been found to correlate significantly with the racial attitude scores from the PRAM procedures (see Table 8-2 in text), and with a measure of fear of darkness (see discussions of Boswell, 1974, study in chapter 3).

MORLAND PICTURE INTERVIEW (MPI)

General Characteristics

The MPI is designed to measure racial acceptance, racial preference, racial bias, perception of racial similarity, and racial classification ability in young children by showing them a set of color photographs about which questions are asked.

There are two parts to the interview. The first, in which there is no mention of race, is designed to find out if the children accept, prefer, and perceive themselves similar to photographic models representing their own or the other race. In the second part, an attempt is made to measure the ability of respondents to apply racial terms correctly to the persons in the pictures, to the interviewer, and to themselves.

There are two versions of the MPI. In one, the models are Afro- and Euro-American; in the other, the models are Chinese and European.

Description of Photographs

The six 8 x 10 color photographs in the MPI were made by a professional photographer. The children and adults who served as models for the pictures were chosen so that there would be variety in skin color and hair form. Nonracial characteristics, including dress and facial expressions, were kept as similar as possible. The children were of ages four through seven, and the adults were of ages similar to those of the parents of the children. There follows a description of the photographs in the order in which they are shown to the child. Note that which photographs are used first and second depends on the race of the child.

Photograph No. 1 / Six children of the respondent's race, three boys and three girls, sitting around a table drinking punch and eating cookies.

Photograph No. 2 / Six children of the other race, three boys and three girls, sitting around the same table, also eating cookies and drinking punch.

Photograph No. 3 / Six men, three of each race, holding cups and looking at a book.

Photograph No. 4 / Six women, three of each race, holding cups and talking with one another.

Photograph No. 5 / Six girls, three of each race, sitting around a table looking at books.

Photograph No. 6 / Six boys, three of each race, sitting around the same table, also looking at books.

Administration of Interview

When the MPI is administered in a nursery school or kindergarten, the interviewer visits the children two or three times before proceeding with the testing. During these visits attempts are made to become acquainted with the children by playing games and sharing refreshments with them. For the actual testing itself each child is invited individually to go with the interviewer to a room in order to "play a picture game." Both the interviewer and the respondent sit at a low table and the interviewer tells the child, "Let's look at some pictures and talk about them." The initial question about each picture is "What do you see in this picture?" This serves as a warm-up question and also reveals any spontaneous use of racial terms. Answers to most of the questions that follow can be made by pointing to persons in the photographs so that even very shy children can respond with ease. If the interview is carried out in the child's home, the interviewer, after a preliminary conversation with other members of the family who might be present, asks to be left alone with the child. Answers to the questions are recorded by the interviewer on a precoded sheet so that very little writing is necessary during the testing. Interviews take from five to ten minutes.

Interview Questions

Part I |
A. *Photograph No. 1*
   1. What do you see in this picture? (This is the initial warm-up question for each of the pictures in the first part of the test. It is also designed to see if there is spontaneous racial awareness, which is indicated if the respondent employs any racial term in his answer.)
   2. Would you like to play with these children? Why or why not? (Answers to these questions are termed Acceptance— if the respondent replies, "Yes"; Nonacceptance—if the respondent replies, "No," and answers the "Why not?" with a nonracial reason; Rejection—if the respondent replies, "No," and answers the "Why not?" with a racial reason.)
B. *Photograph No. 2*
   1. What do you see in this picture?
   2. Would you like to play with these children? Why or why not?
   3. (Pointing to the first and second photographs) Would you like to play with these children, or with these? (This is the first measure of Preference.)
C. *Photograph No. 3*
   1. What do you see in this picture?
   2. Does this man look more like your father (point to a model of the respondent's race), or does this one look more like your father (point to a model of the other race)? Repeat for the other two racial pairs.
   3. (Pointing to all of the men) Which one looks *most* like your father? Why? (These questions form a measure of Perception of Racial Similarity of the parent.)
D. *Photograph No. 4*
   1. What do you see in this picture?
   2. Does this woman look more like your mother (point to a model of the respondent's race), or does this one look more like your mother (point to a model of the other race)? Repeat for the other two racial pairs.
   3. (Pointing to all of the women) Which one looks *most* like your mother? Why? (These questions form a measure of Perception of Racial Similarity of the parent.)

E. *Photograph No. 5*
    1. What do you see in this picture?
    2. (Pointing to a model of the respondent's own race) Would you like to play with this girl? Why or why not? (An Acceptance question.)
    3. (Pointing to a model of the other race) Would you like to play with this girl? Why or why not? (An Acceptance question.)
    4. (Pointing to all of the children) Which one would you *most* like to play with? Why? (A Preference question.)
    5. Which of these girls do you think is the prettiest? (A Racial Bias question.)
    6. Which of these girls do you think is the best student? (A Racial Bias question.)
    7. Which of these girls do you think is the nicest? (A Racial Bias question.)
    *8. (Pointing to models of each of the races) Do you look more like this girl or like that one? (Perception of Racial Similarity question.)
    9. (Pointing to all of the girls) Which one do you look *most* like? (Perception of Racial Similarity question.)
    10. (Pointing to models of each of the races) Would you rather be this girl or that one? (Racial Self-Preference question.)
    11. (Pointing to all of the girls) Which one would you *most* like to be? (Racial Self-Preference question.)
F. *Photograph No. 6*
    1. What do you see in this picture?
    2. (Pointing to a model of the respondent's own race) Would you like to play with this boy? Why or why not? (An Acceptance question.)
    3. (Pointing to a model of the other race) Would you like to play with this boy? Why or why not? (An Acceptance question.)
    4. (Pointing to all of the children) Which one would you *most* like to play with? Why? (A Preference question.)
    5. Which of these boys do you think is the best looking? (A Racial Bias question.)
    6. Which of these boys do you think is the best student? (A Racial Bias question.)
    7. Which of these boys do you think is the nicest? (A Racial Bias question.)
    †8. (Pointing to models of each of the races) Do you look more like this boy or like that one? (A Perception of Racial Similarity question.)

*If the respondent is a girl, continue with the questions; if the respondent is a boy, proceed to Photograph No. 6.
†If the respondent is a boy, continue with the questions; if the respondent is a girl, stop with question 7.

9. (Pointing to all of the boys) Which one do you look *most* like? (A Perception of Racial Similarity question.)

10. (Pointing to models of each of the races) Would you rather be this boy or that one? (A Racial Self-Preference question.)

11. (Pointing to all of the boys) Which one would you *most* like to be? (A Racial Self-Preference question.)

Part II / (Tell the subject that you want him to look at the pictures once more. Beginning with Photograph No. 6, and continuing in reverse order, ask the following questions for each photograph):

A. Racial Classification Ability (For the Afro- and Euro-American Version)

1. Do you see a black child in this picture? Point to the black child.

2. Do you see a white child in this picture? Point to the white child.

3. Do you see a Negro child in this picture? Point to the Negro child.

4. Do you see a Caucasian child in this picture? Point to the Caucasian child.

5. Do you see a Colored child in this picture? Point to the Colored child.

Aa. For Chinese and European Version:

1. Do you see a Chinese child in this picture? Point to the Chinese child.

2. Do you see a Western child in this picture? Point to the Western child.

B. Racial Self-Classification (For the Afro- and Euro-American Version)

(For each of the above terms correctly identified by the respondent, ask the following, without using the photographs):

1. Are you black, or are you white?

2. Are you a Negro?

3. Are you a Caucasian?

4. Are you Colored?

Bb. For the Chinese and European Version

(For each of the above terms correctly identified by the respondent, ask the following, without using the photographs):

1. Are you Chinese, or are you a Westerner?

Scoring

The child's responses to the various types of MPI questions are used to place him in one of two or more categories for each racial concept. For reference, the questions are keyed to the preceding procedure outline.

Racial Acceptance /
A.   Acceptance of Own Race: responses to questions I.A.2,
I.E.2., and I.F.2. Answers are scored "Acceptance" when the
respondent says "Yes"; "Nonacceptance" if the respondent says
"No" for a nonracial reason; and "Rejection" if the respondent
says "No" for racial reasons. If 2 or 3 of the 3 responses receive
the same scoring, the child is so classified. Otherwise, the
classification is "Not Clear."
B.   Acceptance of Other Race: responses to questions I.B.2,
I.E.3, and I.F.3, with scoring the same as that for Part A above.

Racial Preference / Responses to questions I.B.3, I.E.4,
and I.F.4. Answers are scored as "Prefers Own Race," "Prefers
Other Race." If 2 or 3 of the 3 responses receive the same
scoring, the child is so classified. Otherwise, the classification is
"Not Clear."

Racial Self-Preference / Response to question I.E.11 if
the respondent is a girl, or I.F.11 if the respondent is a
boy.

Racial Bias / Responses to questions I.E.5, I.E.6, I.E.7,
I.F.5, I.F.6, and I.F.7. Answers are scored as: "Biased toward
Own Race," or "Biased toward Other Race." If a majority of the
child's answers receive the same score, he is so classified.
Otherwise he is classified, "Bias Not Clear."

Perception of Racial Similarity /
A.   "Similarity to Self": response to question I.E.9, if
respondent is a girl, or to I.F.9, if the respondent is a boy.
B.   "Similarity to Father": response to question I.C.3.
C.   "Similarity to Mother": response to question I.D.3.

Racial Classification /
A.   Racial Classification Ability: responses to the two questions
involving the racial labels with greatest current usage: in recent
studies, white and black; in earlier studies, white and Negro, or
white and Colored. Possible scores are: "High" if respondent is
correct on all twelve of the questions or misses not more than
two; "Low" if the respondent misses more than two of the
twelve questions.
B.   Racial Self-Classification: response to the direct question
asking to what race the respondent belongs.

Other Characteristics of the MPI

When the MPI was first developed in the mid-1950s,
tests were made of the validity and reliability of racial
classification ability (Morland, 1958). Validity was determined

by comparing the respondents' scores on classification ability with their responses to the question regarding the race of the interviewer. Those scoring "High" on racial classification ability were far more likely than those scoring "Low" to be correct in giving the race of the interviewer. Of 157 subjects of high ability, 98.7% made correct responses regarding the race of the interviewer, while of the 70 subjects of low ability, only 30% gave the correct response, a highly significant difference. The reliability of racial classification ability was measured by the split–half method. The responses of 91 subjects to the odd-numbered photographs were compared to their responses to the even-numbered photographs. A correlation coefficient of .98 was found.

Two studies of the race of examiner effect of the MPI, one with Euro- and the other with Afro-American children, were described in chapter 6. In these studies, no statistically significant differences in any of the measures—racial acceptance, racial preference, perception of racial similarity, and racial classification—were obtained by Euro- and Afro-American examiners.

Table B-8. PRAM II Procedure: Picture Descriptions and Stories for the Racial Attitude (RA) and Sex-Role (SR) Items

---

Series A

1. SR—Euro girl and Euro boy, sitting

   Here are two children. One of these children has four dolls with which they like to have tea parties. Which child likes to play with dolls?

2. RA—Afro little boy and Euro little boy, walking

   Here are two little boys. One of them is a kind little boy. Once he saw a kitten fall into a lake and he picked up the kitten to save it from drowning. Which is the kind little boy?

3. RA—Euro little girl and Afro little girl, standing

   Here are two little girls. One of them is an ugly little girl. People do not like to look at her. Which is the ugly little girl?

4. SR—Afro teenage boy and Afro teenage girl, sitting

   Here are two children. They are thinking about what they want to be when they grow up. One of them wants to be a policeman. Which one wants to be a policeman?

5. RA—Euro teenage boy and Afro teenage boy, standing

   Here are two boys. One of them is a friendly boy. He has a lot of friends. Which one is the friendly boy?

6. RA—Afro teenage girl and Euro teenage girl, walking

    Here are two girls. When a lady asked one of them where she lived, the girl gave the wrong answer. Which is the wrong girl?

7. SR—Euro man and Euro woman, walking

    Here are two people. After supper one of these people clears the table and washes all the dishes. Which person washes the dishes?

8. RA—Euro woman and Afro woman, sitting

    Here are two women. One of them is a nice woman. She does nice things for her husband and children. Which is the nice woman?

9. RA—Afro man and Euro man, standing

    Here are two men. One of them is a bad man. He took money out of his children's piggy bank and never put it back. Which is the bad man?

10. SR—Afro teenage girl and Afro teenage boy, standing

    Here are two young people. One of them works at a gas station after school. Which one works at a gas station?

11. RA—Afro man and Euro man, standing

    Here are two men. One of them is a healthy man. He never has a cold or a high temperature. Which is the healthy man?

12. RA—Euro woman and Afro woman, sitting

    Here are two women. One of them is a sad woman. She has been left alone with no one to talk to. Which is the sad woman?

13. SR—Euro woman and Euro man, standing

    Here are two people. One of these people has baked two delicious apple pies. Which person baked the pies?

14. RA—Euro little boy and Afro little boy, standing

    Here are two little boys. One of them is a clean little boy. Whenever he washes his face he also washes behind his ears. Which is the clean little boy?

15. RA—Afro teenage girl and Euro teenage girl, sitting

    Here are two girls. One of them is a stupid girl. She doesn't even know how to spell her name. Which is the stupid girl?

16. SR—Afro man and Afro woman, standing

    Here are two people. When the car won't run, one of them is always able to fix it. Which person can fix the car?

17. RA—Euro man and Afro man, sitting

Here are two men. One of them is a very selfish man. He does not care about anyone except himself. Which is the selfish man?

18. RA—Afro woman and Euro woman, walking

    Here are two women. People say that one of them is a wonderful woman. She can do almost anything. Which is the wonderful woman?

Series B

19. SR—Euro little girl and Euro little boy, standing

    Here are two children. One of them wants to grow up and be a cowboy. Which child wants to be a cowboy?

20. RA—Afro little girl and Euro little girl, sitting

    Here are two little girls. Everyone says that one of them is very pretty. Which is the pretty girl?

21. RA—Euro little boy and Afro little boy, sitting

    Here are two little boys. One of them is a very naughty little boy. He drew pictures on the walls of his house with his crayons and upset his mother. Which is the naughty little boy?

22. SR—Afro little boy and Afro little girl, standing

    Here are two children. One of them likes to dress up in their mother's clothes and pretend that they are grown up. Which child likes to dress up in their mother's clothes?

23. RA—Euro teenage girl and Afro teenage girl, standing

    Here are two girls. One of them is a happy girl. She smiles almost all of the time. Which one is the happy girl?

24. RA—Afro teenage boy and Euro teenage boy, sitting

    Here are two boys. One of them is a cruel boy. When he comes home from school and his dog runs to meet him, he kicks his dog. Which is the cruel boy?

25. SR—Euro woman and Euro man, sitting

    Here are two people. One of them likes to go shopping. When they go shopping they like to buy new dresses. Which person likes to buy new dresses?

26. RA—Euro man and Afro man, walking

    Here are two men. One of them is a mean man. He throws rocks at dogs and cats when they come into his yard. Which is the mean man?

27. RA—Afro woman and Euro woman, standing

    Here are two women. One of them is a good woman. She does things for her neighbors and her children. Which is the good woman?

Table B-8 (continued)

28. SR—Afro man and Afro woman, sitting

    Here are two people. One of them built a barn for their animals to live in. Which person built the barn?

29. RA—Afro woman and Euro woman, standing

    Here are two women. One of them is a helpful woman. Whenever someone is sick she goes to help them. Which is the helpful woman?

30. RA—Euro man and Afro man, sitting

    Here are two men. One of them is an unfriendly man. He will not speak to any of the children playing in his neighborhood. Which is the unfriendly man?

31. SR—Euro woman and Euro man, standing

    Here are two young people. One of them likes to play football every afternoon after school. Which one likes to play football?

32. RA—Euro teenage boy and Afro teenage boy, walking

    Here are two boys. One of them is a smart boy. When the T.V. set breaks, he can fix it all by himself. Which is the smart boy?

33. RA—Afro little girl and Euro little girl, walking

    Here are two little girls. One of them is a dirty little girl. People say she does not take a bath very often. Which is the dirty little girl?

34. SR—Afro teenage boy and Afro teenage girl, walking

    Here are two young people. One of them likes to wear lipstick. Which one likes to wear lipstick?

35. RA—Euro man and Afro man, walking

    Here are two men. One of these men is right. When someone asks him a question, he always knows the right answer. Which man is right?

36. RA—Afro woman and Euro woman, standing

    Here are two women. One of them is a sick woman. She has to stay in the house most of the time. Which is the sick woman?

Table B-9. CMT II Procedure: Description of Test Items

Series A

1. Here are two horses. One of them is a kind horse. He lets Billy pet him and give him apples. Which is the kind horse?

2. Mr. Jones has two pigs. One of them is an ugly pig. He is so ugly that Mr. Jones doesn't want anybody to see it. Which is the ugly pig?

3. Sammy has two bears. One of them is a friendly bear. He likes to play with all Sammy's friends. Which is the friendly bear?

4. Here are two ducks. One of them is a wrong duck. He went swimming right after dinner, even though his Mommy told him not to. Which is the wrong duck?

5. Joey has two mice. One of them is a nice mouse and likes to play with Joey. Which is the nice mouse?

6. Here are two cats. One of them is a bad cat and scratches on the furniture. Which is the bad cat?

7. Here are two chickens. One of them is a healthy chicken and can always go out to play. She never has a cold. Which is the healthy chicken?

8. Here are two lambs. One of them is a sad lamb. He is lost and can't find his Mommy. Which is the sad lamb?

9. Here are two rabbits. One of them is a clean rabbit. He always washes behind his big, long ears. Which is the clean rabbit?

10. Here are two cows. One of them is a stupid cow. She doesn't even know when it's time to come in for supper. Which is the stupid cow?

11. Here are two dogs. One of them is a selfish dog. He won't even share his bone with his friend. Which is the selfish dog?

12. Here are two squirrels. One of them is a wonderful squirrel. She can climb up high in the trees. Which is the wonderful squirrel?

Series B

13. Here are two horses. One of them is a sick horse. He has to stay in the barn and can't go out to play. Which is the sick horse?

14. Farmer Jack has two pigs. One of them is a helpful pig. He helps Farmer Jack keep the yard straight. Which is the helpful pig?

15. Sandy has two bears. One of them is a dirty bear. She got all dirty while Sandy let her out to play. Which is the dirty bear?

16. Here are two ducks. One of them is a happy duck. He swims all day on the pond. Which is the happy duck?

17. Here are two mice. One of them is an unfriendly mouse. He runs and hides when children want to play with him. Which is the unfriendly mouse?

18. Here are two cats. One of them is right. He always knows where the mouse is when they play "hide and seek." Which is the right cat?

19. Here are two chickens. One of them is a naughty chicken. He doesn't come to supper when his Mommy calls. Which is the naughty chicken?

20. Here are two lambs. One of them is a good lamb. She does what her Mother tells her to. Which is the good lamb?

21. Here are two rabbits. One of them is a cruel rabbit. He fights with the little rabbits. Which is the cruel rabbit?

22. Farmer Blake has two cows. One of them is a pretty cow. Everyone likes to come see Farmer Blake's pretty cow. Which is the pretty cow?

23. Here are two dogs. One of them is a smart dog. He can do all kinds of tricks. Which is the smart dog?

24. Here are two squirrels. One of them is a mean squirrel. He steals nuts from the other squirrels. Which is the mean squirrel?

REFERENCES

Adams, Frances M., and Osgood, Charles E. "A Cross-Cultural Study of the Affective Meanings of Color." *Journal of Cross-Cultural Psychology* 4 (1973): 135–56.

Adorno, Theodor W.; Frenkel-Brunswik, Else; Levinson, Daniel J.; and Sanford, R. Nevitt. *The Authoritarian Personality*. New York: Harper, 1950.

Allen, Penny; Crosby, Sallie; and Garrison, Martha. "Racial Awareness of Children in 1958 and 1964." Senior thesis, Randolph-Macon Woman's College, 1964.

Allport, Gordon W. *The Nature of Prejudice*. Cambridge, Mass.: Addison-Wesley, 1954.

Asher, Steven R., and Allen, Vernon L. "Racial Preference and Social Comparison Processes." *Journal of Social Issues* 25 (1969): 157–66.

Ball, Portia M., and Cantor, Gordon N. "White Boys' Ratings of Pictures of Whites and Blacks as Related to Amount of Familiarization." *Perceptual and Motor Skills* 39 (1974): 883–90.

Bartholomew, Suzi; Livingston, Kathy; and Strickland, Martha. "A Comparison of Racial Awareness in Caucasian, Chinese, and Negro Children." Senior thesis, Randolph-Macon Woman's College, 1968.

Baugher, Robert, Jr. "The Skin Color Gradient as a Factor in the Racial Awareness and Racial Attitudes of Preschool Children." Master's thesis, California State University, Fresno, 1973.

Bennett, Paula D. "A Study of the Effects of Racial Composition of Schools on the Racial Attitudes and Self Concepts of Young Black and White Children." Master's thesis, University of Cincinnati, 1974.

Best, Deborah L. "Race of Examiner Effects on the Racial Attitude Responses of Preschool Children." Master's thesis, Wake Forest University, 1972.

———; Naylor, Cecile E.; and Williams, John E. "Extension of Color Bias Research to Young French and Italian Children." *Journal of Cross-Cultural Psychology* 6 (1975): 390–405.

_____; Smith, Suellen C.; Graves, Deborah J.; and Williams, John E. "The Modification of Racial Bias in Preschool Children." *Journal of Experimental Child Psychology* 20 (1975): 193–205.

Blaustein, Albert P., and Ferguson, Clarence Clyde. *Desegregation and the Law: The Meaning and Effect of the School Segregation Cases*. New Brunswick, N.J.: Rutgers University Press, 1957.

Bond, Elizabeth K. "Perception of Form by the Human Infant." *Psychological Bulletin* 77 (1972): 225–45.

Boswell, Donna A. "An Empirical Investigation of Some Theoretical Components of Racial Bias in Young Children." Master's thesis, Wake Forest University, 1974.

_____, and Williams, John E. "Correlates of Race and Color Bias among Preschool Children." *Psychological Reports* 36 (1975): 147–54.

Brace, C. Loring. "Introduction to Jensenism." In *Race and Intelligence*, edited by C. L. Brace, G. R. Gamble, and J. T. Bond. Washington, D.C.: American Anthropological Association, 1971.

Brian, Clara R., and Goodenough, Florence L. "The Relative Potency of Color and Form Perception at Various Ages." *Journal of Experimental Psychology* 12 (1929): 197–213.

Buettner-Janusch, John. *Origins of Man*. New York: John Wiley & Sons, 1966.

Campbell, Donald T., and Stanley, Julian C. *Experimental and Quasi-Experimental Designs for Research*. Chicago: Rand McNally, 1966.

Cantor, Gordon N. "Effects of Familiarization on Children's Ratings of Whites and Blacks." *Child Development* 43 (1972): 1219–29.

Chamberlain, Houston Stewart. *Foundations of the Nineteenth Century*. Translated by J. Lees. London and New York: John Lane Co., 1912.

Chance, Paul. "Reversing the Bigotry of Language." *Psychology Today* 7, no. 10 (1974): 57.

Clark, Kenneth B., and Clark, Mamie K. "Racial Self Identification and Preference in Negro Children." In *Readings in Social Psychology*, edited by T. M. Newcomb and E. L. Hartley. New York: Henry Holt & Co., 1947.

_____. "The Development of Consciousness of Self and the Emergence of Racial Identification in Negro Preschool Children." *Journal of Social Psychology* 10 (1939): 591–99.

Clifford, Eth. *Red Is Never a Mouse*. Indianapolis: Bobbs-Merrill Co., 1960.

Cohen, Rosalie. "The Influence of Conceptual Rule-Sets on Measures of Learning Ability." In *Race and Intelligence*, edited by C. L. Brace, C. R. Gamble, and J. T. Bond. Washington, D.C.: American Anthropological Association, 1971.

Collins, Jeffrey L. "The Effect of Differential Frequency of Color Adjective Pairings on the Subsequent Rating of Color Meaning and Racial Attitude in Preschool Children." Master's thesis, East Tennessee State University, 1972.

Columbia Broadcasting System. *White and Negro Attitudes towards Race Related Issues and Activities*. Princeton, N. J.: Opinion Research Corporation, 1968.

Cowan, Lou, and Leslie, Carlyn. "Racial Acceptance, Preference, and Self-Identification in Nursery School Children." Senior thesis, Randolph-Macon Woman's College, 1959.

Deutsch, Martin. "Happenings on the Way Back to the Forum." In *Science, Heritability, and IQ*. Reprint Series No. 4, Harvard Educational Review. Cambridge, Mass.: Harvard Educational Review, 1969.

Dunn, Lloyd M. *Expanded Manual for the Peabody Picture Vocabulary Test*. Circle Pines, Minn.: American Guidance Services, 1965.

Edwards, C. Drew, and Williams, John E. "Generalization between Evaluative Words Associated with Racial Figures in Preschool Children." *Journal of Experimental Research in Personality* 4 (1970): 144–55.

Ellsworth, Caroline, and Kane, Nancy. "Race Awareness in Negro and White Nursery School Children in Lynchburg, Virginia." Senior thesis, Randolph-Macon Woman's College, 1957.

Epstein, Benjamin R., and Forster, Arnold. *Preferential Treatment and Quotas*. New York: Anti-Defamation League of B'nai B'rith, 1974.

Fagan, J. F., III. "Infant Color Perception." *Science* 183 (1974): 973–75.

Figura, Ann L. "The Effect of Peer Interaction on the Self-Concept of Negro Children." Master's thesis, DePaul University, 1971.

Filler, John W., Jr., and Williams, John E. "Conditioning the Connotative Meanings of Color Names to Human Figures." *Perceptual and Motor Skills* 32 (1970): 755–63.

Floyd, James A., Jr. "Self-Concept Development in Black Children." Senior thesis, Princeton University, 1969.

———. "Self-Concept Development in Black Children." Multilithed, 1973.

Fox, David Joseph, and Jordan, Valerie Barnes. "Racial Preference and Identification of Black, American Chinese, and White Children." *Genetic Psychology Monographs* 88 (1973): 229–86.

Frazier, Edward Franklin. *The Negro Church in America*. New York: Schocken Books, 1964.

Garn, Stanley M. *The Human Races*. Rev. ed. Springfield, Ill.: Charles C. Thomas, 1965.

Gergen, Kenneth J. "The Significance of Skin Color in Human Relations." *Daedalus* 96 (1967): 390–407.

Gobineau, Arthur de. *The Inequality of Human Races*. Translated by Adrian Collins. New York: G. P. Putnam's Sons, 1915.

Goldberg, Faye J. "The Question of Skin Color and Its Relation to Japan." *Psychologia* 16 (1973): 132–46.

_____, and Stabler, John R. "Black and White Symbolism in Japan." *International Journal of Symbology* 4 (1973): 37–46.

Goodman, Mary Ellen. *Race Awareness in Young Children*. Rev. ed. New York: Collier Books, 1964.

Gordon, Lucy H., and Williams, John E. "Secondary Factors in the Affective Meaning System of the Preschool Child." *Developmental Psychology* 8 (1973): 25–34.

Gossett, Thomas F. *Race: The History of an Idea in America*. Dallas, Tex.: Southern Methodist University Press, 1963.

Grant, Madison. *The Passing of the Great Race*. Rev. ed. New York: Charles Scribner's Sons, 1918.

Greenwald, Herbert J., and Oppenheim, Don B. "Reported Magnitude of Self-Misidentification among Negro Children—Artifact?" *Journal of Personality and Social Psychology* 8 (1968): 49–52.

Gregor, A. James, and McPherson, D. Angus. "Racial Attitudes among White and Negro Children in a Deep-South Standard Metropolitan Area." *Journal of Social Psychology* 68 (1966): 95–106.

_____. "Racial Preferences and Ego-Identity among White and Bantu Children in the Republic of South Africa." *Genetic Psychology Monographs* 73 (1966): 217–54.

Gurkin, Sallie G. "The Effects of the Race of the Interviewer in a Study of Race Awareness in Caucasian Children." Senior thesis, Randolph-Macon Woman's College, 1969.

Hagan, Anne Blair, and Watson, Ellie. "A Study of Lynchburg Pre-School Negro Children: Their Acceptance, Preference, Identification, and Recognition of Caucasians, Negroes, and Chinese." Senior thesis, Randolph-Macon Woman's College, 1968.

Harbin, Susan P., and Williams, John E. "Conditioning of Color Connotations." *Perceptual and Motor Skills* 22 (1966): 217–18.

Harrell, David Edwin. *White Sects and Black Men in the Recent South*. Nashville, Tenn.: Vanderbilt University Press, 1971.

Harris, Dale; Gough, Harrison; and Martin, William E. "Children's Ethnic Attitudes: II. Relationships to Parental Beliefs concerning Child Training." *Child Development* 21 (1950): 169–81.

Hays, David G.; Margolis, Enid; Naroll, Raoul; and Perkins,

Dale Revere. "Color Term Salience." *American Anthropologist* 74 (1972): 1107–21.

Hepler, Gladys Ruth. "Children's Perception of the Origin of Child-Directed Evaluative Statements Broadcast Simultaneously from a Black and a White Box." Master's thesis, Georgia State University, 1974.

Hershenson, Maurice. "Visual Discrimination in the Human Newborn." *Journal of Comparative and Physiological Psychology* 58 (1964): 270–76.

Hraba, Joseph, and Grant, Geoffrey. "Black Is Beautiful: A Reexamination of Racial Preference and Identification." *Journal of Personality and Social Psychology* 16 (1970): 398–402.

Isaacs, Harold R. *The New World of Negro Americans*. New York: John Day, 1963.

Jensen, Arthur R. "How Much Can We Boost IQ and Scholastic Achievement?" *Harvard Educational Review* 39 (1969): 1–123.

Jersild, Arthur T., and Holmes, Frances B. *Children's Fears*. Teachers College Child Development Monographs. New York: Columbia University Bureau of Publications, 1935.

Jones, Mary Ellen. "The Effects of the Race of the Interviewer in a Study of Race Awareness in Negro Children." Senior thesis, Randolph-Macon Woman's College, 1968.

Jordan, Winthrop D. *White Over Black: American Attitudes toward the Negro, 1550–1812*. Chapel Hill: University of North Carolina Press, 1968.

Katz, Phyllis A. "Attitude Change in Children: Can the Twig Be Straightened?" In *Towards the Elimination of Racism*, edited by P. A. Katz. New York: Pergamon Press, 1976a.

———. "Perception of Racial Cues in Preschool Children." *Developmental Psychology* 8 (1973): 293–99.

———. "Stimulus Predifferentiation and Modification of Children's Racial Attitudes." *Child Development* 44 (1973): 232–37.

———. "The Acquisition of Racial Attitudes in Children." In *Towards the Elimination of Racism*, edited by P. A. Katz. New York: Pergamon Press, 1976b.

———, and Zalk, Sue Rosenberg. "Doll Preferences: An Index of Racial Attitudes?" *Journal of Educational Psychology* 66 (1974): 663–68.

Koslin, Sandra Cohen; Amarel, Marianne; and Ames, Nancy. "A Distance Measure of Racial Attitudes in Primary Grade Children: An Exploratory Study." *Psychology in the Schools* 6 (1969): 382–84.

Levin, Harry. *The Power of Blackness*. New York: Vintage, 1960.

Lipscomb, Lafayette W. "Racial Identity of Nursery School Children." Master's thesis, University of North Carolina at Chapel Hill, 1972.

Mabe, Paul Alexander, III. "The Correlation of Racial Attitudes as Measured by the Preschool Racial Attitude Measure and Sociometric Choices for Second-Grade Children." Master's thesis, East Carolina University, 1974.

———, and Williams, John E. "Relation of Racial Attitudes to Sociometric Choices among Second Grade Children." *Psychological Reports* 37 (1975): 547–54.

McAdoo, Harriette Pipes. "A Different View of Race Attitudes and Self Concepts in Black Preschool Children." Paper presented at Annual Meeting of Association of Black Psychology, Detroit, Michigan, 1973.

———. "Racial Attitudes and Self-Concepts of Black Preschool Children." Ph. D. dissertation, University of Michigan, 1970.

McAdoo, John L. "An Exploratory Study of Racial Attitude Change in Black Preschool Children Using Differential Treatments." Ph.D. dissertation, University of Michigan, 1970.

McConnell, James V. *Understanding Human Behavior*. New York: Holt, Rinehart, and Winston, 1974.

McMurtry, C. Allen, and Williams, John E. "The Evaluation Dimension of the Affective Meaning System of the Preschool Child." *Developmental Psychology* 6 (1972): 238–46.

Mead, Frank Spencer. *Handbook of Denominations in the United States*. 5th ed. Nashville & New York: Abingdon Press, 1970.

Morland, J. Kenneth. "A Comparison of Race Awareness in Northern and Southern Children." *American Journal of Orthopsychiatry* 36 (1966): 22–31.

———. "Race Awareness among American and Hong Kong Chinese Children." *American Journal of Sociology* 75 (1969): 360–74.

———. "Racial Acceptance and Preference in Nursery-School Children." *Merrill-Palmer Quarterly* 8 (1962): 271–80.

———. "Racial Attitudes in School Children: From Kindergarten through High School." Final Report, Project 2-c009, Office of Education, U.S. Department of Health, Education, and Welfare, November 1972.

———. "Racial Recognition by Nursery School Children." *Social Forces* 37 (1958): 132–37.

———. "Racial Self-Identification: A Study of Nursery School Children." *American Catholic Sociological Review* 24 (1963): 231–42.

———, and Suthers, Ellen. "Racial Attitudes of Children: Perspectives on the Structural-Normative Theory of Prejudice." Multilithed. Paper presented at Southern Sociological Annual Meeting, Washington, D.C., 1975.

———, and Williams, John E. "Cross-Cultural Measurement of

Racial and Ethnic Attitudes by the Semantic Differential."
Social Forces 48 (1969): 107–12.

Osgood, Charles E. "Cross-Cultural Comparability in Attitude
Measurement Via Multilingual Semantic Differentials." In
Readings in Attitude Theory and Measurement, edited by M.
Fishbein. New York: John Wiley, 1967.

———; Suci, George J.; and Tannenbaum, Percy H. *The
Measurement of Meaning*. Urbana: University of Illinois Press,
1957.

Parish, Thomas S. "Changing Anti-Negro Attitudes in
Caucasian Children through Mediated Stimulus
Generalization." Ph.D. dissertation, University of Illinois,
1972.

———, and Fleetwood, Robert S. "Amount of Conditioning and
Subsequent Attitude Change in Children." *Perceptual and
Motor Skills* 40 (1975): 79–86.

Parker, Christopher E. "Total Darkness as an Aversive Stimulus
Condition for the Squirrel Monkey." *Psychonomic Science* 6
(1966): 111–12.

Porter, Judith D. R. *Black Child, White Child*. Cambridge, Mass.:
Harvard University Press, 1971.

Reese, Hayne W., and Lipsitt, Lewis P. *Experimental Child
Psychology*. New York: Academic Press, 1970.

Renninger, Cheryl A., and Williams, John E. "Black-White Color
Connotations and Race Awareness in Preschool Children."
Perceptual and Motor Skills 22 (1966): 771–85.

Ruchames, Louis, ed. *Racial Thought in America: From the Puritans
to Abraham Lincoln*. Amherst, Mass.: University of Massachusetts Press, 1969.

Sattler, Jerome M. "Racial 'Experimenter Effects' in Experimen-
tation, Testing, Interviewing, and Psychotherapy."
Psychological Bulletin 73 (1970): 137–60.

Shanahan, Judith K. "The Effects of Modifying Black-White
Concept Attitudes of Black and White First Grade Subjects
upon Two Measures of Racial Attitudes." Ph.D. dissertation,
University of Washington, 1972.

Simon, Rita James. "An Assessment of Racial Awareness,
Preference and Self Identity among White and Adopted
Non-White Children." Multilithed: University of Illinois at
Urbana-Champaign, 1973.

Simpson, George Eaton, and Yinger, J. Milton. *Racial and
Cultural Minorities: An Analysis of Prejudice and Discrimination*.
New York: Harper & Row, 1972.

Skinto, Susanne M. "Racial Awareness in Negro and Caucasian
Elementary School Children." Master's thesis, West Virginia
University, 1969.

Smith, H. Sheldon. *In His Image, But . . . : Racism in Southern*

Religion, 1780–1910. Durham, N.C.: Duke University Press, 1972.

Snyder, Louis I., ed. *The Idea of Racialism.* Princeton, N.J.: Van Nostrand, 1962.

Spears, William C. "Assessment of Visual Preference and Discrimination in the Four-Month-Old Infant." *Journal of Comparative and Physiological Psychology* 57 (1964): 381–86.

Spencer, Margaret Beale, and Horowitz, Frances Degen. "Effects of Systematic Social and Token Reinforcement on the Modification of Racial and Color Concept Attitudes in Black and White Preschool Children." *Developmental Psychology* 9 (1973): 246–54.

Stabler, John R., and Goldberg, Faye J. "The Black and White Symbolic Matrix." *International Journal of Symbology* 4 (1973): 27–34.

_____, and Johnson, Edward E. "Children's Perception of Black and White Boxes and Bobo Dolls as a Reflection of How They Regard Their Own and Other's Racial Membership." *International Journal of Symbology* 3 (1972): 11–21.

_____; Johnson, Edward E.; Berke, Melvyn A.; and Baker, Robert B. "The Relationship between Race and Perception of Racially Related Stimuli." *Child Development* 40 (1969): 1233–39.

_____, and Jordan, Susan E. "The Measurement of Children's Self-Concepts as Related to Racial Membership." *Child Development* 42 (1971): 2094–97.

Stanton, William. *The Leopard's Spots: Scientific Attitudes toward Race in America, 1815–59.* Chicago: University of Chicago Press, 1960.

Stevenson, Harold W., and Stewart, Edward C. "A Developmental Study of Racial Awareness in Young Children." *Child Development* 29 (1958): 399–409.

Stinchcombe, Arthur L. "Environment: The Accumulation of Events." In *Science, Heritability and IQ.* Reprint Series No. 4, Harvard Educational Review. Cambridge, Mass.: Harvard Educational Review, 1969.

Stoddard, Lothrop. *The Rising Tide of Color against White World-Supremacy.* New York: Charles Scribner's Sons, 1920.

Thomas, Hoben. "Unfolding the Baby's Mind: The Infant's Selection of Visual Stimuli." *Psychological Review* 80 (1973): 468–88.

Traynham, Richard M. "The Effects of Modifying Color Meaning Concepts on Racial Concept Attitudes in Five- and Eight-Year Old Children." Master's thesis, University of Arkansas, 1974.

Vanneman, Reeve D., and Pettigrew, Thomas F. "Race and

Relative Deprivation in the Urban United States." *Race XIII* 4 (1972): 461–86.

Vocke, Jacqueline M. "Measuring Racial Attitudes in Preschool Negro Children." Master's thesis, University of South Carolina, 1971.

Walker, Patricia. "The Effects of Hearing Selected Children's Stories That Portray Blacks in a Favorable Manner on the Racial Attitudes of Groups of Black and White Kindergarten Children." Ph.D. dissertation, University of Kentucky, 1971.

Warner, W. Lloyd; Meeker, Marchia; and Eels, Kenneth. *Social Class in America*. Chicago: Social Science Research Associates, 1949.

Westie, Frank. "Race and Ethnic Relations." In *Handbook of Modern Sociology*, edited by R. E. L. Faris. Chicago: Rand McNally, 1964.

————, and Morland, J. Kenneth. "The Development of Prejudice: Childhood to Adulthood." Multilithed. Paper presented at Southern Sociological Society Annual Meeting, Miami, Fla., 1971.

Whiteside, Robert Reid, Jr. "The Modification of Black/White Color Attitudes and Its Effect upon Racial Attitudes as Measured by the Preschool Racial Attitude Measure II." Master's thesis, East Carolina University, 1975.

Williams, John E. "Connotations of Color Names among Negroes and Caucasians." *Perceptual and Motor Skills* 18 (1964): 721–31.

————. "Connotations of Racial Concepts and Color Names." *Journal of Personality and Social Psychology* 3 (1966): 531–40.

————. "Individual Differences in Color Name Connotations as Related to Measures of Racial Attitude." *Perceptual and Motor Skills* 29 (1969): 711–14.

————; Best, Deborah L.; and Boswell, Donna A. "Children's Racial Attitudes in the Early School Years." *Child Development* 46 (1975): 494–500.

————; Best, Deborah L.; Boswell, Donna A.; Mattson, Linda A.; and Graves, Deborah J. "Preschool Racial Attitude Measure II." *Educational and Psychological Measurement* 35 (1975): 3–18.

————; Best, Deborah L.; Wood, Frank B.; and Filler, John W. "Changes in the Connotations of Racial Concepts and Color Names: 1963–1970." *Psychological Reports* 33 (1973): 983–96.

————; Boswell, Donna A.; and Best, Deborah L. "Evaluative Responses of Preschool Children to the Colors White and Black." *Child Development* 46 (1975): 501–8.

————, and Carter, Dorothy Jean. "Connotations of Racial Concepts and Color Names in Germany." *Journal of Social Psychology* 72 (1967): 19–26.

_____, and Edwards, C. Drew. "An Exploratory Study of the Modification of Color Concepts and Racial Attitudes in Preschool Children." *Child Development* 40 (1969): 737–50.

_____, and Foley, Jackson W., Jr. "Connotative Meanings of Color Names and Color Hues." *Perceptual and Motor Skills* 26 (1968): 499–502.

_____, and McMurtry, C. Allen. "Color Connotations among Caucasian Seventh-Graders and College Students." *Perceptual and Motor Skills* 30 (1970): 707–13.

_____; Morland, J. Kenneth; and Underwood, Walter L. "Connotations of Color Names in the United States, Europe, and Asia." *Journal of Social Psychology* 82 (1970): 3–14.

_____, and Roberson, J. Karen. "A Method of Assessing Racial Attitudes in Preschool Children." *Educational and Psychological Measurement* 27 (1967): 671–89.

_____, and Rousseau, Cynthia A. "Evaluation and Identification Responses of Negro Preschoolers to the Colors Black and White." *Perceptual and Motor Skills* 33 (1971): 587–99.

_____, and Stabler, John R. "If White Means Good, Then Black . . ." *Psychology Today* 7, no. 2 (1973): 50–54.

_____; Tucker, Richard D.; and Dunham, Frances Y. "Changes in the Connotations of Color Names among Negroes and Caucasians: 1963–1969." *Journal of Personality and Social Psychology* 19 (1971): 222–28.

Williams, Kathryn H.; Williams, John E.; and Beck, Robert C. "Assessing Children's Racial Attitudes Via A Signal Detection Model." *Perceptual and Motor Skills* 36 (1973): 587–98.

Wood, Forrest G. *Black Scare: The Racist Response to Emancipation and Reconstruction*. Berkeley: University of California Press, 1970.

Woodward, C. Vann. *The Strange Career of Jim Crow*. Rev. ed. New York: Oxford University Press, 1966.

Yancey, Anna Vance. "A Study of Racial Attitudes in White First Grade Children." Unpublished paper, Department of Education, Pennsylvania State University, 1972.

Zimmermann, Robert R. "Reversal Learning in the Neonatal Rhesus Monkey." *Developmental Psychobiology* 6 (1973): 245–50.

NAME INDEX

A
Adams, Frances, 54–56, 84, 341
Adorno, Theodor W., 278, 341
Agassiz, Louis, 10
Allen, Penny, 170, 172, 191, 197, 341
Allen, Vernon L., 99, 186, 341
Allport, Gordon W., 247, 276, 341
Amarel, Marianne, 345
Ames, Nancy, 345
Asher, Steven R., 99, 186, 341

B
Baker, Robert B., 72, 348
Ball, Portia M., 219n, 341
Bartholomew, Suzi, 172, 175, 180, 202–3, 341
Baugher, Robert, 122–24, 180, 202, 233, 341
Beck, Robert C., 60n, 292–93, 350
Bennett, Paul D., 341
Berke, Melvyn A., 72, 348
Best, Deborah L., 58, 64, 69–71, 77–80, 82–84, 102, 105–9, 112–13, 114–15, 116, 124–29, 139, 143, 159, 161, 216–17, 222, 286, 306, 318, 325, 326, 341, 342, 349
Blaustein, Albert P., 20, 342
Bond, Elizabeth K., 309, 342
Boswell, Donna A., 64, 69–71, 77–80, 85, 86–88, 102, 105–9, 112–13, 116, 121, 124–29, 143, 222, 234, 246–97, 250, 275, 277, 308, 318, 326, 342, 349
Brace, C. Loring, 23, 25, 342, 343
Brian, Clara R., 88, 315, 342
Bridges, M. A., 106
Buettner-Janusch, John, 22, 23, 342

C
Campbell, Donald C., 299, 342
Cannon, Marlene, 292–93

Cantor, Gordon, 219n, 341, 342
Carter, Dorothy Jean, 349
Carter, P. C., 109
Chamberlain, Houston Stewart, 12–13, 14, 21, 342
Chance, Paul, 39, 342
Cheek, Vickie, 293
Clark, Kenneth B., 98–101, 185, 186, 187, 195, 205, 206, 207, 342
Clark, Mamie K., 98–101, 185, 186, 187, 195, 205, 206, 207, 342
Clifford, Eth, 43, 342
Cohen, Rosalie, 26, 342
Cohn, David L., 18
Collins, Jeffrey L., 71, 109, 153, 343
Cooper, James Fenimore, 11
Cowan, Lou, 170, 343
Crosby, Sallie, 170, 172, 191, 197, 341

D
Deutsch, Martin, 25, 343
Dixon, Thomas, Jr., 12
Dunham, Frances Y., 51–52, 350
Dunn, Lloyd M., 343

E
Edwards, C. Drew, 68, 106, 136–39, 146–48, 317, 343, 349
Eels, Kenneth, 183, 349
Ellsworth, Caroline, 195, 343
Epstein, Benjamin R., 31, 343

F
Fagan, Joseph F., III, 33, 343
Feinstein, Carol, 106, 234–35
Ferguson, Clarence C., 20, 342
Figura, Ann L., 68, 343
Filler, John W., 58, 59, 343, 349
Firestone, Carole, 106, 234–35
Fleetwood, Robert B., 154–55, 294, 347

Floyd, James A., Jr., 158–59, 170, 172, 182, 191, 197, 199, 200, 232, 276, 343
Foley, Jackson W., Jr., 60–61, 350
Forster, Arnold, 31, 343
Fox, David Joseph, 99, 100, 186, 195, 206, 343
Frazier, E. Franklin, 9, 343
Frenkel-Brunswik, Else, 278, 341

G
Galton, Francis, 11
Garn, Stanley, 22, 343
Garrison, Martha, 170, 172, 197, 341
Gergen, Kenneth, 40, 41, 344
Gobineau, Arthur de, 13, 14, 21, 344
Goldberg, Faye, 38–39, 45, 240–41, 344, 348
Goodenough, Florence L., 88, 315, 342
Goodman, Mary Ellen, 187–88, 277, 344
Gordon, Lucy H., 84n, 317, 344
Gossett, Thomas F., 5n, 11, 15, 344
Gough, Harrison, 279, 344
Grant, Geoffrey, 99, 100, 186, 206, 345
Grant, Madison, 14, 15, 21, 344
Graves, Deborah J., 71, 102, 105–9, 112–13, 116, 139, 143, 159–60, 161, 163, 318, 342, 349
Greenwald, Herbert J., 99, 100, 186, 195, 344
Gregor, A. James, 99, 100, 186, 195, 344
Gurkin, Sallie G., 184, 344

H
Hagan, Ann Blair, 170, 172, 175, 180, 202–3, 344
Hall, G. Stanley, 11
Harbin, Susan P., 59, 344
Harrell, David E., 28, 344
Harris, Dale, 279, 344
Hays, David G., 34, 344
Hepler, Gladys Ruth, 73, 345
Hershenson, Maurice, 33, 309, 345
Hodges, Wayne, 128
Holmes, Frances B., 262, 345
Horowitz, Frances Degen, 150–57, 348
Hraba, Joseph, 99, 100, 186, 206, 345

I
Isaacs, Harold, 41, 42, 43, 345

J
Jensen, Arthur R., 25–26, 345
Jersild, Arthur T., 262, 345

Johnson, Edward E., 72, 73, 74, 348
Jones, Mary Ellen, 184, 209, 345
Jordan, Susan E., 73, 348
Jordan, Valerie Barnes, 99, 100, 186, 195, 206, 343
Jordan, Winthrop, 5, 6, 345

K
Kane, Nancy, 195, 343
Katz, Phyllis A., 235, 276, 279, 305, 315–16, 345
Keller, K. S., 68, 106
Koslin, Sandra Cohen, 310, 345
Kuhn, Frank, 304–5

L
Leslie, Carlyn, 170, 343
Levin, Harry, 42, 345
Levinson, Danjel J., 278, 341
Lipscomb, Lafayette W., 197, 199, 200, 272, 345
Lipsitt, Lewis P., 309, 347
Livingston, Kathy, 172, 175, 180, 202–3, 341
Lofting, Hugh, 42
London, Jack, 11

M
Mabe, Alex, 128, 189, 217–18, 308, 345, 346
McAdoo, Harriette P., 110–11, 112, 234, 346
McAdoo, John L., 111, 147, 157, 160, 163, 186, 217, 276, 346
McConnell, James V., 263n, 346
Mack, Kinny, 128
McMurtry, C. Allen, 89–90, 136–39, 317, 346, 350
McPherson, D. Angus, 99, 100, 186, 195, 344
Manoogian, Samuel, 142n
Margolis, Enid, 34, 344
Martin, William E., 279, 344
Mattson, Linda A., 102, 105–9, 112–13, 116–17, 143, 219–20, 318, 349
Mead, Frank Spencer, 346
Meeker, Marchia, 183, 349
Minton, Cheryl Renninger, 63
Morland, J. Kenneth, 54, 91–94, 131–33, 170, 172, 178, 181, 182, 183, 191, 195, 197, 199, 200, 201, 205, 208, 209, 212, 334, 346, 349, 350
Morton, Samuel George, 10
Myrdal, Gunnar, 18

N
Naroll, Raoul, 34, 344
Naylor, Cecile E., 82–84, 114–15, 222, 341
Norris, Frank, 11

O
Oppenheim, Don B., 99, 100, 186, 195, 344
Osborn, Henry Fairchild, 14
Osgood, Charles, 46, 54–56, 84, 101, 317, 341, 347
Overholt, Kenneth, 89–91, 92–93

P
Parish, Thomas S., 153–55, 294, 347
Parker, Christopher E., 262–63, 305, 347
Perkins, Dale Revere, 34, 344
Pettigrew, Thomas F., 274, 348
Piaget, Jean, 276
Porter, Judith, 100, 122, 183, 189, 195–96, 206, 274, 295, 347
Priest, Josiah, 8

R
Reckenbeil, Ken, 128
Reese, Hayne A., 309, 347
Renninger, Cheryl, 64, 188, 206–7, 347. *See also* Minton, Cheryl Renninger
Richman, Charles, 305, 309
Roberson, J. Karen, 66–68, 104–6, 207, 222, 233, 317, 350
Rousseau, Cynthia A., 75–76, 223, 350
Ruchames, Louis, 347

S
Sanford, R. Nevitt, 278, 341
Sattler, Jerome M., 307, 347
Selvey, Susan, 305, 309
Shanahan, Judith K., 71, 147–48, 222, 347
Simon, Rita James, 185, 347
Simpson, George Eaton, 274, 347
Skinto, Susanne M., 68, 69, 77, 347
Smith, H. Sheldon, 5n, 7, 9, 347
Smith, Samuel Stanhope, 10
Smith, Suellen C., 109, 139–44, 159, 161, 312, 342
Snyder, Louis I., 5n, 348
Spears, William C., 88, 309, 348
Spencer, Herbert, 11
Spencer, Margaret Beale, 150–52, 348
Stabler, John R., 38, 45, 72, 73, 74, 80–81, 344, 348, 350

Stanley, Julian C., 299, 342
Stanton, William, 5n, 348
Stevenson, Harold W., 188, 206, 208, 348
Stewart, Edward C., 188, 206, 208, 348
Stinchcombe, Arthur L., 26, 348
Stoddard, Lothrop, 14–15, 21, 348
Strickland, Martha, 172, 175, 180, 202–3, 341
Suci, George J., 46, 317, 347
Sumner, William Graham, 11, 18
Suthers, Ellen, 346

T
Tannenbaum, Percy H., 46, 317, 347
Thomas, Hoben, 309, 348
Thompson, K., 105–6
Tillman, Benjamin R., 17
Traynham, Richard M., 71, 109, 125, 148–50, 348
Tse, M., 68, 105–6
Tucker, Richard D., 51–52, 350

U
Underwood, Walter, 54, 350
Ungar, George, 263n

V
Vanneman, Reeve D., 274, 348
Vardaman, James K., 17
Viele, Kay, 170, 172, 191, 197, 199, 200, 209
Vocke, Jacqueline, 76–77, 110–11, 112–13, 222, 234, 349

W
Wade, Wendy, 109, 114
Walker, Patricia, 106, 111, 156–57, 160, 163, 349
Warner, W. Lloyd, 183, 349
Watson, Ellie, 170, 172, 175, 180, 202–3, 344
Watson, Tom, 17
Westie, Frank, 178, 179, 182, 191, 197, 199, 200, 201, 209, 349
Whiteside, Robert Reid, Jr., 152–53, 349
Williams, John E., 48, 50, 51–52, 54, 57, 58, 59, 60–61, 64, 66–68, 69–71, 74–76, 77–80, 82–84, 85, 89–90, 101, 102, 104–9, 112–13, 114–15, 116, 124–29, 136–38, 139, 141, 143, 146–48, 159, 161, 188–89, 206–7, 222, 223, 233, 292–93, 317, 318, 326, 341, 342, 343, 344, 346, 347, 349, 350
Williams, Kathryn H., 292–93, 350

Wister, Owen, 11
Wood, Forrest G., 5n, 350
Wood, Frank B., 58, 349
Woodward, C. Vann, 18, 350

Y
Yancey, Anna Vance, 159–64, 350
Yinger, J. Milton, 274, 347
Young, Barbara, 71, 109, 222, 279–80

Z
Zalk, Sue Rosenberg, 235, 345
Zimmermann, Robert R., 263, 306,
    309, 350

SUBJECT INDEX

A

Affirmative action, and emphasis on race, 31
African Methodist Episcopal Church, emergence of, 9
Afro-Americans
color attitudes of, 48–53, 74–82, 92–94, 241–42
evaluation by of American, Black American, and White American, 131–33
perception of racial similarity by, 194–203
racial acceptance by, 169–74
racial attitudes of, 98–101, 110–13, 125–33
racial classification ability of, 205–10
as racial nomenclature, x–xi, 269–70
racial preference of, 176–77, 179–80, 187–89
racial self-classification of, 211–12
racial self-preference of, 190–91
socioeconomic status of, and racial bias, 273–74
Age, relationship of
to color attitudes, 80, 85–88, 89–94
to perception of racial similarity, 195, 197, 199–202
to racial acceptance, 169–74
to racial attitudes, 119–20, 125–28, 132–33
to racial classification ability, 207–9, 213, 232, 245
to racial preference, 177–79, 181–82, 186, 232, 248
to racial self-preference, 190–92
American, evaluation of by Afro- and Euro-Americans, 131–33
American Indian children, racial attitudes of, 114
Analysis of variance, as a procedure in race/color research, 300–302

Assessment procedures in race/color research, suggested improvements
in forced- and free-choice responses, 290–94
in length of test, 287–89
in measurement of variables, 286–87
in nature of stimulus materials, 289–90
Authoritarian personality of parents, and development of racial bias in children, 278–80

B

Baptists
and slavery, 7, 9
and the Supreme Court decision of 1954, 27
Baylor University Medical School, 263n
Biological make-up of human beings, and color bias, 239–44, 260–62
Black
as a designation of race, x, 34–37, 56–60, 205–10, 243–45, 269–70
and the development of color bias, 239–44, 281–83
and fear of the dark, 264–66
as an unfavorable cultural symbol, 37–45
Black American, evaluation of by Afro- and Euro-Americans, 131–33
Black Codes, 16
Black Identity movement, effect of on race and color attitudes, 38, 46, 51–53, 58–59, 93–94, 157–59, 241–43, 304, 311, 312
Boswell Amendment, 19

C

Caucasian, as a racial designation, 205, 209–10

Chinese
  and racial acceptance, 174–75
  and perception of racial similarity,
    202–3
  and racial preference, 179–80
Clark Doll Test (CDT)
  described, 98
  and perception of racial similarity,
    194–96
  and racial attitudes, 98–101
  and racial classification ability,
    206–10
  and racial preference, 184–87
  relationship of to PRAM, 217
Color. *See also* Color names; Black;
    White
  as cultural symbols, 37–45
  reactions to of adults, 46–56
  relation of to race, 33–37, 56–61
Color attitudes
  of Afro-Americans, 74–82, 92–94
  biological basis of, 239–44
  of Euro-Americans, 66–74, 89–92
  and fantasied color identification,
    223–24
  of French and Italian children,
    82–84
  and IQ, 69, 75, 76
  modification of, 144–56, 258–59
  and pro-Euro bias, 249–53
  relationship of to racial attitudes,
    155, 221–23, 249–51
Color bias. *See* Color attitudes
Color-coding of races, consequences
    of, 34–37, 56–60, 243–45, 269–70
Color differences, sensitivity of hu-
    mans to, 33–34
Colored, as a racial designation, 205–6
Color hues, relation of to color names,
    60–61
Color meaning. *See also* Color attitudes
  outside the United States, 53–56
  shift in among Afro-Americans,
    92–94
  signs and significates of, 60–61
  in the United States, 48–53
Color Meaning Test (CMT)
  and aversion to darkness, 85
  description of, 63–66, 326–29,
    338–40
  in interrelationship studies of racial
    and color concepts, 222–24
  in modification of color attitude
    studies, 145–56
  relationship of to PRAM, 217, 297
  scores on of Afro-Americans, 74–80,
    241

Color Meaning Test (CMT) (*continued*)
  scores on of Euro-Americans, 66–74
Color names. *See also* Black; White
  relation of to color hues, 60–61
  response to by Afro- and Euro-
    Americans, 48–53
Correlation methods, suggested as a
    procedure in race/color research,
    300, 303, 307–8
Counterbalancing, as a way of control-
    ling order effects in research, 296
Cross-cultural studies of race and
    color attitudes, 53–56, 247–48,
    304–5, 311
Cultural factors in color and racial
    attitudes, 37–45, 53–56, 247–49,
    260–62, 267–71, 281–83, 304–5
Cultural pluralism, and renewed em-
    phasis on race, 30–31

D
Darkness, aversion to
  biological basis of, 239–41
  and color attitudes, 85, 121, 264–65,
    281–83
  in monkeys, 262–63
Data analyses, suggestions for
    race/color research, 300–302
Defensiveness hypothesis, as an ex-
    planation of change in bias of
    Afro-Americans, 253
Denmark, color meaning among stu-
    dents in, 54–56
Dr. Dolittle stories, white-black sym-
    bolism in, 42–43

E
Euro-Americans
  color attitudes of, 48–53, 60–61,
    66–74, 85, 89–92
  evaluation by of American, Black
    American, and White American,
    131–33
  modification of racial and color at-
    titudes of, 136–65
  perception of racial similarity by,
    194–203
  racial acceptance by, 169–75
  racial attitudes of, 99–101, 104–9,
    125–33
  racial classification ability of, 205–10
  as racial nomenclature, x–xi, 269–70
  racial preference of, 177–80, 187–89
  racial self-classification of, 211–12
  racial self-preference of, 190–91
  socioeconomic status of, and racial
    bias, 273–74

F
Factor analysis, in race/color research, 300, 303
Family membership, and racial bias, 274–80, 281–83
Father, perception of race of
by Afro-Americans, 198–200
by Euro-Americans, 198–99
Fear of the dark. *See* Darkness, aversion to
Forced-choice in race/color research, 66, 290–94
Free-choice in race/color research, 292–94
French children
color attitudes of, 82–84
racial attitudes of, 114–15, 249

G
Germany, color meaning among students in, 54–56
"Grandfather Clauses," and racial discrimination, 17, 19

H
Hong Kong Chinese
color meaning among, 54–56
pro-Chinese bias of, 247
Human behavior, as a product of both biological make-up and culture, 261–62

I
Identification with one's own racial category
by Afro-Americans, 254–55, 257–58, 270–71
as an American norm, 252–53
by Euro-Americans, 270
India, color meaning among students in, 54–56, 92
Intelligence Quotient. *See also* Peabody Picture Vocabulary Test
and attitudes toward color, 69, 76, 80
and attitudes toward race, 119–20, 130
need for in research design, 295
Interrelationship of racial and color concepts
on measures of affect, 215–24
on measures of cognition and judgment, 224–35
Italian children
color attitudes of, 82–84
racial attitudes of, 114–15, 249

J
Japanese, attitude toward skin color, 45

L
Laws about race, 5, 16–21
Light, preference for over darkness
biologically based, 239–44
in discrimination learning paradigm, 304
and early experience, 264–66
in monkeys, 262–63
in theoretical model of development of racial bias, 280–83
Literary views of race, 11–16
Longitudinal research on race/color concepts, need for, 311–12

M
Methodists
and slavery, 7, 9
pronouncement of against racial prejudice and discrimination, 27
Methodological improvements, need for in race/color research
in assessment procedures, 286–94
in data analyses, 299–302
in research design, 294–99
Modification of color attitudes
by behavior modification techniques, 144–56
effectiveness of and social structure, 258–59
suggestions for future studies of, 312–15
Modification of racial attitudes
by changing color attitudes, 144–56
by direct techniques, 136–44
by special curricula, 156–65
suggestions for future studies of, 312–15
Monkeys, aversion of to darkness, 262–63
Morland Picture Interview (MPI)
description of, 166–67, 329–34
interrelationship of racial concepts in, 220–21, 224–30, 231–32
perception of racial similarity scores on, 196–203
racial acceptance scores on, 167–76
racial classification ability scores on, 203–10
racial preference scores on, 176–84, 248
racial self-classification scores on, 210–13

Mother, perception of race of
by Afro-Americans, 199–200
by Euro-Americans, 201–2
Mother's racial attitude, and racial
attitude of children, 121
Movies, and black-white symbolism,
44
Multivariate designs in race/color research, 297–98

N
National Conference of Christians and
Jews, 27
National Council of Churches
opposition of to racial discrimination, 27
racial representation in, 29
Negro, as a racial designation, x,
205–10

O
Order and sequence effects in
race/color studies, 296
Overcategorization, as a characteristic
of racially prejudiced adults,
276–77

P
Parents, and the development of racial
bias in children, 275–80
Peabody Picture Vocabulary Test
and color attitudes, 69, 75, 76, 77
and racial attitudes, 105–6, 119–20,
130
and theory of racial bias, 248–49
Perception of racial similarity
affective element in, 229–30, 235–36
as a concept, 97, 255
of father, 198–99, 202–3
of mother, 198–201, 202–3
and racial attitude, 219–20
and racial classification ability,
227–28
and racial preference, 228–30
of self, 194–97, 202–3
Philippines, color meaning among
students in, 54–56, 92
Plessy v. Ferguson, significance of,
16–17, 20
Positive-adjective response set,
292–93
Post-only and pre-post designs, in
race/color research, 298–99
Presbyterians, and slavery, 7, 8, 9

Preschool Racial Attitude Measure
(PRAM)
age differences in scores on, 119–20,
125–28, 132–33
description of, 101–4, 317–26,
335–38
interrelationship studies with,
216–20, 222–23, 233–34
IQ differences in scores on, 119–20
modification studies with, 136–44,
147–65
race differences in scores on, 105–15
relationship of to CDT, 217, 297
reliability of, 116–18, 129, 322–24
sex differences in scores on, 118–19
sex-role scores on, 119–20
signal-detection version of, 292
Pro-Euro-American bias
color bias theory of, 249–51
social structure theory of, 247–49
Psychoanalytic explanation of color
bias, 240–41

Q
Questions for future race/color research
concepts to be clarified, 302–4
cross-cultural studies, 304, 311
effects of Black Identity movement,
304
generality of light-dark bias, 304–5
modification studies, 312–15
race of examiner effects, 306–7
relationship of parent-child attitudes, 308
responses of very young and of
older children, 308–12

R
Race
definitions of, 23–24
difficulty in delineation of, 22
laws regarding, 5, 16–21
literary views of, 11–16
present-day emphases on, 28–32,
269
relation of to color, 33–37, 56–61
religious views of, 6–9, 27–28
scientific views of, 10–11, 21–26
Race of examiner effect
with CMT, 68–69
with MPI, 183–84
with PRAM, 106–7, 108, 111,
112–13, 125, 325
suggested research on, 306–7

Racial Acceptance
  of Afro- by Euro-Americans,
    173–74, 187–89
  and age, 169–74, 254
  of Chinese by Americans, 174–75
  as a concept, 96
  of Euro- by Afro-Americans,
    171–72, 187–89
  measured by MPI, 167–69
  of own race, 169–71
  and race of examiner, 184
  relationship of to racial attitude, 254
Racial attitude
  of Afro-Americans, 98–101, 110–13,
    125–33
  and age, 119–20, 125–28, 132–33
  of American Indians, 114
  and aversion to darkness, 121, 266,
    281
  and color attitudes, 221–23
  as a concept, 96
  of Euro-Americans, 99–101, 104–9,
    125–33
  of French and Italians, 114–15
  and IQ, 119–20, 130
  measured by PRAM, 101–4
  modification of, 136–65
  and mother's attitude, 121
  and perceived racial similarity,
    219–20
  and racial acceptance, 254
  and racial classification ability,
    233–35
  and racial preference, 216–19
  regional variation in, 128–29, 249
Racial balance in schools, and re-
    newed emphasis on race, 29
Racial classification ability
  of Afro- and Euro-Americans,
    205–10
  by age, 207–9, 213, 232, 245
  as a concept, 97
  and perceived racial similarity to
    self, 227–28, 256
  and racial attitude, 233–35
  and racial preference, 231–32, 235
  and racial self-classification, 225–26,
    256–57
  and racial self-preference, 231–32
Racial differentiation, emphases on
  in the present day, 28–32
  prior to the 1940s, 4–19
  in the recent past, 19–28
Racial membership, possible influ-
    ences of on racial attitudes, 121,
    272–73

"Racial orthodoxy," triumph of in
    southern churches, 9
Racial preference
  affective element in, 229–30
  of Afro-Americans, 176–77, 179–80
  and age, 177–79, 181–82, 186, 232
  as a concept, 96
  of Euro-Americans, 177–80
  and perception of racial similarity,
    228–30
  and race of examiner, 184
  and racial attitude, 216–20, 246–53
  and racial classification ability,
    231–32, 235–36
  and racial self-preference, 220–21
  and region, 249
Racial segregation
  in churches, 29
  legal support of, 17–18
Racial self-classification
  by Afro- and Euro-Americans,
    210–13
  relationship of to racial classification
    ability, 225–26, 256–57
Racial self-identification. See
    Perception of racial similarity ;
    Racial self-classification
Racial self-preference
  affective element in, 235–36
  as a concept, 96–97
  and racial classification ability,
    231–32
  and racial preference, 220–21
  scores of on the MPI, 189–91
Racial self-rejection by Afro-
    Americans, contested, 82, 257,
    283
Racial similarity. See Perception of ra-
    cial similarity
Racial superiority and inferiority
  cultural messages of, 267–68
  as justification for slavery, 8
  laws promoting belief in, 18–19
  literary views of, 11–16
  questioning of in opinion poll, 26
  as racial orthodoxy in religion, 9
  scientific views of, 10–11, 21–26
Racism, in America, 4, 11
Religion
  and color symbolism, 39–41
  and race, 6–9, 27–28, 29
  and slavery, 6–8
Research design, suggestions for im-
    provement in
  control of order effects, 296–97
  multivariate studies, 297–98
  post-only and pre-post studies,
    298–99

Research design, suggestions for improvement in (*continued*)
 selection of subjects, 294–95
Restrictive covenant, as a form of racial discrimination, 19

S
School curricula
 future research in, 313–15
 and modification of racial attitudes, 156–65
 suggested control for in research design, 297–98
School level, relationship of to race/color awareness. *See* Age, relationship of
Scientific views of race
 in the past, 10–11
 in the present, 21–26
Semantic differential
 and the CMT, 64–65, 101, 317
 description of, 46–48
 and PRAM, 101–4, 317
 in studies of color meaning in adults, 48–61
Sex differences, of subjects
 in MPI scores, 180–81
 in PRAM scores, 118–19, 130
Sex-roles, knowledge of from scores on PRAM, 119–20, 325–26
Skin color
 of MPI models, 167
 of PRAM figures, 101–4
 and racial attitudes, 114–15, 144–45, 151–52, 202, 204, 243–44
 and racial designation, 33–34, 45, 61
 and racial preference, 122–24, 179–80
Slavery
 establishment of in America, 5–6
 religious views of, 6–9
Social class. *See* Socioeconomic status
Social Darwinism, as a support of racial inferiority, 11, 21
Social structure, relationship of to racial bias, 247–48, 267–69
Society of Friends, and slavery, 7
Socioeconomic status
 influences of on racial and color attitudes, 122, 273–74, 295
 relation of to racial preference, 182–83
Subcultural influences on racial bias, 271–80, 281–83

T
"Talking box," use of in color attitude studies, 73, 80

Television, and black-white symbolism, 44
Thailand, color meaning among students in, 54–56, 92
Thunderstorms, and aversion to darkness, 264–65
Toys, choice of by color, 86–88
"Transductive reasoning," as a factor in the development of racial prejudice, 276

U
United States Congress, and civil rights, 19–20
United States Supreme Court, rulings of on race, 16–17, 19–20

W
White
 as a designation of race, x, 34–37, 56–60, 205–10, 243–45, 269–70
 and the development of color bias, 239–44, 281–83
 as a favorable cultural symbol, 37–45
White American, evaluation of by Afro- and Euro-Americans, 131–33
"White primary," and racial discrimination, 17, 19
Williams v. *Mississippi*, and racial discrimination, 17

Y
"Yea-saying" response set
 as a problem in measurement, 292–93
 in racial acceptance, 173–74, 254
Year in school, relation of to race/color awareness. *See* Age, relationship of